Enhancing Teaching and Learning in the 21st-Century Academic Library

Creating the 21st-Century Academic Library
Series Editor: Bradford Lee Eden

About the Series

Creating the 21st-Century Academic Library provides both conceptual information and practical guidance on the full spectrum of innovative changes now underway in academic libraries. Each volume in the series is carefully crafted to be a hallmark of professional practice and thus:

- Focuses on one narrowly-defined aspect of academic librarianship.
- Features an introductory chapter surveying the content to follow and highlighting lessons to be learned.
- Shares the experiences of librarians who have recently overseen significant changes in their library to better position it to provide 21st-century services to students, faculty, and researchers.

About the Series Editor

Bradford Lee Eden is one of librarianship's most experienced and knowledgeable editors. Dr. Eden is Dean of Library Services at Valparaiso University. Previous positions include Associate University Librarian for Technical Services and Scholarly Communication at the University of California, Santa Barbara; Head, Web and Digitization Services, and Head, Bibliographic and Metadata Services for the University of Nevada, Las Vegas Libraries. He is editor of OCLC Systems & Services: *International Digital Library Perspectives* and *The Bottom Line: Managing Library Finances*, and is on the editorial boards of *Library Hi Tech* and *The Journal of Film Music*. He has recently been named associate editor/editor-designate of *Library Leadership & Management*, the journal of the Library Leadership & Management Association (LLAMA) within ALA.

Titles in the Series

Enhancing Teaching and Learning in the 21st-Century Academic Library

Successful Innovations That Make a Difference

Edited by Bradford Lee Eden

ROWMAN & LITTLEFIELD
Lanham • Boulder • New York • London

Published by Rowman & Littlefield
A wholly owned subsidiary of The Rowman & Littlefield Publishing Group, Inc.
4501 Forbes Boulevard, Suite 200, Lanham, Maryland 20706
www.rowman.com

Unit A, Whitacre Mews, 26-34 Stannary Street, London SE11 4AB

British Library Cataloguing in Publication Information Available

Library of Congress Cataloging-in-Publication Data

Enhancing teaching and learning in the 21st-century academic library : successful innovations that make a difference / [edited by] Bradford Lee Eden.
p. cm. — (Creating the 21st-century academic library ; 2)
Includes bibliographical references and index.
ISBN 978-1-4422-4703-1 (cloth : alk. paper) — ISBN 978-1-4422-4705-5 (pbk. : alk. paper) — ISBN 978-1-4422-4704-8 (ebook)
1. Academic libraries—Effect of technological innovations on. 2. Academic libraries—Information technology. 3. Academic librarians—Effect of technological innovation on. 4. Education, Higher—Effect of technological innovations on. 5. Educational innovations. I. Eden, Bradford Lee, editor.
Z675.U5E54 2015
027.7—dc23
2014043551

Printed in the United States of America

Contents

Introduction

Bradford Lee Eden

The second volume of the series *Creating the 21st-Century Academic Library* is centered on the topic of experiments and initiatives in student learning and training, and features thirteen chapters. These chapters reflect the wide range of experimental approaches that are under way on campuses across the country. They range from librarians redesigning the space in the library in order to assume control of the campus bookstore to implementing a MOOC where the problems of providing material to potentially thousands of students taking an online course must somehow overcome copyright restrictions. Or, along another dimension, the iPad has become the delivery mechanism of choice with rich collections of resources that finally begin to reflect the potential of the digital world. These signal that a new era has begun in the definition and design of the academic library, and it promises to be an interesting ride.

In chapter 1, Teri Oaks Gallaway and James B. Hobbs discuss the issues surrounding student retention, a concern that will grow much stronger as the rising costs of a college education continue to escalate. The focus of this chapter is on student textbook costs, and addresses ways they can be reduced. A timely target—the accelerated cost of annual student expenditures for books. During the 2012–2013 academic year they averaged $1,250 at U.S. public and private schools (National Center for Educational Statistics). The authors note that such costs pressure students to buy used texts, borrow texts, or do without them, at the cost of poor grades or dropped courses. The library at Loyola University New Orleans worked with the university administration in piloting an open access textbook initiative as a means of combating these high costs and helping with student retention. As a contrast, James Lund in chapter 2 describes how the bookstore at Westminster Seminary California was placed under library operations, and discusses some of the challenges and opportunities this entailed for the library. New skills are required by the librarian to carry out this function, but there are advantages as well.

In chapter 3, Loren Turner and Jennifer Wondracek discuss the pros and cons of librarians supporting MOOC initiatives within their universities. Typically, a MOOC—a massive, open, online course—is offered by faculty to learners of every variety, unrestricted by geography and for free on an online platform; it is a leading, recent example of how technology is transforming education. The purpose is to provide anyone anywhere a quality education without cost, or at low cost, with 24/7 access to course materials developed by outstanding scholars. This chapter describes how the University of Florida Law School teamed up with librarians to develop a MOOC, and demonstrates how MOOCs provide opportunities to raise the profile of librarians within an academic institution.

Assessment has not been ignored, as shown in chapter 4. Antonio DeRosa and Marisol Hernandez discuss the results of their survey of 119 health sciences librarians on the topic of library educational programs in their medical libraries. They include a review of the literature, which reveals the long-standing challenges faced by health sciences libraries and librarians and serves as background for the survey, which consisted of seventeen questions delivered via e-mail to a select number of library listservs. The survey was made available for four weeks from February 1 through February 28, 2014. Among other results, they were able to conclude that health sciences libraries are still struggling to provide dynamic and robust training sessions as well as increase participation in their educational programs.

In chapter 5, Susan David deMaine, Catherine A. Lemmer, Benjamin J. Keele, and Hannah Alcasid provide a checklist and details for implementing digital badge programs for information literacy skills. Badges in this context represent a form of digital credentialing and offer a contrast to the approaches of gamification, which is treated in chapters 9 and 10. An advantage of badges in this form is that, thanks to projects such as Mozilla's Open Badge Initiative, badges can easily be designed and issued by anyone. The authors weigh concerns about badges competing with traditional educational institutions as a form of credentialing or as a counter to the monopoly formed by accredited schools. They refer to the many benefits of badges and weigh them against pitfalls and unknowns, including authentication, validation, and verification.

In chapter 6, Helen Fallon and Anne O'Brien discuss combining the efforts of special collections and media productions to build an audio archive. They provide an excellent example of how libraries can develop and extend the understanding of Special Collections, in this case a collection of death-row letters. Their work was a collaboration that exploited the talents of many individuals and resulted in increased visibility of the library's Special Collections unit, enriching the experiences of patrons and also encouraging the funding of such efforts—a great example of adding value.

Chapter 7 provides a unique library model enabling academic libraries to serve high school students, motivated by local economic and budget challenges. The authors, Christina Miller and John A. Drobnicki, provide the context and the narrative for incorporating library services to the students and staff of Queens High School for the Sciences at York College. The high school does not have its own library and shares the York College Library with local borrowing privileges at York Library and full access to the Library's online resources, computers, and study rooms.

In chapter 8, Michelle Currier and Michael Magilligan explore how librarians at SUNY Canton, a small technical college in the New York State public higher education system, have transformed their traditional academic library in ways designed to increase student awareness of the library and its services. After building renovations led to changes in the culture and climate on campus, the library felt pressure to revise its mission, vision, and purpose. A key ingredient to the library's transformation was the iPad and its potential for providing alternatives to traditional, high-priced print textbooks. Through the use of iPads, SUNY Canton has changed the way librarians offer services and resources and have created a model that other libraries may find intriguing. Not surprisingly, Canton librarians have found that one of the strongest opportunities for incorporating iPad technology into the academic framework is in the field of digital humanities.

Chapters 9 and 10 describe library applications of gamification, defined by the online Oxford dictionary as "the application of typical elements of game playing (e.g., point scoring, competition with others, rules of play) to other areas of activity, typically as an online marketing technique to encourage engagement with a product or service." See, http://www.oxforddictionaries.com/us/definition/american_english/gamification.

In chapter 9, Cyndi Harbeson and Scott Rice explore how gamification and badges have assisted their library with staff development and training. While establishing a program of continuous technology training, the library included a system of earning badges that was designed to encourage ongoing participation. The project involved creating a number of digital badges, a means of displaying those badges, requirements for earning each badge, and a team of badge experts to monitor the process. By gamifying the technology training program, the authors hoped to increase the levels of motivation and engagement of the staff.

In chapter 10, Diana Parlic, Adam Sofronijevic, and Mladen Cudanov offer an excellent introduction to the concept of gamifying. After tracing the origins of the term to 2002, they provide an overview of its motivation, processes, and outcomes. Their library application is to gamify uses of

DART-Europe, a portal for theses and dissertations from universities in twenty-seven European countries, in order to make it a more engaged and useful resource. Game players are defined to be: authors in the process of writing a master's thesis or doctoral dissertation; authors who have defended their thesis or dissertation; professors; and finally universities as a specific user group. The challenge is to combine these various players in the game of creating, modifying, and using the resources of DART-Europe.

In chapter 11, Alexander Watkins and Rebecca Kuglitsch document how they designed a new science commons at the University of Colorado Boulder, through student-librarian collaborations and partnerships. In this project, the library particularly hoped to harness the synergy between science, technology, engineering, and mathematics, on the one hand, and the arts and humanities, on the other. Their solution was to work with a service learning project in a well-established technical writing course at the university. The approach used in the course was to form design teams from students to help local institutions solve problems. The authors persuasively suggest that other libraries with a need for redesigning their spaces might seek out similar collaborations as those described here. Such projects have much to gain from student participation in the planning, but they also can be assured that students will gain much from the experience as well. Moreover, the authors argue that service learning programs are a mutually beneficial model for librarian-student collaboration in general. The concept of service-learning is already prominent on our campuses, and as it continues to gain leverage, opportunities for library participation in student projects will also grow in importance.

In chapter 12, Rachel Wexelbaum and Plamen Miltenoff explore the world of Web 2.0 technologies and social media, from hashtag to infographics, Facebook, Twitter, YouTube, Slideshare, blogs, Pinterest, on and on. Academic librarians have begun to integrate Web 2.0 and social media into their library instruction, teaching students how to use and evaluate social media for research and real-world problem solving. We are told that "information literacy" covers both media and digital literacy, as well as transliteracy and metaliteracy. The authors suggest that digital-native librarians—those that have been born into the digital age—are very likely to follow blogs and news through Facebook and Twitter, "and to have so many feeds that they will organize them using HootSuite or TweetDeck." Toto, I've a feeling we're not in Kansas anymore.

Finally, in chapter 13, Anthony Holderied and Michael C. Alewine discuss active learning technologies to increase student engagement and learning in library instruction sessions. They define active learning as "instructional activities involving students in doing things and thinking about what they are doing." The three technologies discussed in the article are: interactive whiteboards, clickers, and wireless slates, technologies that we will be hearing a great deal from in the months and years ahead.

It is hoped that this volume, and the series in general, will be a valuable and exciting addition to the discussions and planning surrounding the future directions, services, and careers in the twenty-first-century academic library.

Chapter One

Open Access for Student Success

Teri Oaks Gallaway and James B. Hobbs

INTRODUCTION

The academic library profession has long been concerned with issues of retention and student success. In this chapter a new role for the library as open access textbook curator is described as one potential way to alleviate withdrawal trigger events. A review of the literature of retention triggers, the open access environment, and open access textbooks is provided. A program at Loyola University New Orleans to increase use of commercial textbook alternatives such as open access textbooks is described, including barriers to a successful implementation, new philosophies of collection development, and a dramatic increase in use of physical reserves. Finally, a need for authentic assessment strategies is discussed as a topic of further research.

Loyola University New Orleans is not unlike many private liberal arts institutions in its current attempt to reconcile a challenging employment market, an attack on the value of a liberal arts education, scrutiny of student loan debt, increased emphasis on assessment and productivity, all amid dwindling populations of traditional college students. Not surprisingly, given this climate, Loyola suffered a drop in enrollment, as have many similar institutions in the last several enrollment cycles (Sayre, 2014). As a result, the university undertook a comprehensive self-study of student satisfaction and the higher education marketplace through an ad hoc Student Success Workgroup comprised of faculty, staff, and students from all areas of the university, including the library. This group was charged with identifying problems and solutions to retention issues during a one-semester intensive process.

STUDENT RETENTION AND THE LIBRARY

The library's involvement in university retention efforts is well documented. Two camps of retention rhetoric are revealed throughout the general higher education literature, those that look at actions of the institution and how the institution acclimates students, and another field of literature that looks at the student preparedness and behavior and how it relates to an individual student's likelihood for success. Additionally, several categories of inquiry surface in the library-specific literature including the impact of library materials acquisition, library student employment, information literacy, circulation statistics, use of the library building, and student satisfaction with library services. These studies primarily look for correlations between student behaviors, utilization of resources or services, and the student's likelihood to persist. A less-researched area of emphasis is trigger events that lead to student withdrawal. This idea that isolated events can have a high impact on a student's ultimate decision to transfer or withdraw is largely unresearched in library literature. Library-centric trigger events are identified and discussed here.

In one of the seminal works on retention in higher education, Tinto (1993) examines the impact that institutions have on student retention, how the atmosphere of the campus and services play a part in student departures, and what universities can do to retain their students. "Recurring and widespread dissatisfaction with one or more segments of student life may highlight significant problems in institutional functioning," he offers. "Assessment must, in this sense, be grounded in the common experience of students as they pass through the institution" (p. 7), and "on the informal dimensions of student interactions with other persons in the academic and social communities of the college" (p. 192). The mode of inquiry places the burden with the institution to examine their practices and policies to identify where they have made improvements to retain students; however, Zepke and Leach (2005) report that "This results in an assimilation process, fitting the student to the institution" (p. 47). They warn that the institution should embrace ways to foster student growth with respect for their existing social networks and cultures, rather than identify methods to indoctrinate students into the ways of the university.

In Pierard and Graves (2007), three strategies for libraries to impact retention are described. First, the library needs to be at the table and have representation or a voice in the institutional process of improving retention. Next, the library needs to use information literacy as a platform for engaging students. And finally, libraries should reexamine their physical spaces and how they meet the needs for social and collaborative learning (p. 161). Consistent with this recommendation, the literature of libraries and retention is largely focused on the role of information literacy. Sanabria (2013) describes how

librarians participated in the development of an information literacy component for first-year students as a part of a broader program to improve retention.

Another dominant area of inquiry is the impact of library materials acquisition on student retention and graduation. Hamrick, Schuh, and Shelley
(2004) identified library expenditures as one predictor of student graduation
rates, and encourages using these predictors in resource allocation decisions.
Mezick (2007) also identified correlation between library expenditures and
retention rates using multiyear, multi-institution data from ACRL and
IPEDS.

The use of library materials or library facilities represents another facet in
the research on retention. In an early study in this area, Kramer and Kramer
(1968) showed a correlation between library borrowing and persistence.
More recently, Haddow and Joseph (2010) conducted an analysis of one
entering class (4,661 students) to show that use of the library by new students
within the first weeks of school is a retention predictor. Soria, Fransen, and
Nackerud (2013) also examined library usage patterns by first-year undergraduate students, and found correlation between use of the library building
and services with GPA and fall to spring retention.

As Rushing and Poole (2002) describe, student employment in the library
also may have an impact on retention and graduation. In a longitudinal study
of the graduation rates of library work-study employees, they found positive
graduation and retention indicators. They describe the success of the student
worker program and improving student employment to create a better match
of student/employer expectations. Also important to the article is a discussion of how proximity to library staff and faculty allows development of
mentoring relationships that have a positive impact on student success.

Additionally, student satisfaction with library services and customer service is examined as a retention indicator. Bell (2008) offers ideas for improving retention, including engaging parents and establishing an understanding
of the importance of librarian/student interaction. He recommends that libraries "provide data that links student persistence and satisfaction to the library's services, resources and people—not just collections" and "demonstrate how the library can contribute to a campus-wide effort that uses perks
and incentives to keep students till graduation" (p. 2). In Grallo, Chalmers,
and Baker (2012) a discussion of the nontraditional roles that the library is
filling is presented. Questions unrelated to reference and circulation that
were being asked at the information commons were documented and then
used to develop an FAQ web page for first-year seminar courses. They also
documented a greater need for software support in the library.

Finally, a lesser-explored area of retention literature is the notion of withdrawal trigger events. Hagel, Horn, Owen, and Currie (2012) posit that "Potentially, students who are already more at risk of withdrawing due to their

financial or family circumstances may be triggered to actually withdraw if they believe that the technologies they need to use increase their costs of studying" (p. 220). Furthermore, "for students who are already struggling, it may take little to trigger a withdrawal decision: the failure to receive a requested book in a timely fashion for an off-campus student; difficulties in navigating databases or locating full text articles critical for an assignment; or the receipt of a notification about significant outstanding fines for overdue resources or borrowing encumbrances" (p. 220). Other library-centric triggers could include textbooks or library reserves not being available, computer and printer problems, unavailability of quiet study locations, poor customer service interactions, and confusing library systems. Thus, this chapter explores the notion that the inability to acquire course materials such as textbooks is a withdrawal trigger that libraries can influence through revisions of collection development and reserves policies in addition to leveraging the availability of open access textbook offerings.

THE STATE OF OPEN ACCESS TEXTBOOKS

Textbooks and other costs present a considerable barrier to postsecondary education. During the 2012–2013 academic year, annual student expenditures for books and supplies averaged $1,250 at U.S. public and private schools (National Center for Educational Statistics). One survey found that many students buy used texts, borrow texts, or do without them, at the cost of poor grades or dropped courses (Senack, 2014, pp. 4–5). Perez-Hernandez (2014) found that free electronic and inexpensive print textbooks are one way to reduce school and student costs and help in student success, achievement, recruitment, and retention. Open textbooks (OTs) are rapidly gaining support among students and schools to reduce these costs. Richard Baraniuk, director of the Connexions open textbook repository at Rice University, has said, "If we can capture just 10 percent of the market . . . an estimated 1 million college students in the United States could save $90 million over the next five years" ("Is the End Near for Textbooks?," 2012, p. 72).

The impact of OTs is unclear at this time. There are no definitive numbers on OTs currently available, faculty and students who are using them, or on satisfaction or impact on grades. One study at Virginia State University did find that open textbooks were correlated with higher grades for students in a business course (Feldstein et al., 2012, p. 1).

There are many barriers to achieving the goal of widespread use of OTs. Faculty want "a diversity of choices when they choose a textbook" (Harley, Lawrence, Krzys Acord, & Dixson, 2010, p. 1). The authors also state "there simply are not enough [OTs] currently available in enough disciplines to satisfy the multitude of faculty and student needs in lower and upper division courses; a much wider array of high-quality, easy-to-use, and reliable open textbooks will have to be produced for more widespread faculty adoption . . . open textbooks will likely be only one of many players in the curricular materials market" (p. 2).

In the absence of vetting standards for OTs and the diversity of repositories, faculty may have difficulty locating suitable texts, as there is no central clearinghouse and in most cases no formal university support for selecting OTs. There is no agreement on how to best motivate teachers to write, review, and adopt OTs, though grants, release time, and consideration toward promotion and tenure may serve as motivators.

The Federal Higher Education Opportunity Act (HEOA) of 2008 requires that publishers disclose their prices to faculty when promoting their texts with a list of substantial changes from the last edition, and unbundle CD and online materials from print texts, as well as asks colleges to give students a list of required texts during registration so they can look for the best prices (Student PIRG, 2010); however, there are no enforcement provisions in the law. Creative Commons maintains a listing of current and proposed open education resource legislation and policies from around the world at http://wiki.creativecommons.org/OER_Policy_Registry. Many states have passed laws requiring or encouraging open textbooks. California, Florida, and Washington have taken the boldest steps, each setting up their own OT repositories, with Oregon soon joining them (Garber, 2012; Morris-Babb and Henderson, 2012; Overland, 2011; Chant, 2014). Open textbooks must be adopted by faculty if they are to be successful. Washington State's community colleges had only 75 of 2,722 course sections taught in fall 2013 that used open texts (Biemiller, 2014).

Publishers are responding with lower-cost electronic versions of textbooks. Student acceptance is fairly high, though a 2012 survey found students considered electronic textbooks "clumsy" compared to print (Chen, 2013). Another approach is open textbooks with a low print price (Hilton and Wiley, 2010), such as those from Flat World Knowledge. Open textbooks have been written in the humanities, social sciences, and natural sciences. Many have been collected at websites, such as Rice University's Connexions (http://cnx.org/) and the Community College Consortium for Open Educational Resources (CCCOER) (http://oerconsortium.org/).

Primary hurdles to widespread use of OTs are: 1) sufficient open textbooks for faculty to adopt, 2) faculty selection of open textbooks, and 3) students finding them easy to use. Students will need little encouragement to accept free texts, though they do want sophisticated features in online OTs. Faculty need encouragement to write and to select and teach from OTs: time, money, and credit for promotion and tenure. During this transitional time, electronic OT formats and features are still developing, and there is not a consensus on best practices for OTs. Nor are there sustainable and scalable adoption, creation, and publishing models. It remains to be seen if OTs make profits, and whether traditional print textbook publishers will enter the OT arena more robustly. In some ways the discussion of the viability of OTs echoes the concern with the adoption of MOOCs.

A STUDENT SUCCESS INITIATIVE

At Loyola University New Orleans, a past retention effort by the university in 1998 indicated that multiple academic support services should be located in the library through the development of the Academic (ACE) Center (Rushing & Poole, 2002); the plan never materialized after necessary budget reductions due to Hurricane Katrina. Loyola did develop a learning commons model in 2006, consistent with a large body of literature recommending the library position itself as an academic support hub (Pierard & Graves, 2007), but the services in this have been limited to reference, circulation, printing, and technology troubleshooting, with intermittent tutoring services being provided by the Writing Across the Curriculum (WAC) lab.

Seeking to find meaningful ways to keep students once enrolled, a new provost engaged a new university-wide task force to identify student success initiatives. Eight groups were created to examine current policies and available data. Workgroups included members from diverse areas of the university, not just Academic and Student Affairs personnel. The workgroups focused on:

- Recruitment, Admissions, Financial Aid Packaging, and Marketing to Prospective Students
- Academic Advising
- Academic and Career Support Services
- Pricing Sensitivity Study and Pricing Strategy
- Course Scheduling, Rotation, Frequency of Offerings, and Coordination of Assigning Times for Course Offerings
- Campus Service Areas
- Co-Curricular Programs and Activities, Campus Life, Campus Traditions, and Student Engagement
- Instructional Effectiveness

One initiative of the Academic and Career Support Services workgroup, which was led by the library, was an effort to promote a reduction in student textbook expenses through promotion of open access textbooks. This initiative was largely driven by anecdotal information and shared experiences of frustrated students looking for textbooks at the library's Learning Commons desk. During these interactions, students revealed their frustrations with the traditional textbook model, including their inability to pay for expensive texts, bookstore delays, and waiting to receive books ordered through a discount provider (Amazon.com, for example). This was identified as a potential withdrawal trigger, whereas students who could not acquire the materials needed to succeed in a course would fall further and further behind. Eventually students would have great difficulty catching up if they did acquire or borrow a copy of the required reading materials. Leveraging the library's liaison program, visits were made to departments to speak with faculty about rising textbook costs and solutions, including use of physical and electronic reserves and open access textbooks.

LEVERAGING THE LIBRARIAN LIAISON PROGRAM

The success of the open access textbook initiative rested largely with the librarian liaison program and the relationships that had already been established in departments and colleges. All librarians in the University Library are liaisons to one or more academic departments. The pairing is based on librarians' subject affinities, education, and experience. Each librarian liaison collaborates with their counterpart, the departmental liaison, an instructor in the department, and with other faculty, student majors, and staff. Librarian liaisons engage with members of their department directly or through the departmental liaison in a variety of activities. There is a calendar of suggested activities depending on the flow of work in the school year. Liaison duties include:

1. Communicate and perform outreach.
2. Communicate relevant library news in a timely manner.
3. Promote library resources and services.
4. Form relationships with faculty, students, and staff.
5. Listen and respond to concerns and requests.
6. Participate in relevant student and faculty meetings and events.
7. Welcome new faculty by e-mail and in person.
8. Encourage students to make appointments with librarians regarding their research, follow up with students about their projects after class, and submit collection development requests for purchasing materials to support students' papers and assignments.
9. Provide instruction.
10. Provide research and technology assistance and instruction in the Learning Commons, through appointments and consultations, and in courses.
11. Support online and hybrid courses, including linking library resources and services.

12. Collaborate on new courses.
13. Contribute to curriculum revisions, including the scaffolding of information literacy learning goals.
14. Develop opportunities to participate in intensive instruction commitments.
15. Create and maintain learning objects.
16. Create Research Guides (LibGuides) for liaison areas.
17. Create other specialized learning objects (course guides, tutorials, etc.) as needed.
18. Develop collections.
19. Collect resources (requested and not requested) based on the curriculum and need.
20. Facilitate and track orders for reserves.
21. Participate in professional development.
22. Become familiar with the discipline through learning the language and research tools.
23. Learn the curriculum.
24. Develop information literacy and pedagogical expertise and skills.
25. Develop the ability to communicate information literacy and learning concepts to faculty.
26. Develop and assess activities.
27. Prioritize liaison responsibilities.
28. Develop and assess resources and services.
29. Contribute to program reviews.
30. Use knowledge for fundraising and stewardship.

To facilitate relationship building, there is one meeting each year with all department and librarian liaisons to go over changes in library collections, practices, and policies, and for departmental liaisons to communicate with one another and the library. This is in addition to any independent activities or meetings the librarian liaisons have with their respective departments and programs. Activities continue to evolve as relationships with students, faculty, and staff change with new and developing needs. In creating a community of practice, librarian liaisons meet periodically to share activities and practices.

PRESENTATIONS AT COLLEGES AND DEPARTMENTS

Leading the implementation of the Student Success Forum action plans was the vice-provost for Faculty Affairs. The vice-provost offered support for this initiative by e-mailing the deans to request that they reach out to their department chairs and prioritize a visit by librarian liaisons to upcoming department meetings to discuss the textbook initiative. The librarian workgroup chair then followed up with an e-mail to each of the department chairs to schedule a meeting.

The meetings took place primarily over the course of two months, October and November of 2013. At each meeting the workgroup chair and the departmental liaison were scheduled to speak to the group for fifteen minutes including time for follow-up questions. A one-page color reproduction of an article on open access textbook adoption at California Universities (Domonell, 2012) was provided as a reference and reminder. The discussion with faculty included a real example of a current freshman student's schedule, complete with the costs of the textbooks ($750+), anecdotal information about student requests for textbooks at the library desk, and statistics on the number of current students receiving PELL grants (the financially neediest of students). Faculty were then given an overview of library services that could alleviate the pressure for students to have their textbooks during the first weeks of class, in particular information about scanning a small percentage of a book for e-reserves, selecting articles from the databases to use as course readings, and bringing surplus or donated copies of course textbooks over to the library to place on physical reserve. The librarians also highlighted how utilizing the e-reserves services would position them to be able to continue teaching in the event of a hurricane evacuation at the start of the fall semester, a continuing concern for universities in New Orleans and the surrounding area. In addition to library services, campus services for students with financial hardships, temporary or long term, were also reviewed. These included the availability of short-term bookstore charges and the limited availability of nonrepayable emergency funds from campus units.

In the last portion of the presentation, information about the types of open access textbooks that were available as well as a link to a LibGuide with that information was provided (see http://researchguides.loyno.edu/content.php?pid=524474). Liaisons also explicitly offered their services to review and narrow the field of textbooks that faculty might consider. The remainder of the visit was an opportunity for questions and answers during which faculty offered the librarians and their departmental colleagues ideas on how they might address rising textbook costs. These included allowing students to use older editions of textbooks if they were still available. Problems cited for this solution were the bookstore's policy of not ordering older editions, and difficulties with inconsistencies in numbering of figures, discussion questions, and paginations. One professor described his process of having the first student that requested to use an older edition create a textbook crosswalk for the two editions that could then be posted in the learning management system. There was confusion among many faculty about the difference between library-owned e-book collections, e-book versions of commercial textbooks, and open access textbooks. Throughout the meeting a common concern was the time required to review and select a replacement textbook, and the potential loss of convenient instructor features in commercial textbooks like test banks and discussion questions. Another concerned faculty member cited loss in personal revenues from the textbook that he had authored as a dissuading factor. Faculty were, however, very interested in taking advantage of the library's existing e-reserve and physical reserves services. Several related questions about copyright restrictions were raised in that regard.

A NEW PHILOSOPHY OF COLLECTION DEVELOPMENT

Through these meetings, another common question was why the library would not purchase textbooks and place them on physical reserve. Prior to the campus open access textbook initiative, the library was actively encouraging faculty to not place excess materials on loan due to the limited space for these materials. Several years prior, a policy of allowing permanent reserves was halted to curb the buildup of unused reserved materials. Additionally, the library had a long-standing collection development policy of not purchasing textbooks or borrowing them through interlibrary loan.

Reflecting as a group on how the library could improve student success, the librarian liaisons came to consensus that not only should they actively reach out to faculty to obtain surplus copies of textbooks and to provide scanning services, but that group should identify collection development funds to purchase textbooks on a limited and trial basis. Review considerations for the program included:

- Number of requests by students
- Ability of instructor to provide a copy or older edition of the textbook
- Number of students impacted by purchase
- Expected ability to reuse the same text in subsequent semesters
- Cost

DISCUSSION OF NEEDS FOR ASSESSMENT AND FURTHER INVESTIGATION

While the program at Loyola University New Orleans is in its infancy and limited documentation of success is available, strategies for measuring the impact of the program are being developed. Initial results indicate that the outreach component of the departmental meetings may have had an impact on the utilization of the library reserves program. As shown in table 1.1, a significant rise in utilization in reserves services by both faculty and students is indicated. Fall 2012 and Spring 2013 are referenced as a baseline for the reserves service. Beginning with the departmental presentations, which took place in the Fall 2013 semester, an increase of 30.85 percent was seen in the number of faculty participating in the program and a 58.76 percent increase in student checkouts. Additionally, the number of reserves items increased from 401 in Fall 2012 to 466 in Fall 2013. In the following semester (Spring 2014), further increases in program utilization were documented. Faculty participation was down slightly from Fall 2013 but overall still over 15 percent higher than the prior spring semester. The number of items on reserves reached a new high of 511, or a 29.04 percent increase from the prior spring. Student checkouts of reserves also slowed somewhat from the Fall 2013 semester but were still 35.49 percent higher than the previous spring.

Additional qualitative techniques that are being planned for the program assessment include surveying faculty to see if they are familiar with open access textbooks based on departmental presentations, if they have looked at those already available, if they have selected OTs, if they have used OTs in classes, if they have customized an open textbook, and if they had a positive experience with using an open textbook. Additionally, an online survey is planned for distribution to faculty and students in classes identified to have used an open textbook. The survey will measure the number of faculty who have chosen to adopt open textbooks, the number of classes in which they are used, and the number of students who used open textbooks. It will also be used to measure satisfaction and determine roadblocks to adoption and use. Librarians will include all faculty, those who heard the presentation and those who did not, both full-time and part-time. Participation by those who teach nontraditional students is also welcome. The timing of the survey is important, as it should give participants enough time to have used the text and reflected on its use. Another potentially elucidating approach to assessment of the textbook program is a post-survey follow-up focus group with students and faculty that experienced OTs.

Table 1.1.   Faculty and Student Reserve Service Use

	Fall 2012	Spring 2013	Fall 2013	Spring 2014	Fall to Fall Increase	Spring to Spring Increase
Faculty with Reserves	94	103	123	119	30.85%	15.53%
Items on Reserve	401	396	466	511	16.2%	29.04%
Reserves Checkouts	1,986	2,164	3,153	2,932	58.76%	35.49%

On an ongoing basis, it is anticipated that the survey could be carried out each semester or sent out at the conclusion of the academic year. While the summer is an excellent time to analyze survey results, it may be too late to make significant outreach changes for faculty members in time to influence the following academic year's textbook choices. As acknowledged, the librarian liaison program is an important factor for the success or failure of the program. Working with the liaison group to identify ongoing needs for training and resources is also crucial to instilling momentum in the program. A survey or brainstorming session among library liaisons may also elicit what challenges liaisons face in promoting OTs to the university community and also launch a discussion of potential solutions.

Finally, through conversations with departments and colleges, the library has identified a need for a new role in the negotiation of bookstore contracts and better communication with the bookstore in general. Faculty frustration with the bookstore ordering processes and restrictions could potentially be mitigated by librarian interventions. Working with the bookstore's textbook adoption calendar to determine when best to promote OTs is also a critical component to success. Furthermore, establishing a better partnership with the bookstore could lead to a better ability to conduct quantitative analysis of reductions or increases in textbook expenses. At present, the ability to harvest data on discrete course, discipline, and student expenses is limited to time-intensive manual data collection procedures.

CONCLUSION

Discussions of library impact on student retention include many facets such as strength of collections and instruction programs. Additionally, negative library or bookstore interactions can be viewed as student withdrawal triggers. One such withdrawal trigger event is the inability of students to acquire course textbooks and reading materials. In order to reduce such negative interactions, libraries can expand their services to promote the use of open source textbooks or existing library services like physical and e-reserves. While open source adoptions require a lengthy review process and liaison encouragement, liaisons can support adoptions by creating open source resource guides for faculty. Additionally, promoting e-reserves, physical reserves, and revising collection development policies are promising alternatives.

REFERENCES

American Student Assistance. (2014). "Student Loan Debt Statistics." *American Student Assistance*. http://www.asa.org/policy/resources/stats/.

Angell, Katelyn. (2013). "Open Source Assessment of Academic Library Patron Satisfaction." *Reference Services Review* 41, no. 4: 593–604.

Azevedo, Alisha. (2013). "Pay Nothing? Easier Said Than Done." *Chronicle of Higher Education* 59, no. 21: A18–A19.

Bell, Steven. (2008). "Keeping Them Enrolled: How Academic Libraries Contribute to Student Retention." *Library Issues: Briefings for Faculty and Administrators* 29, no. 1: 1–4.

Biemiller, Lawrence. (2014). "Open Course Library Sees Little Use in Washington's Community Colleges." *Chronicle of Higher Education*, January 31. http://chronicle.com/blogs/wiredcampus/open-course-library-sees-little-use-in-washingtons-community-colleges/50017.

Butcher, Neil. (2011). "A Basic Guide to Open Educational Resources (OER)." Vancouver, BC; Paris, France: *Commonwealth of Learning and UNESCO*. http://unesdoc.unesco.org/images/0021/002158/215804e.pdf.

Chant, Ian. (2014). "Academic: OSU Developing OA E-Textbooks." *Library Journal* 139, no. 9: 14.

Chen, Angela. (2013). "Students Find E-Textbooks 'Clumsy' and Don't Use Their Interactive Features." *Chronicle of Higher Education*, August 22. http://chronicle.com/blogs/wiredcampus/students-find-e-textbooks-clumsy-and-dont-use-their-interactive-features/39082.

Domonell, Kristen. (2012). "Free Textbooks for California: If Funded, Open-Source Digital Textbooks Coming to Public Higher Ed. (BEHIND the NEWS)." *University Business* 15, no. 10: 14.

Feldstein, Andrew, et al. (2012). "Open Textbooks and Increased Student Access and Outcomes." *European Journal of Open, Distance and E-Learning* 2. http://www.eurodl.org/?p=current&article=533.

Garber, Megan. (2012). "California Takes a Big Step Forward: Free, Digital, Open-Source Textbooks." *The Atlantic* (September 30). http://www.theatlantic.com/technology/archive/2012/09/california-takes-a-big-step-forward-free-digital-open-source-textbooks/263047/.

Grallo, Jacqui D., Mardi Chalmers, and Pamela G. Baker. (2012). "How Do I Get a Campus ID? The Other Role of the Academic Library in Student Retention and Success." *The Reference Librarian* 53, no. 2: 182–93.

Haddow, Gaby, and Jayanthi Joseph. (2010). "Loans, Logins, and Lasting the Course: Academic Library Use and Student Retention." *Australian Academic & Research Libraries* 41, no. 4: 233–44.

Hagel, Pauline, Anne Horn, Sue Owen, and Michael Currie. (2012). "How Can We Help? The Contribution of University Libraries to Student Retention." *Australian Academic & Research Libraries* 43, no. 3: 214–30.

Hamrick, Florence A., John H. Schuh, and Mack C. Shelley. (2004). "Predicting Higher Education Graduation Rates from Institutional Characteristics and Resource Allocation." *Education Policy Analysis Archives* 12, no. 19.

Harley, Diane, Shannon Lawrence, Sophia Krzys Acord, and Jason Dixson. (2010). "Affordable and Open Textbooks: An Exploratory Study of Faculty Attitudes." *Center for Studies in Higher Education.* http://escholarship.org/uc/item/1t8244nb.

Hilton, John Levi, and David A. Wiley. (2010). "A Sustainable Future for Open Textbooks? The Flat World Knowledge Story." *First Monday* 15, no. 8 (August 2). http://firstmonday.org/ojs/index.php/fm/article/view/2800/2578.

"Is the End Near for Textbooks?" (2014). BizEd 11.3 (2012): 72–73. Web. June 4. http://www.bizedmagazine.com/features/technology/end-for-textbooks.html.

Kramer, Lloyd A., and Martha B. Kramer. (1968). "The College Library and the Drop-out." *College and Research Libraries* 29, no. 4: 310–12.

"LibQUAL+ ®." (2014). *Association of Research Libraries.* Accessed May 21. http://www.libqual.org/about.

Mezick, Elizabeth. (2007). "Return on Investment: Libraries and Student Retention." *The Journal of Academic Librarianship* 33, no. 5: 561–66.

Morris-Babb, Meredith, and Susie Henderson. (2012). "An Experiment in Open-Access Textbook Publishing: Changing the World One Textbook at a Time." *Journal of Scholarly Publishing* 42, no. 3: 148–55.

Okamoto, Karen. (2013). "Making Higher Education More Affordable, One Course Reading at a Time: Academic Libraries as Key Advocates for Open Access Textbooks and Educational Resources." *Public Services Quarterly* 9, no. 4: 267–83.

"Open Source Software for Online Surveys." (2012). *Leibniz Institute for the Social Sciences.* (September 26). http://www.gesis.org/en/services/study-planning/online-surveys/a-guide-to-survey-software/open-source-software.

Overland, Martha Ann. (2011). "State of Washington to Offer Online Materials as Texts." *Chronicle of Higher Education* (January 9). http://chronicle.com/article/State-of-Washington-to-Offer/125887/.

Perez-Hernandez, Dayna. (2014). "Open Textbooks Could Help Students Financially and Academically." *Chronicle of Higher Education* (January 28). http://chronicle.com/blogs/wired-campus/open-textbooks-could-help-students-financially-and-academically-researchers-say/49839.

Pierard, Cindy, and Kathryn Graves. (2007). "Research on Student Retention and Implications for Library Involvement," in *The Role of the Library in the First College Year*, edited by Larry Hardesty (Columbia: University of South Carolina, National Resource Center for the First-Year Experience and Students in Transition).

Rushing, Darla, and Deborah Poole. (2002). "The Role of the Library in Student Retention," in *Making the Grade: Academic Libraries and Student Success*, edited by Maurie Caitlin Kelly and Andrea Kross (Chicago: Association of College and Research Libraries), 91–101.

Sanabria, Jesus E. (2013). "The Library as an Academic Partner in Student Retention and Graduation: The Library's Collaboration with the Freshman Year Seminar Initiative at the Bronx Community College." *Collaborative Librarianship* 5, no. 2: 94–100.

Sayre, Katherine. (2014). "Loyola University Lays Off 18 Employees in Face of Budget Deficit." *Times Picayune.* February 7. http://www.nola.com/business/index.ssf/2014/02/loyola_university_to_layoff_em.html#incart_river_default.

Senack, Ethan, and the Student PIRGs. (2014). "Fixing the Broken Textbook Market: How Students Respond to High Textbook Costs and Demand Alternatives." *Center for Public Interest Research.* (January). http://www.uspirg.org/reports/usp/fixing-broken-textbook-market.

"Seven Things You Should Know about Open Textbook Publishing." (2011). *Educause.* March 8. http://net.educause.edu/ir/library/pdf/eli7070.pdf.

Soria, Krista M., Jan Fransen, and Shane Nackerud. (2013). "Library Use and Undergraduate Student Outcomes: New Evidence for Students' Retention and Academic Success." *portal: Libraries and the Academy* 13, no. 2: 147–64.

Student PIRGs. (2012). "Federal Textbook Price Disclosure Law." March 16. http://www.studentpirgs.org/resources/textbook-price-disclosure-law.

Student PIRGs. (2010). "New Laws, Free Books and Textbook Rentals Could Help Curb Rising Costs This Fall." Student PIRGs, August 26. http://studentpirgs.org/news/new-laws-free-books-and-textbook-rentals-could-help-curb-rising-costs-fall.

Tinto, Vincent. (1993). *Leaving College: Rethinking the Causes and Cures of Student Attrition.* 2nd ed. Chicago: University of Chicago Press.

"Trends in College Pricing 2013." (2013). *CollegeBoard.* http://trends.collegeboard.org/sites/default/files/college-pricing-2013-full-report-140108.pdf.

Zepke, Nick, and Linda Leach. (2005). "Integration and Adaptation: Approaches to the Student Retention and Achievement Puzzle." *Active Learning in Higher Education* 6, no. 1: 46–59.

Chapter Two

The Library-Bookstore Revisited

James Lund

The fact that the library and bookstore deal with very similar processes tends to strengthen the feasibility of developing a system which uses common staff, space, and methods. Close collaboration between library and bookstore (or complete merger of the two) could do much to solve the immediate problems faced by many small colleges with small library collections and limited budgets.
—Susan Severtson and George Banks, "Toward the Library-Bookstore" (1971)

It is not surprising that experimentation with alternative models of library service would arise in the decade of counterculture and revolution—the Sixties. Severtson and Banks, at the time they published their proposal, were librarians at Franconia College—an experimental college situated in an old resort hotel in rural New Hampshire. Converging with this electric era of experimentation, paperback publishing had reached its zenith, providing mass availability and affordability of books. As a consequence, administrators, librarians, and even publishers began offering different paradigms for library service. If, for instance, the goal of the library is "to make information available in its published form" (Severtson and Banks, 1971, p. 163), then why exclude the retail side of distribution?

Federal City College, formed by Congress in 1966, proposed their new library merge operations and collections with the bookstore, offering any unprocessed, uncataloged library books for sale. Purchasing hardbound books was discouraged, a decision deeply influenced by the low-cost paperback market (Blumenfeld and Jordan, 1968, pp. 36–38). The president of Random House, Robert Bernstein, after criticizing the negative impact libraries have on author and publisher revenue, suggested "creating bookstores in every public library and school in America" (*Library Journal*, 1966, pp.

15

2787–88). No waiting, wider distribution of published materials, and more sustainable and diversified revenue streams for author and publisher were offered as benefits of this new partnership by Mr. Bernstein. Continuing the culture of experimentation, Hampshire College at its founding in 1970 proposed the concept of the "experimenting and extended library" (Taylor, 1970, pp. 135–41). Their objective was to create a model bookstore of the future where management is assumed by the library, and its services complement and enhance those of the library. But this model relationship never came to pass. Instead, they chose the traditional path of contracting bookstore management with "outside concessions." Strikingly, in the report that begins by proclaiming "The whole context of the Hampshire Library Center is to alter the usual posture of the library and to make these two functions (library and bookstore) complement one another," it ends with the abandonment of the vision. This is the path on which every proposed library-bookstore merger, as far as the author can determine, has ended—without implementation. Why the vision without implementation? In Hampshire College's report, they identify several reasons for their decision to outsource instead of integrate library/bookstore service:

1. The difficulty of finding the right kind of bookstore manager is severe—one who knows student cultures, merchandising, accounting and business systems, and sources of supply.
2. A leased operation . . . can obtain better purchasing terms because of centralized buying.
3. The college did not wish to subsidize a store operation, beyond the overhead costs involved. It is doubtful that an internally managed store can begin to cover its own costs before six to ten years of operation, especially in as small an operation as Hampshire College (Taylor, 1970, p. 139).

The report is seminal in that these obstacles to operating a successful bookstore, or any business for that matter, are timeless. So the question remains: Is it feasible for library staff to run a bookstore?

WESTMINSTER SEMINARY CALIFORNIA BOOKSTORE

Westminster Seminary California is a small theological school in Escondido, California, with 150 students, 12 faculty, and a modest library collection of 80,000 volumes. Since moving to its present location in 1983, the seminary has employed a campus bookstore. The original bookstore was leased to a bookseller in San Diego. Inventory at the campus location, situated adjacent to the library, catered mostly to students but with enough inventory to attract the general public. The bookstore enjoyed a twenty-year run on campus before closing in 2003; subsequently, the same lease term was offered to another operator. His tenure lasted just two years. At this point, having lost two operators in three years, the seminary decided to take ownership of the bookstore and operate it under its 501(c)(3) status. Over the next ten years, the seminary's administration tried a number of models to create a sustainable business. But after ten years of significant deficits, the administration could no longer justify the annual subsidy.

Library-Bookstore

The author had already agreed to return to Westminster as theological librarian, a position he had held eight years prior, when he received a call from the president of the seminary. The president had an idea on how to make the bookstore profitable, and it involved the library. In talking about the library taking over management of the bookstore, the option of merging the two operations started making sense for the same practical reasons Severtson and Banks had envisioned forty-two years ago. Both operations acquire, process, account, and check out books. Both provide personal assistance for bookish patrons in need. Yet, the bookstore is a business; the library is not. This distinction is what seems to have stymied the numerous proposals for library/ bookstore merger, as Hampshire College's report illustrated. But for a small academic institution like Westminster Seminary, who still believed having a bookstore was important to its mission, this was an immediate problem that needed a solution. The reward outweighed the risk at this point. If it worked, the merger provided students with a convenient purchasing option for course materials, a unique service to the seminary community, and relief to the budget. If it didn't work, the campus returned to "normal" minus a bookstore. The author decided to take the challenge!

The Move

It was decided early in the planning process that for ease of sales, service, and security the bookstore needed to be moved into the library. Three possible locations emerged (see Figure 2.1):

1. Leave the bookstore in its current location. Create access to the bookstore by cutting a new entrance through the adjacent wall in the library and securing the former outside entrance. Customers shop without staff assistance but would purchase at the circulation desk.
2. Move the bookstore into the periodical room. Customers shop without staff assistance, yet the location is closer to the circulation desk.

3. Move the bookstore into the workroom. The library director and circu-
    lation staff have visible access. All customers would need to pass the
    circulation staff to enter and exit.

As the new bookstore manager, there was little question which option was
best: move the bookstore into the library workroom. First and most importantly, the library needed to create as many points of personal customer
contact as possible. Passion for this human-centric service philosophy came
while working retail grocery at an upscale vendor and was subsequently
incorporated into public library service (Lund, 2012, pp. 23–25). By being
located in the workroom, bookstore customers engage with two natural
points of contact with staff: outside the bookstore at the circulation desk, and
inside the bookstore at the library director's office. The two alternative locations were essentially self-service hubs with little or no natural points of
contact until the final transaction. Second, the workroom space was the right
size to create an inviting environment and provided adequate space for shelving. Third, it was available. The space was initially created to store new
materials while waiting for cataloging. Having streamlined cataloging, the
space was available, except for IT, which occupied a section of the room.

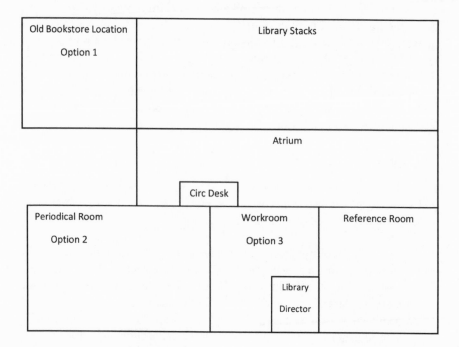

Figure 2.1.   Options for the New Bookstore.

Three office moves later, the workroom was vacant. Library staff executed the bookstore move mid-June 2013, and the store opened two weeks later. (See Figure 2.2.)

Making sales

Thankfully, the library had a couple summer months to practice making sales on a trickle of unsuspecting customers. The QuickBooks Point of Sale (POS) register (computer, receipt printer, scanner, cash drawer) assumed computing tasks at the circulation desk. With a web-based ILS, there was no need for locally installed ILS applications or Citrix. The QuickBooks POS interface is intuitive. After a week of sales, staff had a good grasp on how to execute standard transactions, look up inventory, troubleshoot, etc. Training new staff to make sales was a breeze. Credit cards are accepted and make for quick transactions that account for 97 percent of sales! Every morning staff reconcile the cash drawer and run the end-of-day report in QuickBooks. The end-of-day report provides a record of the previous day's transactions for the business department to reconcile.

Reducing costs

A walk-up sale is a simple transaction that can be processed by library circulation staff already stationed at the desk. An online sale, on the other hand, is labor-intensive. It is simply not profitable for a small local retailer to

Figure 2.2.   The New Bookstore.

compete with large warehouse online resellers. Online sales accounted for only 12 percent of annual sales, yet 35 percent of a bookstore staff's time is spent on processing these sales. The library's goal was to hold labor costs steady when absorbing bookstore tasks, so labor-intensive online sales were terminated, except for a simple online store promoting faculty titles.

Keeping labor costs to a minimum when confronted with such narrow profit margins was the key to profitability. Library circulation staff can absorb light bookstore duties (reader's advisory and sales transactions) into their job descriptions without additional compensation, which makes profitability possible. The only labor charged to the new bookstore was a managerial stipend for the library director. In total, the new bookstore was able to reduce personnel costs by 83 percent.

Additional cost savings came from rent-free space (the seminary did not charge the previous operators rent, but this practice is not the norm), eliminating food and drink items, and canceling a dedicated Internet connection. Credit card fees are an irritation, but research shows accepting credit cards significantly increases sales (Intuit, 2012).

Profit margins and inventory

Keeping costs in line is only one aspect of creating a profitable retail business. Purchasing desirable inventory that generates high profit margins is another essential component. The bookstore's customer base is and always has been predominantly students; yet, in prior years the bookstore tried to appeal more broadly, and the inventory reflected that philosophy. Although that inventory sold well, it just didn't generate the needed profits when aggressively priced at or below Amazon.com's prices. Amazon casts a shadow over every bookstore. Walk-up bookstore customers shop with their smart phones, and if the price is higher than what they find online, the sale is lost. It's that simple. In this retail environment, there is little loyalty toward independent booksellers. Price is king for customers, and booksellers must price at low-margin Amazon levels to make a sale. According to the Retail Owners Institute benchmarks, bookstores need a gross margin around 43 percent to be profitable (ROI, 2014). The National Association of College Stores reports the average gross margin of all bookstore sales is 29 percent (NACS, 2013). The seminary's bookstore is right in line with reported average gross margins of 25 to 30 percent. Generating profits at this rate positioned the previous seminary bookstore in a perpetual state of deficit. What action was taken to increase profitability?

In the first semester of managing the new bookstore, little attention was paid to margins. Sales were the focus. Fall purchasing centered on required course materials and little else. Most of the orders were placed with academic presses, who are not fond of giving generous discounts and free shipping.

Materials hitting the shelf had high per-unit costs and low prices—Amazon.com low prices. The gross margin for fall sales came in at 19 percent, and the shelves were still flush with unsold inventory. The library purchased too much at too high a price and generated too little in sales. Not a good start.

Thankfully, the seminary's curriculum is stable from year to year, so the excessive fall inventory can be held for sale until the following academic year. But, there is another way to manage excessive inventory: return it! This was a surprising revelation serendipitously discovered while talking to a publisher. As long as the item is still in print, most publishers will accept returns and credit the account or cut a check for the invoice price minus shipping. It is the shipping costs, however, that make this option less appealing. One-way shipping for fifty textbooks costs $50–$60. Absorbing that cost twice (first on delivery and then on return) increases unrecoverable expenditures quickly. The solution is to learn how to order the right amount and judiciously control inventory. This is not easy, and there is no formula to follow. One needs to study the purchasing behaviors of students, which in today's multi-option marketplace is tough to pattern. Adjusting baseline quantities (copies for 80 percent enrolled) in light of what students value (inexpensive essential titles) will help hone one's orders. When choosing to pursue the policy of matching Amazon.com pricing, it is inevitable that some academic press books will be sold at or just above cost due to low discounts. In general, these academic press books (or any book) priced at $30 or more do not sell well. Buying less of these titles has proven to be a good business decision, even though you may disappoint a few customers.

The standard discount offered by larger publishers to bookstores is generally 40–50 percent. Academic presses, as mentioned above, are stingier at 30–40 percent or less. That said, discounts are not standardized, and each publisher has their own thresholds, sales, and promotional offers. Asking for and negotiating the best discount, as uncomfortable as it may be, is a must to increase profitability. Annually, the bookstore buys books from three hundred different publishers. That is three hundred different discounts to remember, and they constantly change. No point in remembering or taking notes. Just ask the salesperson for the discount thresholds (buy a case and get 50 percent off, etc.) to make the best deal possible without over-ordering . . . which is always a temptation! Shipping is also negotiable. Free shipping is a rare perk, but utilizing media mail can lower shipping costs by 60 percent. There are risks involved with using media mail. It takes significantly longer, and the package is not traceable. Is saving $30 worth the risk of losing a $1,500 order? For less expensive orders, media mail is a fine option. For other orders, traceable delivery via standard shipping is best.

Inventory valuation affects profitability. This concept is as difficult to explain as it is to understand. QuickBooks POS adopts the weighted average inventory accounting method to determine the cost of goods sold and to assign a final valuation to the remaining inventory. This method divides the total average cost of all items by the total number of items resulting in an average cost per unit. This number can then be applied to each item to determine a final valuation. The net change in valuation from year to year is entered either as an increase or decrease to the cost of goods in the current fiscal year (in this case, the book expense line item). The end of the year adjustment accounts for the cost of merchandise purchased in previous fiscal years but sold in the current (increase cost of goods sold), or for the cost of merchandise purchased but not sold in the current fiscal year (decrease cost of goods sold). Simply put, the cost of an item sold must be accounted for in the financials for the fiscal year that it was sold—even if it was purchased years prior. This lesson in accounting tempered enthusiasm during spring semester. Unlike fall semester when there was little leftover inventory, spring semester's shelves were full of the previous year's books. Sales were strong and purchasing was light, so the budget report at first glance showed a huge profit. The business manager, hearing of the perceived windfall, took the opportunity to educate staff on the fundamentals of business accounting. What appeared to be a $25,000 profit, before accounting for the cost of old inventory sold, fell to $8,000. Still, much better than showing a $20,000 loss!

Tax concerns

Having turned a profit, the time had come to determine whether or not the bookstore's income was taxable—a concern never before confronted. A non-profit can bring in more money than it spends to conduct its business (in this case educational). This profit is exempt from corporate income tax. For profits from the bookstore to be tax exempt, the bookstore's activity needs to be closely related to the seminary's purpose. The Code of Federal Regulations §1.513-1 helps define a related activity:

> Trade or business is *related* to exempt purposes . . . only where the conduct of the business activities has causal relationship to the achievement of exempt purposes . . . and it is *substantially related* . . . (Reg. 1.513-[1][d][2])

The IRS also has identified additional activities that will be tax exempt even if they are not related to the nonprofit's purpose:

> Any trade or business carried on by an organization described in section 501(c)(3) or by a governmental college or university . . . primarily for the convenience of its members, students, patients, officers, or employees . . . (Reg. 1.513-[1][e][2])

The bookstore's primary activity is described on its resale certificate: "Textbooks and theological books for classes at Westminster Seminary California." The activity is clearly "substantially related" and "primarily for the convenience of its . . . students . . ." Based on these criteria, profits from the bookstore are not subject to tax from unrelated business activities. But, if the bookstore expanded its activity into the rare book business, for example, buying from other retailers and reselling to the public, that income is unrelated to the seminary's nonprofit activity of educating pastors and would need to be reported.

CONCLUSION

Is it feasible for library staff to run a bookstore? For small colleges and graduate schools like Westminster Seminary California, the answer is yes. Managing the bookstore, library, and actively participating as a faculty member looks like a big job on paper, but the academic year provides stretches of low student activity so as to pursue all three activities and do them well. The three reasons identified in the Hampshire College report for not going forward with the library-bookstore (finding a good manager, purchasing terms, overhead costs) are not insurmountable. Library professionals with a little entrepreneurial spirit and a workable location can make it happen. Intuitive out-of-the-box software guides purchasing, sales, and inventory control. Publishers in the Amazon.com era have a renewed affection for the independent bookseller and provide good terms for purchase. Personnel costs can be controlled by library staff absorbing a few extra duties, many of which are common to their library tasks. Location is rent free in the library, cutting costs further. The library-bookstore is feasible, profitable, and advances the status of library services as essential within the academic institution. Besides, it is a lot of fun!

REFERENCES

Blumenfeld, Catherine, and Robert T. Jordan. (1968). "Federal City College Media Center: A Plan for an Active Service." *Library-College Journal* 1 (Spring): 31–39.
Internal Revenue Service. (2014). *Electronic Code of Federal Regulations*. Washington, D.C.: U.S. Government Printing Office. Accessed April 17, 2014. http://www.ecfr.gov/cgi-bin/text-idx?SID=babc3e9493f3df8e903897e43482ca6f&node=26:7.0.1.1.1.0.3.86&rgn=div8 .
Intuit. (2012). *GoPayment Survey Estimates $100 Billion in Missed Sales for Small Businesses that Deny Plastic*. California: Intuit Inc. Accessed April 17, 2014. http://about.intuit.com/about_intuit/press_room/press_release/articles/2012/GetBusinessGrowing.html.
Library Journal. (1966). "Put Books in Libraries, Says Random House President." 91 (June): 2787–88.
Lund, James. (2012). "Let Them See Change." *The Bottom Line: Managing Library Finances* 24, no. 2: 185–86.

National Association of College Stores. (2013). *2011–2012 College Store Margins*. Ohio: National Association of College Stores. Accessed April 17, 2014. http://www.nacs.org/ research/industrystatistics/collegestoremargins.aspx.

Retail Owners Institute. (2014). *Book Stores Gross Margin Percent Trends*. Washington: Outcalt & Johnson: Retail Strategists, LLC. Accessed April 17, 2014. http:// www.retailowner.com/Benchmarks/RecreationLeisureActivitiesStores/Book-stores.aspx#287932-gross-margin.

Severtson, Susan, and George Banks. (1971). "Toward the Library-Bookstore." *Library Journal* 96, no. 2 (January): 163–66.

Taylor, Robert S. (1970). *The Making of a Library: The Academic Library in Transition*. Washington, D.C.: Office of Education. ERIC, ED 047742.

Chapter Three

Librarians and MOOCs

Loren Turner and Jennifer Wondracek

INTRODUCTION

Are you intellectually curious or professionally ambitious? Have you ever wanted to take a class about paleontology or art history or thermodynamics or constitutional law without having to pay for course credit or sit in a classroom? Do you have access to the Internet? If you answered yes to any of these questions, then join a MOOC! You have nothing to lose.

WHAT IS A MOOC?

A massive, open, online course (MOOC) is a class offered by faculty members of elite universities to adult learners all over the world for free on an online platform. MOOCs are the most recent example of how technology is transforming adult education. They provide quality education without cost, the flexibility of 24/7 access to course materials, and a global network of scholars. Additionally, MOOCs provide opportunities to raise the profile of librarians within an academic institution and internationally through librarian/faculty collaboration, advocacy of information literacy, and when possible, research skills training.

MOOCs were developed by three computer science professors at Stanford University who recognized that advancements in artificial intelligence and robotics made it possible for computers to grade students' homework assignments and respond to common student mistakes (Schrag, 2014, p. 85). Without the hassle of grading, exporting education to students on a grand scale was a natural progression. And so was the impetus to capitalize on the discovery. Both MOOC platforms, designed by the Stanford University professors—Coursera.org, and Udacity.com—were founded as for-profit companies (although making money from MOOCs is still an ongoing experiment, as discussed below). Harvard and MIT, in response to Stanford and citing open-access, open-source, altruistic ideals, created an alternative, not-for-profit MOOC platform, edX.org. To date, edX, Coursera, and Udacity remain the leading MOOC providers, expanding their individual brands through strategic partnerships with educational institutions and nongovernmental organizations around the world.

MOOCs have the potential to democratize education. They deliver expert instructors to every student with an Internet connection anywhere in the world—for free. Students can register for MOOCs without entrance exams, prerequisites, recommendations, or any other formal educational requirements. Additionally, MOOCs offer a great amount of flexibility. Students can take MOOCs from the comfort of their own homes or favorite cafés, as a replacement or supplement to traditional coursework, and most importantly, at their own pace, viewing and reviewing course materials whenever convenient, any time day or night. MOOCs also connect students to each other through embedded discussion forums, encouraging an international web of knowledge sharing and social interaction.

For participating educational institutions, nongovernmental organizations, and expert faculty, MOOCs provide unique marketing advantages. Exposure to a global audience creates celebrity status for particularly engaging professors and a heightened interest in the institutions that employ them. Promotional videos of upcoming classes reinforce institutional branding mechanisms. And MOOC platforms provide a canvas to advertise degree programs from the host institution for those students interested in continuing traditional, formal study. Given the potential for high rewards with practically zero risk, institutional policies actively encourage faculty participation in MOOCs.

On the other hand, MOOCs certainly have their share of critics. Some say MOOCs are simply the latest technological/instructional fad and not a viable method of educational reform (Greenstein, 2013). They cite high dropout rates (Adams, 2013), low student/professor interactions (Wetterstrom, 2014), and inconsistent quality standards (Freedman, 2013). They question whether MOOCs actually democratize education or further reinforce economic, geographic, and gender-based hierarchical structures (Christensen et al., 2014). It doesn't help that the majority of MOOCs are currently only available in the English language, although closed-captioning translations and partnerships between MOOC platforms and foreign institutions are becoming more common. For example, edX just welcomed Sorbonne Universités as its thirty-sixth charter member.

While the debate about the future of MOOCs wages on among academics and venture capitalists, the question for librarians is: Does it matter whether MOOCs exist twenty years from now? The answer: no! MOOCs are happening now, and they represent an opportunity for librarians to actively participate in MOOC development and design for the benefit of their institutions, their profession, and their own professional development.

LIBRARIAN ROLES IN A MOOC

Librarians involved with MOOCs have played one or more of the following roles, depending on institutional culture and faculty/librarian relationships: professor/instructor, faculty support, institutional support, student support, and technologist.

Librarian as Professor/Instructor: UF Law Case Study

This section gives an example of librarians taking on the role of "professor/ instructor" (hereafter, professor) in a MOOC and also provides an outline of the steps involved in the creation of a MOOC through a case study of the University of Florida's Levin College of Law's MOOC (UF Law's MOOC) titled "The Global Student's Introduction to U.S. Law," which ran from May 1, 2014, to June 26, 2014, on the Coursera platform. Since UF Law's MOOC was an ensemble effort, the librarians included on the team played roles in addition to that of professor. Details of the responsibilities associated with those additional roles are examined in separate sections below. This section highlights the unique challenges of MOOC professors, including duties associated with identifying course objectives and class schedule, creating course materials and assessment tools, and receiving student feedback. It also provides insight to the value of carefully crafted research assignments embedded within substantive lessons and the latest attempts of for-profit MOOC providers to cement a lucrative and sustainable business model.

Initial Efforts

In September 2012, Coursera announced it had recruited the University of Florida (UF) into the MOOC experiment. To encourage faculty involvement, with funding from Coursera, UF reconfigured a few administrative offices into a Coursera studio equipped with green screen technology and provided support staff including instructional designers to help develop a MOOC from start to finish.

Law schools have not been as quick to embrace distance learning, in general, or MOOCs, in particular, as have undergraduate and other graduate programs. The Center for Computer-Assisted Legal Education offered a Topics in Digital Law Practice MOOC in early 2012, but that effort inspired only five more law-related MOOCs within the following two years (Sampson &

Street, 2014, p. 9). Citing market demand, MOOC providers began soliciting law school administrators for a greater supply, which is how UF Law agreed to create its MOOC with Coursera.

Given the global audience MOOCs provide, the UF Law faculty and administration quickly recognized the value of using the MOOC as a vehicle to advertise and recruit students for its L.L.M. Comparative Law Program. The administration, however, invited all faculty members—not just comparative law scholars—to join the team. Eventually, a group of eight committed faculty members assembled, including three librarians: Claire Germain, Jennifer Wondracek, and Loren Turner. Claire Germain joined as associate dean for Legal Information; and Clarence J. TeSelle, Professor of Law, joined as a professor of substantive law, given her comparative law scholarship. Jennifer Wondracek and Loren Turner joined as research professors stemming from their interests in distance education and comparative/international law.

Identifying Course Objectives and Class Schedule

The team's preliminary duties included identifying course objectives and class schedule. After several meetings and the invaluable guidance of an experienced instructional designer supplied by the UF/Coursera partnership, the group decided to create an introductory-level eight-week class that explored the legal subject areas and interests of the faculty involved in the project. Professors Pedro Malavet, the director of the UF Law L.L.M. Comparative Law Program, and Claire Germain agreed to compare the common law and civil law systems and discuss U.S. civics over the initial two weeks of class. Professor Lyrissa Barnett Lidsky opted to tackle the topic of freedom of expression during the third week. Professor Sharon Rush agreed to cover other topics within the realm of constitutional law during the fourth week. Professor Kenneth Nunn opted to explore criminal law in weeks five and six of the course, and Professor Jeffrey Harrison consented to cover general principles of contract law in the remaining weeks seven and eight. Professors Jennifer Wondracek and Loren Turner decided to teach legal citation and embed legal research assignments within the substantive weeks of the course.

Within the discussion of course objectives, the team had to select the "tracks" the course would offer to global students. At present, regardless of platform, MOOC students have options as to their level of serious study. The vast majority of students embark on the MOOC journey with little to no intent of serious study. For those students who want to commit themselves further, MOOC platforms offer two types of certificates. The exact title varies depending on platform, but the first type of certificate is generally known as a "certificate of completion," and the second type is a "certificate of completion with distinction." MOOC platforms allow professors to decide whether to offer these certificates as part of a course. They also permit professors to define the criteria for satisfaction of the certificates, should they be offered as part of a course. The UF Law MOOC team decided to offer both certificates. To satisfy the first type, students had to receive an overall score of 70 percent or higher on weekly quizzes and discussion forum posts. To satisfy the second type, students had to achieve a score of 80 percent or higher on weekly quizzes, discussion forum posts, and completion of at least one research assignment (see below for further details).

MOOC providers are still currently offering these certificates without cost to students who satisfy the criteria; however (and here is where MOOC providers hope to capitalize on the great MOOC investment), MOOC platforms offer a paid service to students who want to prove to current or future employers that they have successfully completed a MOOC (with or without distinction). Again, the actual title varies depending on provider, but this service is generally known as a "verified" feature, which costs anywhere between $30 and $100 and requires students to photograph themselves using their webcams at the start of the course and at every assessment thereafter. Somehow (the exact details are not yet public) MOOC providers compare the photograph submissions to verify student identity. The service hopes to combat concerns of student cheating while simultaneously establishing a base worth of the certificates to employers. Professors that create MOOCs are encouraged to offer a "verified" track through monetary incentives. Approximately 192 students out of 19,526 joined the verified signature track of UF Law's MOOC.

Inventing Course Materials

Copyright law is a massive concern affecting the creation of course materials for a MOOC. A detailed explanation of the role of librarians as copyright experts and publisher-faculty intermediaries follows in the "Librarian as Faculty Support" section below. For now, suffice it to say that MOOC professors are limited in the types of course materials they may assign a global audience.

For the UF Law MOOC, professors opted against assigning copyrighted reading material and instead committed to a class consisting entirely of video lectures, weekly quizzes, and optional research assignments. All professors recorded on-camera video lectures standing in front of PowerPoint slides of their own creation, utilizing the green screen technology available at the designated "Coursera studio" on campus (for readers who need a visual image: think of a television personality standing in front of a weather map and predicting the day's precipitation levels . . . and now add some legalese). The process was much more nerve-racking than expected for those who struggled to meet the "eye" of the camera while attempting to remember the words of a script written in one's mind! Yet, video lectures facilitated the learning objectives of MOOC students because they gave students the power to stop, start, view, review, slow down, or speed up lectures depending on their individual intellectual and linguistic capabilities. Although each week consisted of ten or more video lectures, each video lecture was approximately only ten minutes in length, so students did not become overwhelmed with manipulating the pace to personalize the experience. As for the intellectual property rights to those PowerPoint slides and video lectures, professors retain ownership, granting Coursera only the license for the course itself (and any feature enhancements provided by Coursera, including closed captioning).

Creating Assessment Tools

As with any class, the team spent a great deal of time deciding how to assess student learning and satisfaction of course objectives. Again, with the expert guidance of the instructional designer, who explained the types of assessment tools students expect when taking a MOOC, the team decided to require weekly quizzes for students electing to obtain certificates for their study.

Additionally, as mentioned briefly above, the team agreed to require completion of a research assignment for students opting to receive a certificate of distinction. The research professors, Jennifer Wondracek and Loren Turner, determined the number, content, and assessment of research assignments offered as part of the MOOC. There were primarily two stages at which Wondracek and Turner developed research assignments for the MOOC: (1) the creation stage, and (2) the maintenance stage. Each stage was associated with its own set of duties and challenges.

In the creation stage, Wondracek and Turner focused on the number and topic areas of research assignments, the method of research instruction, the access capabilities of students to legal research databases, and the development of an appropriate rubric to grade research assignments. Wondracek and Turner began this stage with the decision to embed research assignments into weeks four (freedom of expression), six (criminal law), and seven (contract law) of the MOOC, based on predicted interest levels in these topics and support from the substantive professors of those modules. The research assignment for week six is included as appendix I below. Next, Wondracek and Turner committed to instructing students on statutory and case law research utilizing Camtasia screencasting software to capture their research strategies on selected databases. A fuller description of the Camtasia software and of Wondracek and Turner's efforts to use it is included in the "Librarian as Technologist" section below. As for the selection of legal research databases from which to demonstrate effective research strategies, Wondracek and Turner elected to highlight the free databases of Cornell Law's Legal Information Institute (for U.S. statutes and cases) and Google Scholar (for U.S. case law). Despite the authenticated legal documents hosted by U.S. government websites, Wondracek and Turner opted against examining them in the MOOC, due to a warning from Coursera that these websites were often blocked by foreign government filters. The last step in the creation stage was developing a rubric for the research assignments. Due to the large numbers of students taking MOOCs, assignments are not graded by MOOC professors. Students grade each other; however, MOOC professors must provide students with a rubric from which to grade. With the advice of the experienced instructional designer assigned to the UF Law MOOC, Wondracek and Turner created a rubric that identified five objective measurements of student assessment and awarded one point per measurement. The rubric is included as appendix II below. Students committed to obtaining the certificate of distinction from UF Law's MOOC would need to achieve at least three points out of five for successful completion of the research assignment. If a student opted to complete more than one research assignment, he or she could apply her highest score.

The maintenance stage of the research assignment development required Wondracek and Turner to monitor MOOC discussion forums to react to student difficulties with the research assignments. Despite attempts to curtail global access problems with the selected legal research databases for the research assignments, a few foreign students wrote in to the discussion forums during week six. One Chinese student was completely unable to access Google Scholar (probably due to government filters). Another student, this one from India, wrote into the forums seeking an explanation for why his Google Scholar home page differed from "the look" of the Google Scholar home page captured in Wondracek and Turner's Camtasia videos. To explain his predicament, he inserted a screen clipping of his image into the forum, which showed that he only had access to articles on the Google Scholar database—which did not include case law, as was required for the research assignment. A German student responded with an anecdote that she experienced the same dilemma until she followed a link in the corner of her screen that said, "Google Scholar in English." Despite the German student's advice, the student from India was still not able to access case law on Google Scholar. In response, to provide students without access to Google Scholar with an alternative database for case law, Wondracek and Turner decided to create an ad hoc Camtasia video highlighting another free legal research database, the Public Library of Law. The video was uploaded onto the MOOC platform immediately after completion. Without monitoring these discussion posts in the maintenance stage of research assignment development, Wondracek and Turner would not have known of these various Google Scholar interfaces, which proves that professors have just as much to learn from their students in MOOCs as they do in traditional classes!

Receiving Student Feedback

As with any course, particularly inaugural ones, student feedback for improvement is crucial if professors have any intention of repeating the class. To solicit feedback for the UF Law MOOC, a simple question was posed to the discussion forums: Did you enjoy class? The post received 248 responses, the vast majority of which were overwhelmingly positive. Many students praised the opportunities for student interactions with professors and/or teachers' assistants (TAs). The UF Law MOOC team decided early in the development process to hire TAs to flag substantive questions in the discussion forums and divert them to the appropriate faculty, but the professors also took an affirmative duty, for professional reasons and personal curiosity, to establish an online presence in the forums throughout the duration of the course.

The feedback for the research assignments was especially congratulatory. The following are direct quotes from a handful of the 2,202 students who submitted a research assignment for the UF Law's MOOC:

- "I was a bit wary about the research exercises, at least at first, as I have never done something like this before, but the videos were very good and helpful and I have quickly discovered that I like both researching and reading legal texts—something that will come into handy when I start studying law in a few months."
- "I found the research assignments to be very interesting, educational, and fun to do. Navigating the LII and Google Scholar databases to find statutes and cases regarding criminal law was very interesting. Locating a case that discussed whether a business has the right to freedom of speech was also challenging. I completed all three assignments and I especially enjoyed week 7, contract law, because that was the subject reason I enrolled in this class. As a final grade I would give this course an A plus."
- "I loved the course! I couldn't believe we actually got to research real cases. I'm excited to go back and do some more research in the databases."
- "It seems to be a consensus view that this was an excellent introductory course to US law, a view I fully endorce [sic]. Aspects I particularly liked: little prior legal knowledge was assumed, making it suitable for a wide audience, basic practical exposure to legal tasks like legal research. . ."
- "I learned a lot of new and important things by doing this class!!!! I just loved this course! But, I would say that one thing that I liked a lot was how to research case law! It was so great and I'm using the technic (sp) in my own work!"

The most common criticism from the forums with regard to the research assignments related to the rubric. A few students were frustrated with (what they felt was) a rubric that was too objective and didn't leave any room for evaluators to award more points to those students who put in more of an effort than others. Of particular concern for these evaluators involved the prevalence of plagiarism. All MOOC providers have an honor code, but plagiarism does not have a universal definition. A few students objected when peers copied the language of a case word for word as satisfaction of the research assignment (rather than summarize the case in their own words). Yet, as one frustrated evaluator recognized: *"I know that whatever job a person did he knows more about how to research now than he did before and I guess that was the main aim."*

Although it may not be feasible for every librarian to assume the role of professor in a MOOC, due to funding and time constraints, librarians should grasp at the chance to do so whenever possible. MOOCs provide an international soapbox from which librarians can advocate for the dissemination of knowledge. Through the development of MOOCs, librarians can support and advertise reliable, open-access databases and teach the world's students how to conduct effective research for the benefit of all.

Librarian as Faculty Support

Another important role that a librarian can have for a MOOC is faculty support. Professors have a great deal of experience creating course content in traditional settings, but are often unaware of the unique challenges in creating course content for MOOCs. One of the most important roles that a librarian can have for a MOOC is faculty support. Professors are the ones who create the course content, but they are often unaware of the differences in MOOCs and regular courses, which removes many materials that are traditionally used in the classroom.

Copyright Concerns

Perhaps one of the biggest and most difficult changes is the use of copyrighted materials. Title 17 of the U.S. Code provides specific rights to authors, including the distribution and creation of derivatives of their works [17U12]. For decades, teachers at all levels have utilized the Fair Use exception [17U121], which allows for the use of copyrighted materials without obtaining author permission in certain circumstances, such as classroom use. Code 17 U.S.C. § 107 provides four nonexclusive factors that the courts look at when considering fair use:

1. The purpose and character of the use, including whether such use is of a commercial nature or is for nonprofit educational purposes,

2. The nature of the copyrighted work,
3. The amount and substantiality of the portion used in relation to the copyrighted work as a whole, and
4. The effect of the use upon the potential market for or value of the copyrighted work.

Other sections of the federal statutes, such as the TEACH Act codified in 17 U.S.C. § 110, also support the use of copyrighted materials in the classroom. MOOCs, however, do not generally have the same protections.

Due to its not-for-profit status, edX may satisfy factor 1 of the Fair Use test, but Coursera and Udacity, as for-profit MOOC providers, would likely fail. Regardless of for-profit status, all MOOC platforms face the issue of distributing materials to large numbers of people, most of whom are not actually students of the institution providing the instruction. For example, UF Law's MOOC attracted over eighteen thousand students. This generally leads to the belief that MOOC students do not meet the definition of traditional students [Bye12], which means that some laws, such as the Family Educational Rights and Privacy Act (FERPA), do not apply [Uni13]. It also brings into question whether MOOCs can be considered classrooms or educational environments under the copyright laws. If they do not meet the definition of classrooms, factor 1 becomes less likely to favor fair use. One also then has the problem of distributing copies to a large enough number of people to affect the market or value of the work.

The for-profit MOOC providers often err on the side of caution and restrict the works that can be delivered through their platform. Public domain works tend to be preferred under these circumstances. Alternatively, if the author gives permission, either expressly or through a standard means, such as a Creative Commons license, the works are likely able to be used. Commercial products, such as textbooks and traditional journal articles, are usually precluded from use in MOOCs.

One exception to the textbook preclusion took place when Coursera and Chegg tried a pilot program with several large publishers [New13]. Under this program, the publishers would provide access to pertinent portions of texts through the Chegg platform, which would then be integrated into select Coursera courses. The full texts would be offered for a discount to the MOOC students, with the assumption that they would want to read further on the MOOC topic.

The professors of the UF Law MOOC wanted to use a textbook titled *Law 101: Everything You Need to Know about American Law* (hereafter, *Law 101*), published by Oxford University Press (Feinman, 2010). The UF Law librarians worked through the process of determining which sections the professors wanted to use, and applied for permission to use the book. Everything was on track until the pilot program was suddenly canceled with only two months to spare before the start of the UF Law MOOC. There was then a scramble to replace the readings. Interestingly, when students requested additional readings during the duration of the UF Law MOOC, professors still recommended *Law 101*, leading many students to purchase the book anyway.

No matter how the need for readings arises, as a MOOC professor tries to locate readings that will work within the copyright laws, proactive librarians can shine. Librarians are experts at locating relevant materials. Adding in the additional requirement that the readings be either in the public domain or available for access with the author's permission brings this search into the librarian's realm even further.

Content Delivery

An additional faculty-support issue that librarians can assist with is content delivery. MOOC students, especially those in foreign countries, are often accessing the course on mobile devices, such as cell phones. This means that course materials are being viewed on small screens, often smaller than an index card. While some MOOCs will have instructional designers to assist with this process, the designer is often juggling multiple courses and does not have the time to review a professor's materials, unless specifically asked to review a particular item. Librarians can use this as an opportunity to embed themselves in the course.

The UF Law librarians reviewed some of the professors' materials, such as slides, prior to publication. This allowed the librarians to make suggestions, such as reducing the amount of text on slides, to make the materials more mobile friendly. Additionally, the librarians were then able to identify potential copyright issues, such as copyrighted pictures, and assist the professors in locating alternate materials.

Faculty Reference

Sometimes faculty support will not be so structured. It can be as simple as responding to a reference request at the reference desk that turns out to assist a MOOC. For instance, the UF Law reference desk received two requests for "publicly accessible" laws, which turned out to be for a non-law MOOC. When it was determined that the resources were for a MOOC, the UF Law librarians were able to make informed choices on which sources to recommend and to advise the professor that a PDF of the laws, which are in the public domain, may be more appropriate than a link, which some people may not be able to access due to country access restrictions, as discussed under the "Librarian as Student Support" section.

Professors working on MOOCs come up with new requests on a regular basis. Many will offer librarians the opportunity to embed themselves in specific MOOCs. This will often take some proactive attempts on behalf of the librarian to make it known to professors that they have skills and experiences that will benefit the professor as they prepare for the MOOC. Alternatively, librarians may seek out the office that coordinates the MOOCs for their institution and articulate why it would be beneficial to incorporate librarians into the institution's MOOCs.

Librarians as Institutional Support

Institutional support is also a possible role for librarians when it comes to MOOCs. Many of the opportunities involved in faculty support can be enlarged to incorporate the entire institution. For instance, librarians' copyright expertise and information skills can be put to work for the entire institution.

Copyright Expertise

At UF, the Scholarly Communications Librarian, Christine Fruin, was consulted on the copyright portion of the overall Coursera contract. Ms. Fruin worked with the UF General Counsel Office to negotiate the copyright provisions by which all UF courses held on the Coursera platform would operate. In general, when copyright questions arose that were not specified by the contract, Ms. Fruin was consulted.

Information and Preservation Specialties

At Harvard, librarians from almost every department of the library have become involved in the MOOCs provided by edX. Even the libraries are being highlighted in various MOOCs, such as The History of the Book, which will include a segment on the efforts the Harvard libraries undertake to preserve their special collections. As Harvard law librarian Kyle Courtney states regarding library involvement, *"Where do the resources exist?* Ask the library. *We need articles and journals for courses?* Ask the library. *We need copies from books?* Ask the library. *We need digital images for slides?* Ask the library"* (Courtney, 2013, p. 514). These questions implicate a variety of library departments including: reference, course reserves, document delivery, scholarly communications, rights clearance, and potentially even technical services. At UF Law, it was determined that it would be a good idea to acquire a copy of the book *Law 101* for any UF students or library patrons who may wish to access the readings. The e-book version was acquired before the Coursera-Chegg program fell apart. This caused the UF Law e-services and cataloging departments to become involved in the MOOC.

Public Relations Efforts

Another way to support the institution is to assist with marketing the institution both in mentioning the MOOCs to interested parties and in talking to MOOC students about the benefits of the institution. For instance, in the UF Law MOOC, several students who were foreign attorneys asked about U.S. tax law. One of the law librarians responded to the questions by pointing the students to the law school's institutional repository (http://scholarship.law. ufl.edu), which includes many works by UF Law tax professors. The librarian was also able to promote the law school's advanced tax degrees, which rank number two in the United States.

The method of promotion should be considered carefully, however. UF Law, as mentioned above, was interested in using the UF Law MOOC to promote its L.L.M. Comparative Law Program, which accepts only foreign attorneys. When one of the UF Law administrators sent an e-mail to the UF Law MOOC team about strategies involved in promoting the L.L.M. Program, she also accidentally included all 18,000+ students enrolled in the MOOC as recipients. Disclosure of the students' personal e-mail addresses led to about thirty unnecessary (and belligerent) responses. The access issues were discovered quickly, and the individual e-mail addresses were not revealed to anyone other than one of the MOOC professors who was trying to diagnose and fix the problem. It was a learning moment for the UF Law MOOC team, fortunately without dire permanent consequences.

Librarian as Student Support

Librarians can also play the role of student support in a MOOC. This role can involve monitoring MOOC discussion forums to address student questions about access to information, or proactively posting messages on the discussion forums educating students about reliable sources for knowledge acquisition. The role can also include creating a research guide embedded within or supported outside of the MOOC platform (Sampson & Street, 2014, p. 11). Of course, librarians also assume the role of student support for any person taking any MOOC whenever that person approaches a librarian for access or research help—even when the librarian is not involved in the MOOC directly.

Librarian as Technologist

Librarians can also play the role of technologist. There is a great deal of technology involved in creating a MOOC. Some of the technologies include:

- Green screen recording—where a lecturer stands in front of a green-colored screen and presents their information. A picture, slide show, or other visual element can then be inserted behind the lecturer. Well-known uses of the green screen technology include weather forecasting on the television and making Christopher Reeve fly in *Superman* [Ric78], *Superman II* (Donner & Lester, 1980), *Superman III* (Lester, 1983), and *Superman IV* [Sid87].
- Video recording—recording of video and audio by professionals or by amateurs. Professional video is often used for official lectures. Amateur video is used more frequently for spontaneous videos, such as weekly check-ins. Amateur video can be created with a regular video camera, a webcam, or a cell phone.
- Screencasting—recording activity on a computer screen and converting it to video. This may or may not include narration of the activities, and is often used in software and database tutorial videos. Wondracek and Turner used Camtasia screencasting software to teach students completing the UF Law MOOC's research assignments about effective research stategies.
- Screenshots—still images from a computer screen. This technology can be used to illustrate a concept and can also be annotated to point out specific features.
- Audio recordings—recording of just audio/no video. This can be used for lectures that do not require visuals, for visually impaired students, or for musical compositions. Files may be streamed through the MOOC platform or provided as downloads for use on mobile devices, such as mp3 players.
- Slide presentations—combination of writing, imagery, and sometimes multimedia in a presentation format with multiple screens. This is a traditional technology used in both face-to-face and online teaching.
- Written materials in electronic format—this can be anything in written format, from journal articles and textbooks to the professor's class notes. PDF, RTF, TXT, and HTML are common forms used in online education, including MOOCs. Professors must carefully consider format selection, as some formats require software that may not be accessible to all students (for example: Microsoft Word .docx files).

Some librarians may feel comfortable enough with these and other technologies to take on a technologist role in a MOOC. This could be as simple as recommending specific formats for certain types of materials being presented or as complicated as instructing MOOC creators on technology use. Librarians can also sometimes be technology troubleshooters.

For instance, for the UF Law MOOC, Wondracek served as a technology consultant to all of the professors. As mentioned above, all professors opted for green screen recording for their substantive lectures. Additionally, some mini-lectures or topic introductions were recorded by the professional UF video team in a variety of locations around the law school. Professors were also encouraged to create spontaneous "check-in" videos to respond to questions raised by a student or students in the discussion forums. These videos were often taken with cell phones, as many of the professors traveled for personal or professional reasons during the course of the MOOC.

Librarians serving as technologists may be limited by institutional restrictions. Often, however, librarians can become involved with the technology to some extent, depending upon their skill level and interest.

Tips to Involve Oneself in the Development of a MOOC

The theory of working with a MOOC is fantastic, but actually getting involved can be difficult. Here are some suggestions to help you get started:

- Find the department/office in your institution that supports faculty/staff initiatives to develop MOOCs. If there isn't one, find out which faculty members have previously developed a MOOC or have the desire to do so.
- Determine your preferred scope of involvement. Do you want to teach the MOOC yourself or with your peers? Provide faculty support? Provide student support? Before offering to assist with a MOOC, you have to confront your own time and skill capabilities. MOOCs take a long time to develop. UF Law's MOOC took over one year to develop before the course launched. Your time commitment may be significant depending upon how involved you become.
- Sell yourself and your library's resources to the appropriate institutional department/office/faculty member. Do not assume that the person you are contacting knows the value librarians provide to a MOOC. If your institution does an open call for interested parties, speak up.

CONCLUSION

MOOCs are still in their experimental phase, which means that no one has yet identified with any clarity a "right way" or a "wrong way" to develop or support a MOOC. The ambiguity is both liberating and terrifying for those brave enough to make a concentrated effort. When it pays off (figuratively, if not literally), it feels incredibly rewarding—even when one can think of a million ways to improve upon the effort on the next attempt. For librarians, it doesn't matter whether MOOCs exist twenty years from now. Regardless, they still provide an opportunity to raise our profile within our individual institutions and around the world, because they provide the vehicle to promote our value and our values to a global audience. MOOCs are merely the latest way to refine our instructional, support, and technology skills. Let's jump in and learn from one another to create a better product for our current and future patrons.

APPENDIX I: RESEARCH ASSIGNMENT FOR WEEK SIX

Assignment: Your lectures this week focused on the types of homicide (first-degree murder, second-degree murder, manslaughter) and the justifications (defenses) of the use of force. Let's see if you can locate additional resources on this topic. Watch the research video for tips on how to navigate the Legal Information Institute and Google Scholar databases. Then, use your skills to locate the following:

- Find the section of the U.S. Code that defines "murder" (use the Legal Information Institute to find the correct section) and
- Find a case from 2014 that cites the statute you found (above) and discusses the issue of self-defense (use Google Scholar to find a relevant case).

To receive full credit for this assignment, you must:

1. Use the databases mentioned in the research lectures.
2. Identify a relevant statute and/or case.
3. Explain how you located the relevant statute and/or case on the database(s).
4. Provide the following citation information:

   - For the statute: give the title number and the section number of the U.S. Code, and a web link to the statute.
   - For the case: give the case name and date, the name of the court that issued the opinion, and a web link to the case.

5. Summarize your case in one to two paragraphs. What happened in the case? What, if anything, did the court say about the murder statute? Did the court find that the defendant's claim of self-defense was reasonable? Why or why not?

APPENDIX II

Table 3.1. MOOC Research Rubric

Answer these questions regarding your classmate's assignment:	Yes 1 pt	No 0 pts
Did your classmate use one (or more) of the following databases for their research: • Legal Information Institute (cases and statutes), • Google Scholar (cases), • FDsys (cases and statutes), • CISG Database?		
Did your classmate explain how he/she located the case or statute on one of the databases above?		
Did your classmate find a primary legal resource (statute or case) that is relevant to the research topic? Note: if asked to find a case, the case should not be one of those discussed in the class lectures—it should be a new case.		
Did your classmate provide the citation information requested, including the web link to the case or statute?		
Did your classmate summarize the rule of the case or statute?		

REFERENCES

Accredible. (June 21, 2013). "5 MOOC Professors to See before You Die." Accredible blog: http://blog.accredible.com/5-mooc-professors-to-see-before-you-die/.

Acemoglu, D., D. Laibson, and J. A. List. (2014). "Equalizing Superstars: The Internet and the Democratization of Education." *American Economic Review Papers and Proceedings*. http://economics.mit.edu/files/9452.

Adams, S. (December 11, 2013). "Are MOOCs Really a Failure?" *Forbes*. http://www.forbes.com/sites/susanadams/2013/12/11/are-moocs-really-a-failure/.

Arnold, S. E. (2013). "Gadzooks, It's MOOCs: The Fuss over Open Source Learning." *Online Searcher* 37, no. 1: 10–15.

Baggaley, J. (2013). "MOOC Rampant." *Distance Education* 34, no. 3: 368–78.

Barnes, C. (2013). "MOOCs: The Challenges for Academic Librarians." *Australian Academic & Research Libraries* 44, no. 3: 163–75.

Billsberry, J. (2013). "MOOCs: Fad or Revolution?" *Journal of Management Education* 37, no. 6: 739–46.

Byerly, A. (October 29, 2012). "Formerly Known as Students." *Inside Higher Education*. http://www.insidehighered.com/views/2012/10/29/essay-how-moocs-raise-questions-about-definition-student.

Cavaliere, F. J. (2014). "Online Alternatives for Legal Education: MOOCs." *The Practical Lawyer* 60, no. 1: 9.

Christensen, G., et al. (2014). "The MOOC Phenomenon: Who Takes Massive Open Online Courses and Why?" *Social Science Research Network*. http://papers.ssrn.com/sol3/papers.cfm?abstract_id=2350964.

Christensen, G., and B. Alcorn. (2014). "A Lesson in Learning." *New Scientist* 221, no. 2959: 24–25.

Colbran, S., and A. Gilding. (2014). "MOOCs and the Rise of Online Legal Education." *Journal of Legal Education* 63, no. 3: 405–28.

Courtney, K. (November 2013). "The MOOC Syllabus Blues: Strategies for MOOCs and Syllabus Materials." *College & Research Libraries News* 74, no. 10: 514–17.

Donner, R. (Director). (1978). *Superman* [Motion Picture].

Donner, R., and R. Lester. (Directors). (1980). *Superman II* [Motion Picture].

Feinman, J. (2010). *Law 101: Everything You Need to Know about American Law*. 3rd ed. New York: Oxford University Press.

Fowler, G. A. (October 8, 2013). "An Early Report Card on Massive Open Online Courses." *Wall Street Journal*. http://online.wsj.com/news/articles/SB10001424052702303759604579093400834738972.

Freedman, J. (November 25, 2013). "MOOCs: Usefully Middlebrow." *Chronicle of Higher Education*, "The Chronicle Review." http://chronicle.com/article/MOOCs-Usefully-Middlebrow/143183/.

Frey, T. (May 11, 2012). "The Rise of the SuperProfessor." FuturistSpeaker.com. http://www.futuristspeaker.com/2012/05/the-rise-of-the-superprofessor/.

Furie, S. J. (Director). (1987). *Superman IV: The Quest for Peace* [Motion Picture].

Greenstein, D. (July 1, 2013). "Innovation Exhaustion and a Path to Moving Forward." *Inside Higher Education*. http://www.insidehighered.com/views/2013/07/01/essay-need-focus-higher-ed-reforms-right-goals-not-just-quick-change.

Lester, R. (Director). (1983). *Superman III* [Motion Picture].

Liyanagunawardena, T. R. (2013). "MOOC Experience: A Participant's Reflection." *SIGCAS Computers and Society* 44, no. 1: 9–14.

New, J. (May 8, 2013). "Partnership Gives Students Access to a High-Price Text on a MOOC Budget." *Chronicle of Higher Education*, "Technology." http://chronicle.com/article/Partnership-Gives-Students/139109/.

Pappano, L. (September 13, 2013). "The Boy Genius of Ulan Bator." *New York Times*. http://www.nytimes.com/2013/09/15/magazine/the-boy-genius-of-ulan-bator.html?_r=0.

Pappano, L. (November 2, 2012). "The Year of the MOOC." *New York Times*. http://www.nytimes.com/2012/11/04/education/edlife/massive-open-online-courses-are-multiplying-at-a-rapid-pace.html?pagewanted=all&_r=0.

Sampson, S., and L. Street. (2014). "MOOCs and the Role of Law Librarians." *AALL Spectrum* 18, no. 4: 9–11.

Schrag, P. G. (2014). "MOOCs and Legal Education: Valuable Innovation or Looming Disaster?" *Villanova Law Review* 59, no. 1: 83–134.

Smith Jaggars, S. (2014). "Democratization of Education for Whom? Online Learning and Educational Equity." *Diversity & Democracy* 17, no. 1. http://www.aacu.org/diversitydemocracy/vol17no1/jaggars.cfm.

Tickle, L. (May 14, 2012). "So You Want to Be the New Brian Cox? How to Become a Celebrity Academic." *The Guardian*. http://www.theguardian.com/education/2012/may/14/celebrity-academic-radio-tv-funding?CMP=.

University of Illinois at Urbana–Champaign, Office of the Chancellor and Office of the Provost, MOOC Strategy Advisory Committee Interim Report (November 2013). http://mooc.illinois.edu/docs/MSAC-Interim-Report-2013-11-11.pdf.

Wetterstrom, Luke. (January 28, 2014). "The Year after the Year of the MOOC." *The Gate*. http://uchicagogate.com/2014/01/28/years-after-mooc/.

Chapter Four

Trends in Medical Library Instruction and Training

A Survey Study

Antonio DeRosa and Marisol Hernandez

INTRODUCTION

The success of a health sciences library educational program depends on a number of factors such as setting, staff, time, interest from users, and the variety of content being offered, just to name a few. Information professionals in these libraries face the challenges head-on while coming up with innovative and creative ways of keeping their users engaged in their instructional sessions. Unfortunately, however, this is not always the case, and more and more health sciences libraries are closing up shop on traditional bibliographic instruction.

The authors surveyed 119 health sciences libraries nationwide to get their insights and gain their knowledge on the status of their educational programs. The term "educational program" throughout this chapter is used loosely to define any instruction performed by a librarian or information specialist/ professional for any individual, department, group, class, or curriculum. Many libraries have formal programs while others take a more workshop- or walk-in-like feel to their instruction initiatives. No matter the mode or context, the authors were interested in learning more about the specific challenges plagued by health sciences librarians today.

LITERATURE REVIEW

Health sciences libraries have undergone many transformations throughout the decades, and so have their educational programs. Librarians have learned to adapt to their changing environments, and continue to thrive in an unknown future. Whether they be from a special or research library, an academic setting, or a hospital library, information specialists from all areas are tasked with educating and instructing clients in areas like research methods, evidence-based medicine, literature searching, database searching, bibliographic management, and emerging technologies. A review of the literature reveals the challenges faced by health sciences libraries and librarians in offering innovative, timely, fresh, and successful training endeavors to their clients.

Assessing library instruction through a historical lens reveals that teaching has been an integral part of library services since the late nineteenth century, mainly in academic libraries. "The introduction of graduate level education drove the creation of much larger libraries. This in turn created a need to educate patrons in how to use these larger, more complicated collections" (Lorenzen, 2001). This was further supported when some in the field of higher learning advocated for librarians to educate students. A number of librarians at the time were also university professors. By the late 1800s "academic librarians were also lecturing in the classroom" (Lorenzen, 2001). It would not be long before the first college credit course in bibliography would be offered at the University of Michigan. This course would serve as a model for future library instructional sessions at other universities.

In addition to courses in bibliographic resources, librarians also began to see book talks and orientation tours. By the early twentieth century, instruction included the organization of the library as well as the history of the book. Instruction by librarians continued to grow in the areas of reference sources, study habits, and as independent research.

The literature becomes scarce on the topic of library instruction between the 1930s and the 1960s. It's not until the 1970s, with the establishment of Library Orientation Exchange (LOEX), "a non-profit, self-supporting education clearinghouse" (Lorenzen, 2001), that library instruction resurfaces with momentum. LOEX had its first conference in 1973, and it continues to be held today. The LOEX collection contains a number of resources that include bibliographies, audiotapes, instructional videos, and CD-ROMS.

Partnerships between academic librarians and faculty were greatly encouraged in the 1970s as more and more universities made library skills a requirement for their students. The next couple of decades would bring about major changes to the information world. The development of online systems and the Internet would present a great number of opportunities and challenges for librarians and information specialists.

Expectations of information seekers have had an impact on the delivery of library instruction throughout the years. "Academic libraries must reach beyond their physical facilities to meet the expectations of freshmen users" (Robertson & Jones, 2009). Furthermore, "contemporary 17- to 19-year-olds bring unique learning style preferences and worldviews with them when they come to libraries' information literacy classes" (Manuel, 2002). Therefore, libraries need to provide multiple modalities of instruction that include the latest trends in social media, social networking, and digital gaming, among others.

Aside from social networks and gaming rising in popularity, libraries and librarians are facing increased pressure to deliver instruction in an ever-growing virtual world in regard to distance learning in recent years. Many libraries are already developing and sharing online video tutorials with their users in an effort to reach them anywhere, at any time. The problem is that these videos "tend to go stale fairly quickly as database vendors make changes to their interfaces, and in terms of user success . . . some students tend not to do well in this platform" (Barnhart & Stanfield, 2011). Most students still need the in-person interaction to be successful learners, or something more similar to it than a static video tutorial.

Barnhart and Stanfield (2011) discuss their experiences with a web conferencing service (Wimba) to reach distance learners at the University of West Georgia. A major challenge noted in the article is the issue of the web conferencing software's technical glitches. There was disruptive feedback heard in certain situations, unusual connection speed, and lag time in others (Barnhart & Stanfield, 2011). Also noted was that the amount of content covered in an online session tends to be less than a face-to-face session. This is not only due to technical issues but also because questions typically take longer to answer in a virtual setting as opposed to an in-person classroom; however, librarians at the University of West Georgia noted that Wimba offers an alternative to in-person instruction, especially during a library renovation (Barnhart & Stanfield, 2011).

The Clairoux et al. case study (2013) is an exemplar paper showcasing one university's unique experience with implementing and maintaining an educational program. Librarians and technicians at the Université de Montréal (UdeM) are embedded in the health sciences curricula, teaching both undergraduate and graduate students on MEDLINE, PubMed, library resources, evidence-based practice, EndNote, copyright, and pharmaceutical patents. Some challenges they face throughout their teaching sessions include information retention, relevance of content, and linear online education tools.

Regarding information retention, Clairoux et al. state that "although 71 percent of students successfully completed workshop exercises, 2 weeks later very few demonstrated that they could utilise new tools and apply new research skills to a new topic, or that they could incorporate new knowledge of resources and searching techniques into their final projects" (Clairoux, Desbiens, Clar, Dupont & St-Jean, 2013). UdeM's way of handling this problem was to collaborate with faculty to ensure that library instruction take place before any research projects. Keeping instructional content relevant to users is another challenge reported in this case study. Based on feedback via student evaluation forms from a pharmaceutical patents workshop, the session changed from a two-hour lecture to a 2.5-hour hands-on format. Meeting the needs of users is imperative for keeping an educational program current. UdeM has also looked into the possibility of offering more robust web-based library instruction to its users, although this is an ongoing project due to static page formats and limited staff to upgrade web pages. Again, feedback from users is a pivotal role in providing content that is current and appealing to users. This is evident in the overhaul of their Drug Development subject guide after receiving numerous comments from faculty members.

Methodology

An online survey was created using the Survey Monkey application. The survey consisted of seventeen questions and was delivered via e-mail to a select number of library listservs. These included: MEDLIB-L, METRO (Metropolitan Library Council) Hospital Libraries List, BQSI/MB (Brooklyn, Queens, Staten Island, Manhattan, and the Bronx) Health Sciences Libraries, and MLA (Medical Library Association) New York–New Jersey chapter.

The survey was made available for four weeks from February 1 through February 28, 2014. A total of 119 respondents representing hospital, academic, and special research libraries completed the questionnaire. The following is a featured selection of survey responses displayed in graphical and tabulate format. The remaining question responses will be explained in the discussion section of this chapter. Please refer to the appendix below for the full survey.

In what health sciences library setting do you work?

A total of 119 responses were recorded for this question with thirty-eight (31.9 percent) being from academic libraries, seventy (58.8 percent) from hospital libraries, six (5 percent) from special libraries, and five (4.2 percent) respondents reporting from other settings. Note that four out of the five *other* responses fall into one of the three categories of library settings offered in the question answers. The responses were as follows: specialty hospital and cancer research institute, teaching hospital, academic medical center, academic health sciences library. The truly *other* respondent reported coming from a medical publisher.

Do you offer training to staff within the organization?

This was a mandatory question, and 115 (96.6 percent) institutions answered *yes* to currently offering training to staff within their organization, one (0.8 percent) answered *no*, zero people marked *not at this time*, and three (2.5 percent) responded *other*. The *other* responses: *I am recently hired, but intend to teach*; *sometimes, but it really depends on the topic*; and *a tiny bit with our market research databases*.

If yes, what type of training do you offer? (Select all that apply)

For those respondents who answered yes to the previous question about offering training at their organization, the more detailed follow-up question regarding type of training came next. The highest ranking type of training being offered by these respondents is *database searching* with a total of 116 responses (97.5 percent). Next came *library orientation/new hire orientation* at ninety-seven (81.5 percent), then *bibliographic management* at fifty-nine (49.6 percent), *information literacy* at fifty-three (44.5 percent), *research methods* at thirty-five (29.4 percent), *technology trends* and *other* topics at nineteen (16 percent) each, and finally *Microsoft Office* at three (2.5 percent). The *other* topics listed by respondents ranged from specific databases and resources that they perform instruction on, to evidence-based medicine principles/theory (eight write-in responses), grants and funding, advanced Google, and data management. Figure 4.1 shows the distribution of responses in tabular form.

How often do you offer scheduled training workshops to your users?

The recurrence of workshop training sessions could be a useful bit of information for determining the challenges of an educational program. Another mandatory question, this one was interesting because seventy-six (63.9 percent) responses were *other*, the majority of which were write-ins to the effect of ad hoc, as needed, or by request training to staff within an organization/ university. Based on these results, more than half of medical information professionals who took this survey are no longer scheduling training workshops for their clients. Rather, they are waiting for their clients to come to them, or are offering training as the need presents itself. As for the rest of the results, ten respondents (8.4 percent) schedule training weekly or quarterly and twenty-three (19.3 percent) schedule on a monthly basis.

DeRosa and Hernandez

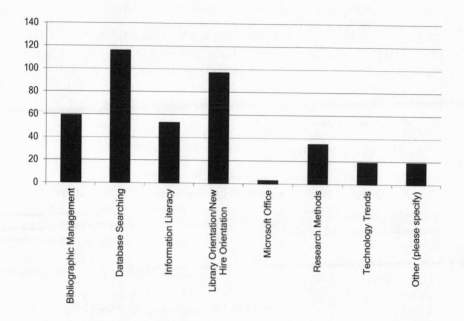

Figure 4.1. Types of training offered.

What forms of communication do you use to promote your workshops or training programs? (Select all that apply)

Another key component to any successful training program is effective communication and marketing to potential persons of interest. The survey respondents provided some insights into how many medical librarians and information specialists are going about this. Not surprising, the top mode of communication is *e-mail* with ninety-five (79.8 percent) responses. This includes individual e-mails as well as PDLs (personal/public distribution list). There was also a significant number of respondents who marked *other* for this question: forty-one (34.5 percent). Most of these responses can be summarized as newsletters, departmental/group meetings, word of mouth, and outreach events. Figure 4.2 shows the results in tabular form.

In what settings do you offer training? (Select all that apply)

The place in which a workshop or class is held, whether it be virtual or physical, can be a deciding factor for participants when it comes to attendance. The survey participants mostly partake in individual or one-on-one training with their clients for a total of 110 (92.4 percent) responses. The runner up with 101 (84.9 percent) responses was the classic classroom/lecture-style instruction. A healthy number of respondents reported offering

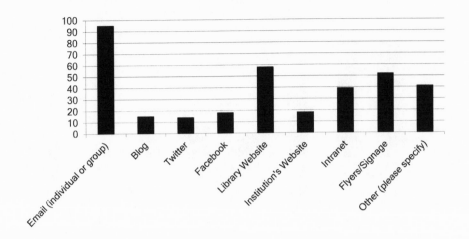

Figure 4.2. Forms of communication to promote training.

video tutorials and *online self-paced tutorials* to their clients: twenty-seven (22.7 percent) and twenty-three (19.3 percent), respectively. Surprisingly low was the number of responses for webinar-based instruction at a mere nine (7.6 percent) responses. Figure 4.3 shows the results in tabular form.

From the list provided, what tools do you utilize for instruction? (Select all that apply)

Of interest in this question are the *other* responses by survey participants. Some supply very specific tools not listed as an answer to the question, such as BrainShark, Guide on the Side, Videoscribe, Jing, Articulate Studio, polle-verywhere.com, and ZOOM meeting software. The top tool for presentation is PowerPoint at ninety-seven (81.5 percent) responses, with LibGuides coming in next (after *other*) with forty-four (37 percent) responses. It seems many information professionals are beginning to leverage LibGuides for their training abilities like surveys, feedback forms, comment boxes, and file/document download features. Figure 4.4 shows the results in tabular form.

Please share one challenge you've faced in your training initiatives.

Another required survey question and perhaps one of the most important, the number one challenge faced by medical information professionals who completed the survey is getting clients to attend training sessions. This lack of participation could be for a number of reasons: medical staff is pressed for time, library educational sessions are unappealing to clients, times of scheduled training does not work for medical staff schedules, no buy-in from medical staff, creating more robust and engaging presentations, and poor

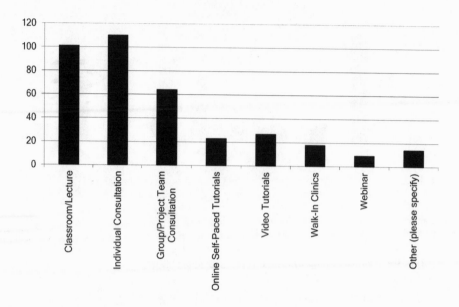

Figure 4.3.   Types of settings in which training sessions are offered.

advertising strategies. Other challenges reported include IT limitations, ac-
commodating appropriately for distance learners, and lack of time and/or
resources to develop instructional sessions.

Discussion

The number one challenge faced by medical librarians in regard to training,
suggested by the survey results, is the lack of attendance or interest on the
part of medical staff and students. Many information specialists are having
difficulty getting clients to attend their training workshops and seminars for a
number of reasons. The major reasons reported are time (both on the part of
the librarian and the medical professional), lack of appeal of educational
sessions (presentation itself or session as a whole), poor marketing strategies,
and the lack of resources to develop educational programs.

Poor Marketing Strategy

Getting medical professionals and students to perceive librarians as educators
is no easy task. A big part of accomplishing this feat is marketing. Librarians
need to think of new modes of communicating with their clients in a way
that's most appealing to them, especially for scheduled instruction sessions.
Many survey respondents noted receiving an increase in their training numbers over time, but this is largely due to an increase in customized training

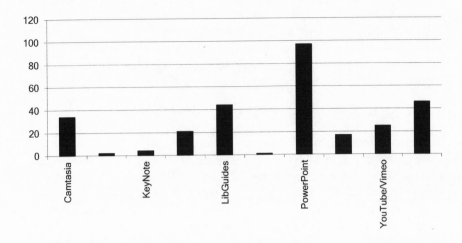

Figure 4.4. Tools for delivery instruction.

requests at these libraries. These respondents also mention having a strong presence at institutional events, during committees, and other departmental meetings. McAdoo states, "This is a good way to build rapport. . . . Increasing your approachability in this way increases the likelihood of students seeking you out when they do need more formal instruction" (2012). Similarly, some survey respondents report an upswing in the amount of one-on-one training sessions provided at their institutions. Again, this is credited to the libraries' outstanding presence during extracurricular opportunities.

These libraries and librarians are doing a fine job of marketing themselves to their clients and it seems to be working for them, but this strategy doesn't easily translate to every institution. For instance, an effective way to personalize an advertising strategy is with some clear follow-up after any teaching point or interaction with a client (McAdoo, 2012). This is not so evident in these comments from the survey:

- *Time and staffing do not allow for follow-up.*
- *This is very important and we have long been waiting for our clients to contact us back if they need further assistance. We need to be more proactive.*
- *I hadn't considered the need for follow-up.*

Librarians and information specialists performing training are not overtly against following up with their students or training attendees; they either haven't thought of it as a marketing opportunity, don't have the time, or it's not standard practice in their library. Most information professionals would agree that marketing is imperative to ensure a successful educational and instruction program in their libraries (Estall & Stephens, 2011). Libraries need to be seen by higher administration as providing a valuable service to the institution and its staff members. Taking on a more businesslike model of advertising training services may not be such a bad idea when it comes to increasing statistics in this functional area of the library.

Lack of Resources: Budget and Staffing

Perhaps the most inhibiting factor to running an effective educational program is budget restraints. Not only does a diminishing budget affect a collection, but it also affects the number of hours a staff member is available to give instruction, for example. It can also determine how much time an information professional can devote to developing educational programs for her or his users. Another survey study conducted in 2012 reports that "the economic downturn had affected the nature or number of departmental bibliographic instruction sessions . . . the downturn had led to staffing reductions or concerns, and these resulted in a reduced number of instructional sessions" (Reynolds, 2012). It's imperative to note, however, that these findings reflect the responses of only two special collection libraries that were surveyed. Nonetheless, it represents the struggle that some libraries are facing in regard to exceeding budget cuts and instruction. Below are some comments from the survey:

- *Having my hours cut in half—a definite challenge.*
- *Time and project management. I am solo librarian and one staff.*
- *As a solo librarian, training is vital, yet challenging because of time constraints.*

Both time constraints and staff hours being cut are contributing factors that make successful training in medical libraries a challenge. Again, the Reynolds survey offers an astute insight into this challenge by pointing out the direct relationship between staff for instruction and faculty interest: "Staffing pressures and levels of faculty interest emerged as the top two issues from responses relating to challenges and concerns. This points to a potential dilemma for librarians who wish to see greater use of their services and resources, including instructional sessions, but who realize that such an increase will likely result in a need for additional staff to meet these goals (Reynolds, 2012). How are librarians expected to meet the growing needs of their faculty with less staff members to do the instructing? This is a key question to consider when it comes to budgeting for educational programs in a health sciences library.

Time Factor and Good Presentations

As identified in the survey, libraries face a number of challenges surrounding the issue of instruction. Two additional challenges include the time factor and the ability to create appealing and engaging training sessions for users. In a busy medical facility, clinical staff will often find it difficult to attend library training workshops because of the rigorous demands of clinical scheduling and other professional responsibilities.

Before embarking on providing a library training program, librarians should keep in mind the following tips for providing library instruction:

- User-initiated instruction—where individuals simply request training at the library
- Faculty-, department head–, clinical manager–initiated training—when an assignment requiring library resources is needed and staff are designated for training to complete the specified project
- Librarian-initiated instruction—where library staff identify gaps in learning via observation or user assessment

Training sessions can be scheduled or can be provided ad hoc. For scheduled sessions where a high attendance is desired, it is advisable that librarians consider the following:

- Availability of library instructors—have more than one librarian available to teach the session, in the event of personal illness or emergency.
- Flexibility when scheduling—users may want to take sessions on their lunch or dinner breaks.
- Be informed of major organizational events so as to avoid scheduling conflicts.
- Choose a comfortable teaching setting where lighting and temperature are optimal for learning.

While these recommendations may strengthen one's teaching program, it by no means ensures well-attended workshops. Another challenge to address is the delivery of diverse and engaging training presentations. First, pay close attention to the following items:

- Understand your audience, and know their expectations.
- Pace yourself when speaking.
- Combine lecture with hand-on exercises.
- Follow up with users after the training session.

Moving away from Powerpoint slides may be a very good first step. Consider alternative platforms such as:

- LibGuides—a content management system to share information in a variety of formats that include text, images, videos (also mobile and tablet friendly)
- Prezi—a virtual whiteboard that allows you to share information via a canvas presentation, and Prezi is also a mobile app
- Jing & Screencast—an excellent online tutorial tool for brief but informative learning tips
- Gamification—using game techniques to engage users and help them solve problems
- MOOC—Massive Open Online Course where there is unlimited participation to a variety of subjects in an open-access environment

These tools allow for a variety of presentation materials: handouts, images, videos, chat, and more. One may also engage remote users via Skype and/or FaceTime. Tools that have mobile capabilities are another option for providing short instructional tips to your clients. "Improved teaching methods help participants feel welcome in the online space and effective co-streaming of classes depends on engaged participants. Best practices include things as simple as uploading a welcome slide that participants see when they log into the online space" (Hayes, Handler, & Main, 2011). In addition, one may also get participants "used to communicating through the chat window, the primary communication for students participating online" (Hayes, Handler, & Main, 2011). Today's technological options allow for a wider reach of users at any given time while enhancing the user learning experience.

CONCLUSION

Despite the increase in options of instructional modalities, health sciences libraries are still struggling to provide dynamic and robust training sessions as well as increase participation in their educational programs. The many constraints include busy clinical staff, unappealing educational sessions, budget cuts, IT limitations, and resources available to develop instructional sessions. Open sources such as MOOC and other cost-effective online communication tools like Skype may provide better options. It is also recommended that these online tools provide several modalities of engagement and that they may be archived for accessibility at any given time. Getting to know the user's expectations is a key element to successful training. Ensuring that staff are trained and are available for instruction is also important. Finally, assessing user preferences and the user environment along with the points made in this survey study should be the starting point for a successful training initiative.

APPENDIX

Survey questions:

1. In what health sciences library setting do you work?
2. Do you offer training to staff within the organization?
3. If yes, what type of training do you offer?
4. What instructional workshops have you retired from your program, if any? Please state why.
5. How often do you offer scheduled training workshops to your users?
6. How long have you had a training program in place?
7. What forms of communication do you use to promote your workshops or training programs?

   - E-mail (individual or group)
   - Blog
   - Twitter
   - Facebook
   - Library website
   - Institution's website
   - Intranet
   - Flyers/signage
   - Other/please specify

8. Your training numbers (number of attendees) have increased over time.

   a. disagree
   b. agree
   c. neither agree nor disagree

9. Please give one reason why you made your selection in question #8.
10. In what settings do you offer training?

    - Classroom/Lecture
    - Individual consultation
    - Group/Project team consultation
    - Online self-paced tutorials
    - Video tutorials

- Walk-in clinics
- Webinar
- Other/please specify

11. After a user attends one of your training workshops/sessions, what do you do?

    a. No follow-up
    b. Follow-up after 1 week
    c. Follow-up after 2 weeks
    d. Follow-up after 3 weeks
    e. Follow-up after 1 month
    f. Follow-up after more than 1 month

12. If you answered NO FOLLOW-UP to question #11, please give one reason why you made your selection.
13. From the list provided, what tools do you utilize for instruction?

- Camtasia
- Gaming
- KeyNote
- Learning Management System (Moodle, BlackBoard)
- LibGuides
- MOOC courses
- PowerPoint
- Prezi
- YouTube/Vimeo
- Other/please specify

14. Do you have any educational initiatives planned for the future?
15. How do you keep your clients interested in your training program? Please provide one unique example below.
16. Please share one challenge you've faced in your training initiatives.
17. From the survey response, we might have additional questions. Please provide us with your contact information if you don't mind us following up with you.

REFERENCES

Barnhart, A. C., and A. G. Stanfield. (2011). "When Coming to Campus Is Not an Option: Using Web Conferencing to Deliver Library Instruction." *Reference Services Review* 39, no. 1: 58–65.

Clairoux, N., S. Desbiens, M. Clar, P. Dupont, and M. St-Jean. (2013). "Integrating Information Literacy in Health Sciences Curricula: A Case Study from Quebec." *Health Info Libr J* 30, no. 3: 201–11. doi: 10.1111/hir.12025.

Estall, C., and D. Stephens. (2011). "A Study of the Variables Influencing Academic Library Staff's Attitudes toward Marketing." *New Review of Academic Librarianship* 17, no. 2: 185–208. doi: 10.1080/13614533.2011.610217.

Hayes, B. E., L. J. Handler, and L. R. Main. (2011). "Co-streaming Classes: A Follow-up Study in Improving the User Experience to Better Reach Users." *Med Ref Serv Q* 30, no. 4: 349–56. doi: 10.1080/02763869.2011.609037.

Lorenzen, M. (2001). "A Brief History of Library Information in the United States of America." *Illinois Libraries* 83, no. 2: 8–18.

Manuel, K. (2002). "Teaching Information Literacy to Generation." *Journal of Library Administration* 36, no. 1–2: 195–217.

McAdoo, M. L. (2012). *Fundamentals of Library Instruction*. Chicago: American Library Association.

Reynolds, M. C. (2012). "Lay of the Land: The State of Bibliographic Instruction Efforts in ARL Special Collections Libraries." *RBM: A Journal of Rare Books, Manuscripts, and Cultural Heritage* 13, no. 1: 13–26.

Robertson, M. J., and J. G. Jones. (2009). "Exploring Academic Library Users' Preferences of Delivery Methods for Library Instruction." *Reference & User Services Quarterly* 48, no. 3: 259–69.

Chapter Five

Using Digital Badges to Enhance Research Instruction in Academic Libraries

Susan David deMaine, Catherine A. Lemmer,
Benjamin J. Keele, and Hannah Alcasid

INTRODUCTION

Digital badges are an electronic means of communicating credentials or achievements. They have a visual element, similar to an icon or a scouting badge, which creates an initial indication of the credential. With a click, badges then convey metadata about the learning path required to earn the credential and can provide access to more information or work product. They are "instantly accessible portals to evidence of a person's accomplishment, like internships and portfolios of work" (Carey, 2012, Nov. 2). At their best, badges can create a sort of interactive e-résumé. Thus far, they have proven particularly popular in computer-oriented fields such as programming, web design, and game design, but they are making headway in other academic areas as well.

Librarians—whether in academic libraries, public libraries, or specialized libraries—do extensive amounts of education, but rarely do they have mechanisms to acknowledge student achievement or be acknowledged themselves for the teaching they provide. Digital badges offer new opportunities for librarians to add value to existing educational systems and be acknowledged as educators. Take the following example: a librarian may partner with a humanities professor whose students must write a research paper by the end of the semester. Typically, the librarian may be invited into the classroom, or the students may be sent to the library for a single research lesson on data-

59

bases and search terms—not enough for truly high-quality research. A better alternative may be that the professor require the students to complete a series of badges—designed, implemented, and managed by the librarian—that build thorough research skills and ultimately produce a better paper (for example, University of Central Florida [UCF] [2014]). The badge program adds value to the humanities course without much additional cost to the university, better research is conducted, student achievement is recognized, and teaching by librarians in their area of expertise is acknowledged and validated. In addition, not only would the badges enable students to communicate their research competencies digitally, but they would also act as an incentive for further training.

This chapter explores the nature and potential of badges, their technical aspects, and the institutional issues involved in establishing digital badge programs in academic libraries.

THE NATURE AND APPLICATION OF DIGITAL BADGES

Badges come in many forms and have been used for centuries as indicators of credentials, achievements, and rank. As Halavais (2012) points out, badges have also been used to mark people as belonging to a group (for good or ill), to indicate authority (military ranks), or to simply communicate a viewpoint (bumper stickers and political buttons).

Badges hearken back at least as far as the Middle Ages, where pilgrims wore badges to communicate which holy sites they had visited (BBC, n.d.), and servants, retainers, and followers wore badges indicating their loyalty to a particular nobleman (Fox-Davies, 1907, p. 14). The United States military has been issuing badges since the Revolutionary War (Washington, 1782), though the system of military badges expanded considerably in the twentieth century to indicate skills, identity, and rank (Navy Personnel Command, 2011). Of course, scouting organizations have long used badges as signs of achievements. Sir Robert Baden-Powell included identification and proficiency badges in *Scouting for Boys*, the 1908 publication that gave rise to modern scouting organizations (Baden-Powell, 1908/2007, p. 37). Other examples include police badges and martial arts belts (Halavais, 2012).

More recently, badges have been popularized by the video and online gaming communities. Badges and similar indicators are used to reward and communicate progress or achievement in a game. Research indicates that incentives, progress, and rewards—even when they are only ephemeral—are vital characteristics of successful games (Zichermann & Cunningham, 2011). A good example of this is SuperBetter (n.d.), a website that encourages players to improve their health and increase their personal resilience by mapping their own goals, incentives, and rewards in a gamelike environment.

Likewise, skill-based incentives in a learning process have been identified as a means to motivate beginners and even those with intermediate skills when other forms of promotion are not available or not relevant. As Halavais explains,

> Badges of achievement do more than just celebrate a particular victory or ability. From very early on, it became clear that they encouraged excellence and the development of particular skills, or even just participation in a collective action. While a trophy or medal is one way of inducing competition among a group to see who might become the most skilled, this does little to motivate the neophyte. As a result, indications of more discrete skills, and of levels of skill, have frequently been adopted as a way to shape behavior. (Halavais, 2012)

Because of this potential to motivate all kinds of learning, educators are interested in digital badges. They are being implemented by K–12 teachers (Ferdig & Pytash, 2014), the Smithsonian Institution (Waters, 2013), and institutions of higher learning including Purdue University, Carnegie Mellon University, and the University of California, Davis (Carey, November 2, 2012).

According to Brent Herbert-Copley of Canada's Social Sciences and Humanities Research Council, the ideal college graduate is now "T-shaped," combining a broad set of skills such as information literacy, writing, communication, and teamwork (the horizontal stroke) with in-depth knowledge in a particular area (the vertical stroke) (Herbert-Copley, 2013). Badges provide students seeking these horizontal skills with structure for their learning, recognition of their achievement, and the means to communicate their skills to potential employers.

Enthusiasts point to several aspects of digital badges that make them flexible and informative. Perhaps the biggest advantage is that badges have the capacity to convey far more information about the learning path than traditional grades or transcripts. Someone seeing an "A" on a typical transcript cannot readily know what earning that "A" actually entailed. A list of classes taken or a degree granted can give some impression of a body of knowledge, but the impression is built on nothing more than course titles or the degree major. In contrast, badges are "talkative" (Rughinis, 2013). They can carry with them all the information about the requirements involved in earning the badge, who issued the badge and what their level of expertise is, what the student accomplished, when the badge expires (if applicable), and how the accomplishment relates to other learning experiences and other badges. Badges can also provide a portal to a work product created in pursuit of the badge. In short, they provide evidence-based documentation of an achievement (Casilli, 2012).

A second advantage of badges is that, thanks to projects such as Mozilla's Open Badge Initiative, badges can easily be designed and issued by anyone. Although this may seem threatening to traditional educational institutions that have long dominated the credentialing market (Carey, 2012, March 13), a more open system of credentialing through badges may well benefit society at large. Erin Knight, senior director of Learning at Mozilla, sees badges as an opportunity to counter the monopoly accredited schools have on education that "counts" (Carey, 2012, Nov. 2).

Digital badges are also highly portable. People collect badges in portfolios—called backpacks, wallets, passports—that can include badges from multiple issuers. Figure 5.1 offers an example of a Mozilla Open Badge Backpack. Badge issuers may be traditional educational institutions or alternative sources of learning, but together they can give a fuller picture of a person's commitment to learning and expertise. Badges can be organized into different portfolios, such as one for a job search, one for a graduate school application, and one for a hobby. Badges can easily be communicated via social media, e-mail, and personal or professional websites, all at no cost to the badge earner. "[B]adges may be not just an alternative to traditional résumés and transcripts but an improvement on them" (Carey, 2012, Nov. 2).

In addition, research instruction itself would likely benefit from the use of badges. Research and information literacy classes typically develop a student's skills in a few discrete areas, each limited by the time available and the

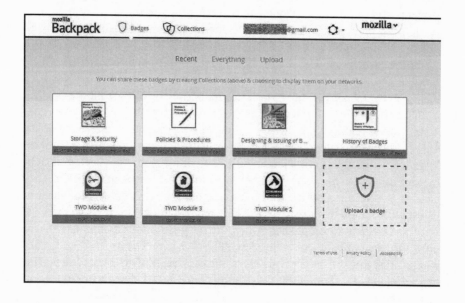

Figure 5.1.   Mozilla Open Badge Backpack.

readiness of the students. These limitations keep instructional librarians from delving deeply into these skills, thereby limiting the instruction all students receive. Offering optional badges would let librarians provide advanced instruction to those students seeking greater expertise without pushing up against the limits of time, interest, and readiness on the part of an entire group. The self-selection for advanced badges would also give students control over their individual educational goals and needs.

This idea of a series of badges leads to the notion of metabadges. Metabadges are simply badges that indicate completion of multiple related badges. This can help communicate both iterative progress as well as mastery, similar to a progression of courses taken to complete a major or a graduate degree. The University of Central Florida's information literacy badge program offers a good example. At the basic level, students who complete any of the library's information literacy instruction modules and score at least 80 percent on the module's quiz earn a digital badge. If a student goes on to earn all five badges in the "Gather" series, he or she gets the "Gather Information" metabadge. Similarly, earning all four badges in the "Evaluate" series results in the "Evaluate Information" metabadge, and so on. Adding another layer, if a student earns all three second-tier metabadges (which requires earning all fourteen first-tier badges), they earn the grand prize: the top-tier "Information Literacy" metabadge (University of Central Florida, 2014). In a comprehensive system like this, not only do the badges build on one another in substance, but they can also be designed to be visually coherent: distinguishable from one another yet with similarities that tie the whole together. The overall effect is attractive and clearly communicates both iterative learning and overall advancement. Figure 5.2 gives an illustration of what badges from a three-tiered system might look like.

Although badges have many benefits, there are some potential pitfalls and plenty of unknowns. Authentication (determining that the badge has not been altered) and validation/verification (checking that the badge has actually been earned and issued by the stated issuer) are major concerns. It is also important, particularly in the academic context, to make sure that the badge does not come to replace the learning it represents. A badge is a symbol that other skills and knowledge exist in this individual's portfolio of skills and talents. Therefore, badges awarded in the educational context must reflect time and effort and be based on vetted standards, or they will become empty symbols (Edwards & Green, 2014).

Educators also worry about badges setting up a system of external motivation when they would prefer students to be intrinsically motivated. In fact, it may well be this fear of extrinsic motivation that makes people leery of the idea of "gamification" in learning (Edwards & Green, 2014). Pure intrinsic motivation may be unrealistic, though, and a well-structured badge program can offer a reasonable balance between extrinsic and intrinsic motivation. On

Expand Your Research Badge (first tier)

Collect Information Metabadge (second tier)

Research Skills Metabadge (top tier, combining all second tier badges)

Figure 5.2.   Three-tiered badges example.

the one hand, people enjoy the sense of accomplishment when they acquire a symbol of their achievements; on the other hand, badges can be designed to build layers of learning, with one badge pointing to the next level of instruction and enticing the learner with suggestions as to how useful that new knowledge will be (Rughinis, 2013; Kim, 2012).

Well-designed badges hold promise for learning. Research on the overall effectiveness of badges in higher education is still sparse (Domínguez et al., 2013), but with the continued growth of online education, social media, and electronic résumés, it is likely that badges in some shape or form will continue to be developed and promoted.

CONSIDERATIONS IN DEVELOPING A BADGE SYSTEM

Digital credentialing recognizes "learning of many kinds which are acquired beyond formal education institutions . . . ; it proliferates and disperses authority over what learning to recognize; and it provides a means of translation and commensuration across multiple spheres" (Olneck, 2012, p. 1). This dispersion of authority challenges the norms of mainstream higher education. Dan Hickey, associate professor of learning sciences and a research scientist for Indiana University's Center for Research on Learning and Technology, warns that adopting badges at the university level presents many challenges, because early adopters may not fully anticipate the impact that badges have on "the whole ecosystem" of higher education (Raths, 2013). Getting institutional buy-in for a badge program will require convincing administrators and faculty that the opportunities presented by digital badges outweigh the challenges.

University digital badge projects are rarely a top-down undertaking. Typically, digital badge programs arise from collaborative efforts "of people agitating from the middle" (Raths, 2013). If you are a mid-level agitator, what challenges do you need to anticipate and prepare to resolve if you want to bring your badge program to fruition?

An important first step is to understand where the university lies on the spectrum of technology adoption and innovation. A starting point might be to assess the institution's view of instructional technology and online education. If the institution prides itself on educational innovation, it may grant greater latitude than an institution that is not an early adopter. For example, Hickey notes that Indiana University, where he works, has allowed projects to move forward with the understanding that policy issues will be resolved later (Raths, 2013). Elsewhere, however, and with no small amount of irony, the digital environment is perceived as riskier, and institutions that previously paid no mind when academic units handed out paper certificates evidencing the completion of specialized learning opportunities may be alarmed by digital badges. To alleviate concerns, a badge program proposal will need to address the following questions.

1. What skills or experiences are students seeking to enhance their portfolios or résumés? In what areas do they need encouragement for further learning?

At the Agriculture Sustainability Institute at the University of California, Davis, faculty implemented a badge program for undergraduate majors in Sustainable Agriculture and Food Systems. Students were acquiring valuable skills outside the traditional curriculum, and faculty wanted to help students document these activities. The badges recognize outside-the-classroom activities that align with the Institute's core competencies of "systems thinking, experimentation and inquiry, understanding values and interpersonal communication" (Buell, 2013).

This University of California, Davis program is an example of a badge system driven by student activities. Badges can also be driven by instructor or librarian identification of areas in which more learning is needed, achievements could be better recognized, and incentives are lacking. What employers want can also be highly relevant in determining what skills should be emphasized in a badge program.

2. What institution or academic unit is standing behind the badge?

The value of a badge depends in large part on the reputation of the issuer. Students are likely to want the full value of their institution behind the badge to impress potential employers. On the other hand, universities and colleges need to be protective of the value of their brand. They may require institutional approval of the badge criteria, and want to be assured of the validity of any badges issued under their auspices. A proposal will need to speak to concerns of authentication and fraud and how the selected technology addresses these issues.

Seeking the backing of the institution is important on the front end. The university's crest on the badge may or may not be a motivator for all students; however, those students for which the crest is a motivator will cry foul if their newly earned badge does not have the status of the university behind it when they expected otherwise.

Because the politics and personalities within colleges and universities vary, the need to align with an academic unit may vary as well. In one institution, a badge program might be most successful if it stays within a single academic unit, while elsewhere it will work best to cross disciplinary lines and seek multiple bases of support. Considerations might include subject expertise, responsibility for the workload, technological confidence, relationships with students, and ties to the professional development office.

3. Does the badge program support or enhance existing curriculum, and if so, how? Or does it supplant existing curriculum opportunities, and if so, why will the badge program be an improvement?

In the University of California, Davis, example, student experiences outside the classroom provided the impetus for the badge program, and the badges in turn support the existing curriculum. What happens if your badge program seeks to replace a traditional course? Badges that replace existing curriculum options will probably face greater resistance. Replacing existing curriculum can raise questions about accreditation and may have an impact on tuition revenue. A badge program proposal will need to speak to why allowing students to earn a non-tuition or reduced-tuition badge makes sense.

Massive open online courses (MOOCs) may have already laid the supporting groundwork for badge programs that supplant specific coursework. Some universities are allowing students to complete MOOCs and earn completion certificates. Are these completion certificates appearing on transcripts? Are MOOCs being seen as an equivalent rather than a watered-down version of the for-credit curriculum? Are MOOCs allowed to stand in for introductory credit-bearing courses? If yes, it makes sense that digital badges could gain a similar foothold.

4. How will the criteria for earning the badge be determined and vetted?

A badge system is more likely to be successful when the content of the badges is well designed and supported by an interested community (Carey, 2012, April 8). Developing criteria for a badge is familiar to instructors; the questions are those that any instructor addresses when developing a new course. Who should be involved in developing the criteria? Does some university unit, such as an academic affairs committee, need to approve the criteria? Will the criteria be measured against outside standards? What are the learning outcomes the students should achieve? How will satisfaction of the criteria be measured?

For academic librarians wanting to issue badges for research skills, this community already exists and has agreed-upon general standards (Association of College & Research Libraries, n.d.). Standards exist in specialty areas as well, such as the *Principles and Standards for Legal Research Competency* issued by the American Association of Law Libraries (American Association of Law Libraries, 2013).

While aligning badges to vetted standards is recommended, each badge system can still be unique, with its specific steps, expectations, and parameters determined by the issuer. This leaves room for both professional creativity and tweaking of standards so that diverse forms of learning can be recognized and valued. Historically, credentials have fulfilled two roles in education: recognition of learning and recognition of desirable learning behaviors (Halavais, 2012). An "A" on an exam and extra credit points awarded for participation in class are both symbols of achievement, the "A" recognizing mastery of content and the extra credit points recognizing a particular education-enhancing behavior. A badge system can be unique in its implementation of these two roles, because it can reward both in one iteration and communicate both achievements via its metadata.

5. What metadata will be included, and how will it be maintained?

The purpose of metadata is to provide sufficient evidence for a badge viewer (a potential employer, a supervisor, an admissions officer) to comprehend and value the individual's accomplishment. Unlike metadata, transcripts and résumés have limited qualitative and comparative value. A transcript includes only the basics such as a course name and number, the date the course was taken, and the grade earned. Similarly, a résumé lists dates of employment with a particular employer and provides only a brief description of the position prepared by the résumé owner.

Badge metadata is largely unconstrained. In addition to providing the date the badge was earned and the issuing organization, metadata can detail the work produced to earn the badge. Badge metadata typically includes the criteria used to evaluate the learner, but more is possible. It could include access to the actual lesson as well as work product such as a capstone project or student portfolio. It is this ability to link to actual evidence of experience or knowledge that moves badges far beyond the traditional résumé or transcript in providing information useful in fully evaluating the individual's accomplishments. The connections possible with digital badges are exciting, but they do raise questions about student privacy, which are discussed below.

Badge metadata raises two other issues, both related to the longevity of the badge. First is the question of expiration. Some credentials, such as diplomas, never expire. Others, such as professional licenses, require continuing education or annual fees. Then there are credentials that expire after a stated time, such as CPR certification. Some research skills are relatively timeless and universal—planning, devising search terms, documenting your findings, and avoiding plagiarism. Other skills are more susceptible to changes in technology. Digital badges for these latter skills run the risk of growing stale and may merit an expiration date.

The second issue is maintenance of the metadata. Once a badge exists, most of its data should be static—name and description of the badge, name of the earner, issuer, date—and remain intact as long as the host remains in business. Links to outside materials, however, are susceptible to link rot. For example, if you design a badge with a link to the course syllabus, one small change in the filename for that syllabus breaks that link and undermines the badge's value. Persistent links and reliable hosting of materials are crucial.

6. How is scalability built into the badge program so that it can expand to meet demand?

It is important to have a sense of the entire scope of the project even if you do not intend to roll it all out at once. If you anticipate that the learning opportunities can expand over multiple levels, it is smart to design multiple badges that build on each other on the front end just as you would map out courses that build on each other. The level one badge should adequately prepare the student for the level two badge, and so on. At the same time, the design of the badge program, if done with care, can allow students to gain valuable skills at every level, making it possible to piece together an individualized learning path. A badge program that is initially designed to scale both up and down is better in the long run for both the badge earners and for those administering the badges.

7. How will you build faculty support for and student interest in the badge program?

The fortunate badge program will have a powerful advocate and an interested student base. As an advocate, a librarian designing a badge program will need to articulate the value and need for the badge program. The story will need to be compelling in order to generate time and funding commitments. It will fall on the advocate to explain the benefits, design a prototype to help people understand how a badge works, survey students as to their level of interest, prepare a marketing campaign, and reassure faculty that the badges enhance rather than threaten instructional offerings.

Employer expectations are likely to be key to buy-in. The advancement and acceptance of badges will depend on the "information needs of employers, the validity of the information conveyed by badges, the efficiency and practicality of prospective employees acquiring badges, and the efficiency and practicality of prospective employers utilizing them" (Olneck, 2012, p. 4). Institutions of higher education that understand this equation will be able to participate in the badge phenomenon without risking their own role in continuing to deliver education.

A digital badge program does not have to be an "us versus them" situation. As demonstrated by both Purdue University, where badges have been used to teach nanotechnology and other science-related subjects to students around the world, and the Agriculture Sustainability Institute at the University of California, Davis, digital badge programs can easily coexist with traditional educational efforts and expand rather than threaten our view of learning. In these instances, the institutions identified skills desired by students and employers along with experiences that arose naturally out of the current educational programs. As these programs demonstrate, digital badge programs do not need to replace existing traditional educational efforts; rather, they bring "more people, more activities, and more kinds of learning, doing, and being within the embrace" of higher education (Olneck, 2012, p. 6).

8. What technology is involved, and how does it work?

In September 2011, the MacArthur Foundation, along with Mozilla and the Humanities, Arts, Science, and Technology Alliance and Collaboratory (HASTAC, pronounced "haystack"), announced the Digital Media & Learning Competition. This two million dollar competition was designed to encourage the development of badges across diverse organizations. Simultaneously, Mozilla announced development of its Open Badge Infrastructure (OBI) (Mozilla, n.d.). In their press release, Mozilla stated, "Open Badges is a response to this trend: an open specification and APIs that provide any organization the basic building blocks they need to offer badges in a standard, interoperable manner" (Surman, 2011). The MacArthur Foundation press release added, "Mozilla is creating an Open Badge Infrastructure—a decentralized online platform that will house digital badges and can be used across operating platforms and by any organization or user. This approach will help to make digital badges a coherent, portable and meaningful way to demonstrate capabilities. It will also encourage the creation of 'digital backpacks' of badges that people will carry to showcase the skills, knowledge and competencies they have gained" (MacArthur Foundation, 2011).

API stands for "application programming interface." API is generally used to refer to a collection of functions that determine how computer applications interact with each other. With the OBI, Mozilla has standardized the functions of how badges can be issued, authenticated, and verified, thus enabling portability and consistency across various platforms. An API also determines how badges can be displayed in places other than a hosted storage space. Having created this "ecosystem" for digital badges, Mozilla's Open Badges has become the preeminent open-source framework for digital badge creation, storage, and management. A number of platforms, including Achievery, Badge Forge, Credly, and Sash, operate on the OBI standard (University of Southern California, The Center for Scholarly Technology, 2013).

When awarded to a learner, badges are pushed into a storage space for the learner to manage and make available for display in other digital spaces, such as a blog or social media sites. In Open Badges, this storage space is called the Backpack (see Figure 5.1). With programming knowledge, custom badge systems can be made, but staying within the OBI ensures portability, allowing the badges to be communicated to broader communities.

The visual element of a badge can be created in any type of image editing software, including Adobe Fireworks, Adobe Illustrator, Microsoft Paint, or even Microsoft PowerPoint. Any software that can generate a .png (portable network graphics), .jpg (joint photographic experts group), or .gif (graphics interchange format) file is suitable for creating a badge. When working with

Mozilla's Open Badges, the image must be a .png file, and the standard file size is 256KB or less. Other badge hosting systems may allow other file types and sizes.

Since creators of badges may not possess the skills needed to create these optimized image files, open-source image libraries of badges are available. Mozilla even built a badge design studio where a badge creator can design and export badges made by navigating through drop-down menus and choosing from preselected templates, patterns, and images (Chicago Summer of Learning, 2013). A similar service called, not surprisingly, Open Badge Designer is offered by MyKnowledgeMap. Here, badge creators can devise a badge while also having the ability to choose a workflow that integrates other software that will seamlessly encode the image with metadata (MyKnowledgeMap, 2014).

As discussed above, common metadata designated for badges are the date of issue, name of recipient, title and affiliation of the person who verified the work needed to achieve the badge, scores, and access to assessments such as exam questions. With Mozilla's Open Badges, this metadata is specified in a .json (java script object notation) file. If using custom programming, this data may also be specified in an .xml (extensible markup language) file or other script that can be interpreted and embedded into the image file.

Once the badge image and necessary metadata have been prepared, the metadata has to be associated with the image. Mozilla refers to this process as "baking" in the metadata. It happens in one of two ways: (1) taking the metadata of the unique learner and baking it into the badge's image file, or (2) using an issuer API to bake the metadata into the badge upon verification and push it into the Backpack. Currently, baking can be done through Mozilla's "baking service." This service interprets the .json file and encodes the image, producing a new .png containing a link. When a viewer clicks on the badge, a window will open, displaying the specified metadata in a user-friendly format. Figure 5.3 provides a basic example of badge metadata as displayed when a user clicks on a badge.

Mozilla's OBI has two support features that can confirm a badge's legitimacy: the authentication channel and the verification channel. The authentication channel assures viewers that the badge was actually issued to the learner, is not expired, and has not been altered since it was issued. The verification channel is used by an issuing organization or individual to add an encrypted signature. Though this is not a required step, it does make the badge more trustworthy. When a badge is verified, the administrator of a badge storage space can communicate with the issuing organization to make certain the badge carries the signature.

Ongoing work is being done to further streamline the workflow of creating, encoding, building requirements or tasks for achievement, evaluating, issuing, and storing digital badges. In March 2014, Mozilla released a limited

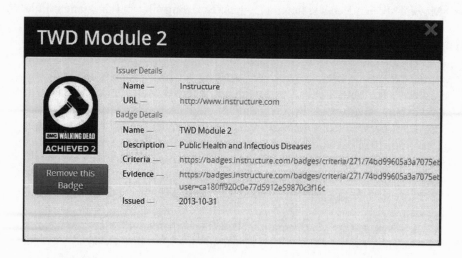

Figure 5.3.   Example of basic badge metadata.

beta version of an Open Badges application and API called BadgeKit. This will create a more user-friendly interface for badge creators, tools for creating badges, and ease in interacting with badge earners.

9. What will the badge program cost?

Badge projects on university campuses tend to begin with collaborative efforts of subject experts, and some aspects of a badge program can be done at no to very low cost. For example, you can design a simple badge icon and house it through Mozilla's Open Badge Initiative for free. At some point, however, instructional design, graphic design, and technological support may be required. A budget might include costs of professionally designed visuals, the assistance of an expert in instructional design if there are online lessons, and tech support for both instruction and management of the badge metadata. If available, costs from comparable projects would be helpful in proposing a budget.

10. What legal concerns need to be addressed?

• *Privacy concerns*

Badges may implicate federal privacy laws dealing with educational records. The Family Educational Rights and Privacy Act of 1974 (FERPA) requires educational institutions that accept federal funding to permit students to access their education records, petition for corrections, and control disclosure of certain records. If the student is a minor, then the parents have these rights. Violating a student's rights under FERPA can lead to unpleasant investigations from the U.S. Department of Education and, at worst, jeopardize federal funding. In general, libraries issuing badges should have thorough records access and disclosure policies to ensure compliance with FERPA and to uphold librarianship's long-standing privacy protection ethos.

FERPA applies to "educational records," so the initial consideration is whether a badge is an educational record. For purposes of FERPA, educational records are those that contain information directly related to a student and are maintained by an educational institution or someone acting on their behalf. Since a badge earned by a student contains information directly related to that student, it is likely to be deemed an educational record. In addition, even if an academic library hires a company to maintain its badge program, the badges would still be educational records since the outside company would be acting on behalf of the educational institution.

Since most badges are likely to be educational records under FERPA, a badge program must take into account FERPA requirements. Yet badges are specifically designed to facilitate open communication about student achievements, and pieces of metadata cannot be turned on and off at will once they are baked in. The entire badge can be hidden, but then it has no value. How can we resolve this tension between privacy requirements and the "talkativeness" of badges?

One possible resolution is offered by the FERPA exception for "directory information." Directory information is a student's name, address, telephone number, date and place of birth, major, participation in officially recognized activities and sports, dates of attendance, degrees and awards received, and last school attended. Directory information can be disclosed if the school has: (1) issued a public notice detailing what information can be released as directory information, and (2) given students an opportunity to instruct that their directory information not be released. Under the directory information exception, libraries could display badges (typically in something like OBI's Backpack but perhaps also in congratulatory website postings or alumni newsletters) that include a student's name in the metadata and the nature of the award represented by the badge. At the same time, libraries should not include grades or assessment scores in the metadata because that information does not fall under the directory information exception.

Relying on the directory information exception is essentially an opt-out system; the library will disclose only basic student information in badge metadata unless the student opts out, in which case the library or its vendor would not display the badge. This places responsibility for display of the badge on the institution, subject to notification of the student's wishes.

Given that badges are generally designed so that communication of them is controlled by the badge earner, a more workable option is to seek student consent at the outset. Under FERPA, any educational record can be released with the student's written consent. When a student signs up for a badge program, the library can require the student to sign a consent form releasing the badge as an educational record. This opens up the metadata possibilities by removing the badge from the directory information exception, and aligns much more readily with the way badges and badge portfolios work. It grants the student control over the badges in their portfolio, and leaves room for the library to communicate its badges for publicity purposes.

Although written consent allows the release of any record, libraries should still consider carefully what information will be included in a badge's metadata. For instance, if students must pass an exam as part of the requirements for earning a badge, should the badge's metadata include the actual test score? Or is the issuance of the badge enough information? As discussed earlier, badges are powerful in part because there are few limits on the information they could communicate, but too much information may infringe on librarianship's ethos of privacy and may make student consent hard to gain. Depending on the nature of the work, some students may be uncomfortable with making a badge publicly accessible. For example, disclosing test scores may raise students' defenses while sharing portfolio work may not. The value of a badge is greatly reduced if it is not shared publicly, so it is best to include enough assessment information in the badge metadata to support the badge award but not so much that students feel exposed. For instance, the metadata could include a link to the badge requirements and a statement that those requirements have been satisfied. If someone later wants access to more detailed assessment information, requests for those records can be handled like other educational records and require written consent from the student.

Also, the badge itself may inadvertently disclose assessment information that is too specific. For example, issuing a "gold" version of a badge that requires a particular score or grade may be disclosing information that the library would not normally include in metadata. Different levels of badges can be highly effective, but consider each level carefully so as not to inadvertently disclose information the library deems too confidential.

• *Trademark concerns*

When designing the image that will visually represent a badge, it may be tempting to use a recognizable logo. For example, a badge indicating mastery of a particular computer program could display the program's logo, or a badge issued by a unit within an educational institution could display the institution's crest. Succumbing to such temptation is legally very risky. Many educational institutions and companies closely control use of their logos and other distinctive markings, especially if they have registered the marks as trademarks protected under the federal trademark law.(See Trademark Act of 1943.)

Trademark law is designed to help prevent confusion in the marketplace as to who is responsible for a product or service (Dinwoodie & Janis, 2007, p. 1599). If a badge uses a logo that could indicate that connection to or endorsement by the trademark owner, the badge may attract some unwanted attention. There are some exceptions that permit using trademarks without the owners' permission, but prudent badge design involves avoiding use of trademarks, obtaining permission from the trademark owner, or eliminating any suggestion that the trademark owner endorses or is affiliated with the badge.

Academic institutions are often just as protective of their trademarks and visual identities as businesses are. Academic libraries may be able to obtain permission to use a university trademark, but there may be specifications that must be followed to help maintain the school's brand. The University of Texas's Wordmark guidelines are a good example of this (University of Texas at Austin, n.d.). Before adding an institutional seal or well-known mark to a badge, check for visual identity or trademark use policies.

11. What are the measures of success for the badge program?

The success of a badge program depends on delivering the desired learning outcomes and accruing benefits to the students earning the digital badges. A badge program design should include ways of tracking student achievement and following up with students to find out how useful the badge program was for them. Generally, statistics on participation, completion, and short-term feedback will provide the baseline, but planning the means to contact badge earners about the usefulness of the program after six months or a year would be remarkably valuable.

In the end, be prepared for the long haul. Collaborative projects, especially those attempting to address challenging and complex questions with innovation, require time to hear all parties and respond to and resolve concerns at multiple levels. As a result, digital badge programs do not happen overnight. Most programs take over a year to launch. For example, the University of California, Davis, badge program was in development for eighteen months (Arizona State University, 2013; Raths, 2013). As in all new ventures and projects, the success of a digital badge program lies in part in the detail and depth of the proposal. Cutting short the planning process may significantly damage the ultimate success of the program.

CONCLUSION

Badges have long been used as indicators of credentials, achievements, and rank in many arenas. The advent of academic credentialing through digital badges issued by a multitude of players opens many possibilities for recognizing and validating learning outside the traditional classroom. In addition, digital badges present academic librarians, often unacknowledged for their many teaching efforts, with an opportunity to move the recognition of their teaching and their impact on students' educational experiences into the limelight. Although badge programs are challenging to develop and implement, courageous and inventive librarians can seize this exciting and innovative opportunity to validate their students' efforts and their own contributions to higher education.

NOTE

The authors are colleagues at the Indiana University Robert H. McKinney School of Law, Ruth Lilly Law Library. Susan David deMaine, J.D., M.S.L.S., and Benjamin J. Keele, J.D., M.L.S., are Research and Instructional Services Librarians. Catherine A. Lemmer, J.D., M.S.L.I.S., is Head of Information Services, and Hannah Alcasid, B.A., is the Electronic Information and Data Support Technician.

REFERENCES

American Association of Law Libraries. (2013). "Principles and Standards for Legal Research Competency." http://www.aallnet.org/main-menu/Leadership-Governance/policies/Public-Policies/policy-legalrescompetency.html.

Arizona State University. (2013). "Digital Learning Badges: Project Plan/Proposal." http://www.educause.edu/sites/default/files/library/presentations/EC141/PS04/DigitalBadgesin-HigherEdCertifyingResearchSkillsforSelf-DirectedOnlineLearningFacultyFutureEmployers-ExampleProjectPlanandTimelin.pdf.

Association of College and Research Libraries. (n.d.). "Information Literacy Competency Standards for Higher Education." http://www.ala.org/acrl/standards/informationliteracycompetency.

Baden-Powell, R. (1908/2007). *Scouting for Boys: The Original 1908 Edition*. http://books.google.com/books?id=R2lJgMD9MRAC.

BBC. (n.d.). Medieval Pilgrim badge. http://www.bbc.co.uk/ahistoryoftheworld/objects/nMwqDkEfSV6DUUEldDLCXA.

Buell, C. (2013, Aug. 30). "Using Badges to Quantify Learning Outcomes at UC Davis." *edcetera*. http://edcetera.rafter.com/using-badges-to-quantify-learning-outcomes-at-uc-davis/.

Carey, K. (2012, March 13). "The Higher Education Monopoly Is Crumbling As We Speak." *The New Republic*. http://www.newrepublic.com/article/politics/101620/higher-education-accreditation-MIT-university.

Carey, K. (2012, April 8). "A Future Full of Badges." *The Chronicle of Higher Education*. http://chronicle.com/article/A-Future-Full-of-Badges/131455/.

Carey, K. (2012, Nov. 2). "Show Me Your Badge." *New York Times*. http://www.nytimes.com/2012/11/04/education/edlife/show-me-your-badge.html.

Casilli, C. (2012, July 31). "Mozilla Open Badges: The Ecosystem Begins to Take Shape." *Persona.* http://carlacasilli.wordpress.com/2012/07/31/mozilla-open-badges-the-ecosystem-begins-to-take-shape/.

Chicago Summer of Learning. (2013). Badge Studio. https://web.archive.org/web/20140821191514/http://badgestudio.chicagosummeroflearning.org/

Dinwoodie, G. B., and M. D. Janis. (2007). "Confusion over Use: Contextualism in Trademark Law." *Iowa Law Review* 92: 1597–667.

Domínguez, A., et al. (2013). "Gamifying Learning Experiences: Practical Implications and Outcomes." *Computers & Education* 63: 380–92. http://dx.doi.org/10.1016/j.compedu.2012.12.020.

Edwards, E., and A. Green. (2014, Feb. 24). "Confusion, Trends & Possibilities with Gamification for e-Learning." *e-Learning Leadership Blog.* http://info.alleninteractions.com/bid/101522/Confusion-Trends-Possibilities-with-Gamification-for-e-Learning.

Family Educational Rights and Privacy Act of 1974. 20 U.S.C. § 1232g.

Ferdig, R., and K. Pytash. (2014). "There's a Badge for That." *Tech & Learning.* http://www.techlearning.com/features/0039/theres-a-badge-for-that/54727.

Fox-Davies, A. C. (1907). *Heraldic Badges.* http://books.google.co.uk/books?id=HKMrAAAAIAAJ.

Halavais, A. M. C. (2012). "A Genealogy of Badges: Inherited Meaning and Monstrous Moral Hybrids." *Information, Communication & Society* 15: 354–73. http://www.tandfonline.com/doi/abs/10.1080/1369118X.2011.641992

Herbert-Copley, B. (2013, May 1). "Ditch the Resume and Pick Up a Badge, They're Not Just for Boy Scouts." *The Globe and Mail.* http://www.theglobeandmail.com/news/national/education/ditch-the-resume-and-pick-up-a-badge-theyre-not-just-for-boy-scouts/article11639205/.

Kim, B. (2012, Aug. 7). "Why Gamify and What to Avoid in Library Gamification." *ACRL TechConnect Blog.* http://acrl.ala.org/techconnect/?p=1633.

MacArthur Foundation. (2011). Press release. "Digital Media & Learning Competition Provides $2 Million for Innovations in Digital Badges." http://www.macfound.org/press/press-releases/digital-media-learning-competition-provides-2-million-for-innovations-in-digital-badges/.

Mozilla. (n.d.). Open Badges. Retrieved from http://www.openbadges.org/.

MyKnowledgeMap. (2014). Open Badge Designer. https://www.openbadges.me/.

Navy Personnel Command. (2011). "Identification Badges/Awards/Insignia." http://www.public.navy.mil/bupers-npc/support/uniforms/uniformregulations/chapter5/Pages/default.aspx.

Olneck, M. R. (2012). "Insurgent Credentials: A Challenge to Established Institutions of Higher Education?" http://www.hastac.org/files/insurgent_credentials__michael_olneck_2012.pdf.

Raths, D. (2013, June 20). "How Badges Really Work in Higher Education." *Campus Technology.* http://campustechnology.com/Articles/2013/06/20/How-Badges-Really-Work-in-Higher-Education.aspx?Page=1.

Rughinis, R. (2013). "Talkative objects in need of interpretation. Re-thinking digital badges in education." In *CHI '13 Extended Abstracts on Human Factors in Computing Systems,* 2,099–2,108. http://dx.doi.org/10.1145/2468356.2468729.

SuperBetter. (n.d.). About SuperBetter. https://www.superbetter.com/about.

Surman, M. (2011, Sept. 15). "Mozilla Launches Open Badges Project." *The Mozilla Blog.* http://blog.mozilla.org/blog/2011/09/15/openbadges/.

Trademark Act of 1946. 15 U.S.C. § 1051.

University of Central Florida. (2014). Badges. http://infolit.ucf.edu/students/badges/.

University of Southern California, Center for Scholarly Technology. (2013). "Digital badge platforms." https://cst.usc.edu/files/2013/07/TechTeamBadgesfinal.pdf.

University of Texas at Austin. (n.d.). "Wordmark." http://www.utexas.edu/brand-guidelines/visual-style-guide/wordmark.

Washington, G. (1782, Aug. 7). "General Orders." In *The George Washington Papers at the Library of Congress, 1741–1799.* http://memory.loc.gov/cgi-bin/query/r?ammem/ mgw:@field%28DOCID+@lit%28gw240544%29%29.

Waters, J. K. (2013). "Everything You Ever Wanted to Know about Badging in the Classroom: Our Definitive Guide." *T.H.E. Journal.* http://thejournal.com/Articles/2013/05/30/Every-thing-You-Ever-Wanted-to-Know-about-Badging-in-the-Classroom-Our-Definitive-Guide.aspx.

Zichermann, G., and C. Cunningham. (2011). *Gamification by Design: Implementing Game Mechanics in Web and Mobile Apps.* Sebastopol, CA: O'Reilly Media.

Chapter Six

The Librarian and the Media Producer

Creating an Audio-Archive Based on a Unique Collection

Helen Fallon and Anne O'Brien

INTRODUCTION

The Ken Saro-Wiwa Audio Archive is one example of how libraries can develop and extend the understanding of Special Collections, in this case a collection of death-row letters.

Librarians need to give more thought to how to add value and understanding to Special Collections, and audio archives provide one possible route. There was extensive learning for both of the authors in the process; for the librarian, it was a journey of discovery into the world of sound; for the media producer, it was a journey through the sometimes complex area of Special Collections and Archives. Through collaborations, such as the one described below, libraries can maximize the visibility and use of their archives and special collections. Increasing visibility of such resources may help to acquire funding for new special collections, and may also encourage people to donate collections, knowing that the library is open to exploring avenues to widely promote such collections.

In November 2013, Dr. Owens Wiwa, brother of the late Ken Saro-Wiwa, Nigerian writer and international environmental rights activist, launched the Ken Saro-Wiwa Audio Archive in the Library at National University of Ireland Maynooth (NUIM). The launch of the audio archive and a book of letters by Ken Saro-Wiwa (Corley, Í., et al., 2013) marked the eighteenth anniversary of the execution of Saro-Wiwa and eight others (the Ogoni Nine) by the then Nigerian military government. The audio archive, created by NUI Maynooth Library and Kairos Communications, contains extensive recordings of people connected with Ken Saro-Wiwa. This chapter recounts the experiences of the two authors—a librarian and a media producer—in creating the audio archive. Following background information, it goes on to discuss the making of the recordings, hosting the audio archive in SoundCloud, and subsequent marketing and promotion. It concludes with a reflection by the two authors on the process.

BACKGROUND

An Irish Missionary

In November 2011, Sister Majella McCarron, a member of the religious congregation Our Lady of Apostles (OLA), donated a collection of twenty-eight letters and twenty-seven poems written by Ken Saro-Wiwa, artifacts and ephemera relating to Saro-Wiwa to the NUI Maynooth Library. McCarron had corresponded extensively with Saro-Wiwa during his two years in military detention, prior to his execution.

McCarron grew up in rural Fermanagh, in Northern Ireland. An avid writer from an early age, as a young girl she wrote away for books and a violin, sent letters with money for the "black babies," and at age twelve wrote to a religious order in response to an advertisement for religious vocations. After completing a science degree at University College Cork, she went on mission to Nigeria in 1964; she was to remain there for thirty years, teaching science at a secondary school and later teaching education at the university. She first met Saro-Wiwa in 1990. Nigerian universities had frequent strikes at that time, and during one such period she was asked by her Institute (Our Lady of Apostles) to identify activities by European businesses that were having an adverse effect on Nigeria. The Africa Europe Faith and Justice Network (AEFJN)—of which Our Lady of Apostles was a member—offered to lobby on behalf of such groups at the European Union (EU) level. McCarron was aware of the oil pollution problem in the Niger Delta caused by the activities of the international petrochemical industry and Saro-Wiwa's nonviolent campaign against Royal Dutch Shell, and began to discuss the issue with him.

Movement for the Survival of the Ogoni People (MOSOP)

Saro-Wiwa was a well-established businessman, writer, and television producer when he met McCarron. He had authored children's books, novels, plays, poetry, and articles/books on political/environmental issues. He produced and directed *Basi and Company*, a television sitcom that ran from 1985 to 1995 on Nigerian television, and which was later syndicated to stations across Africa.

Saro-Wiwa was a member of the Ogoni ethnic group. Ogoni is in the Niger Delta in southwestern Nigeria, an area with extensive oil reserves. While the then Nigerian military regime received massive revenues from the petrochemical industry, in Ogoni there was no piped water, no electricity, no hospitals, and schools were almost nonexistent. Alongside this, the environmental impact of the unchecked oil exploration had devastated the land. Water was contaminated, fish stocks depleted, the atmosphere poisoned with carbon dioxide and monoxide, farmland lay crusted in crude oil, and rain fell as acid rain. Against this background, Saro-Wiwa began a peaceful campaign against Royal Dutch Shell and the Nigerian government to challenge the state of affairs in Ogoni. He established the Movement for the Survival of the Ogoni People (MOSOP) in 1990, and began a peaceful protest to highlight the issues. McCarron worked with him on planning leadership training programs based on the psychosocial method of Paulo Freire, a Brazilian adult educator. Within three years of the establishment of MOSOP, on January 4, 1993, over three hundred thousand Ogonis, from a total population of half a million, protested in marches across each of the six kingdoms that comprise Ogoni. A small ethnic group managed, through peaceful protest, to defy one of the largest armies in Africa and force one of the most powerful corporations in the world to withdraw from Ogoni.

Government Backlash

But there was a price to pay. Following the marches, the Nigerian government, led by then military dictator Abacha, began to take Saro-Wiwa's campaigning seriously, afraid that MOSOP's protests would spread to other areas of the Niger Delta and threaten oil revenue. Saro-Wiwa was harassed, detained, and arrested on a number of occasions. In July 1993 Ogoni was blockaded by military checkpoints, villages were surrounded and attacked; hundreds were slaughtered. The government blamed the violence on local ethnic conflict. McCarron was active in the relief effort, helping to secure funding from Trócaire (an Irish-Catholic Church Aid Agency), who worked with Irish sisters from the Daughters of Charity in Port Harcourt running refugee camps to feed, clothe, and house the thousands of displaced survivors and to subsequently rebuild the devastated villages. The first letter in the collection is a letter from Saro-Wiwa thanking her for her efforts, and lending his support to funds being channeled through the Catholic Church (NUI Maynooth Ken Saro-Wiwa Archive).

Detention and Trial

Following the murder of four local chiefs in May 1994, Saro-Wiwa was arrested and accused of encouraging the killings. He and fourteen others were placed in military detention and held without charge. He continued to run MOSOP from detention, writing letters that were smuggled out in food baskets.

In August 1994, McCarron returned to Ireland for a sabbatical, having decided not to renew her contract at the University of Lagos where she had taught for thirteen years. She planned to work on the Northern Ireland conflict. The conversations begun in Nigeria continued on paper, and twenty-six of the twenty-eight letters written by Saro-Wiwa to Sister Majella date from 1994–1995. In these letters Saro-Wiwa writes about family, the Ogoni struggle against Royal Dutch Shell, and his conditions in detention. In an interview with the authors McCarron commented: "Ken saw me as a contact with the outside world; a way of getting his ideas and ideals out to a wider audience."

Back in Ireland, McCarron campaigned actively to save the lives of Ken Saro-Wiwa and eight others (the Ogoni Nine). Despite her efforts and international protest, he was hanged with eight others on November 10, 1995.

THE KEN SARO-WIWA ARCHIVE

Following the deaths of the Ogoni Nine, McCarron continued to work on environmental justice issues, as a table observer of the Northern Ireland Garvaghy Road conflict and the Irish Shell to Sea Campaign, a movement that opposes the construction by Shell of an overland gas pipeline and the establishment of an oil refinery in Erris, a coastal district in County Mayo in the west of Ireland. In 2010, NUI Maynooth student John O'Shea interviewed McCarron while working on his MA thesis, which related to Irish media coverage of the Shell to Sea Campaign. She told him about the Saro-Wiwa letters and poems, and expressed an interest in finding an appropriate home for this material, knowing the value it would have for present and future generations of scholars and activists. He contacted the library, who acquired the collection. (See Figure 6.1 for sample items.) Shortly after its receipt and processing, Dr Íde Corley, a lecturer in Post-Colonial Studies at NUI Maynooth, this author, the deputy university librarian, and Dr. Laurence Cox, a lecturer in social movements at NUI Maynooth, edited the letters, publishing them alongside the poems and contextual essays as *Silence Would Be Treason: Last Writings of Ken Saro-Wiwa* (Corley, Í., et al., 2013). While this was ongoing, the NUI Maynooth Library was approached by Kairos Communications—an Irish media company—with a view to creating an audio archive relating to Saro-Wiwa. The company is located near the NUI

Figure 6.1.   A cap that belonged to Ken Saro-Wiwa, an Ogoni flag with Ken Saro-Wiwa's signature, two letters written by Ken Saro-Wiwa to Sister Majella McCarron. *Copyright: National University of Ireland Maynooth. Photograph by Alan Monahan.*

Maynooth Campus and is involved in delivering undergraduate and postgraduate programs in media studies. They offered to do the recording on a pro bono basis.

Producing the Audio Archive

While the archive of letters and images that McCarron donated to the library is immensely valuable, and the book *Silence Would Be Treason* offers an astute analysis of Saro-Wiwa's work from a variety of perspectives, neither the archive nor the book entirely tell his story. The audio archive was designed to set out a more detailed and direct account of that story. Usually the hardest part of creating an audio archive is deciding on where the story is to be found. This was not the case with the Ken Saro-Wiwa audio archive, as the people who had the story were quite obvious, available, and willing to participate. In this case the story was most closely observed from an Irish perspective by McCarron, and from a personal perspective by Saro-Wiwa's brother, Owens Wiwa. The audio archive also contains an interview with Dr. Íde Corley on postcolonial African literature; Helen Fallon talking about the importance of the letters and other materials in the collection; and Dr. Laurence Cox addressing the environmental issues. Their recordings complement their input to the written volume of letters and poems.

Arguably, it is the unique contribution of the audio archive that two of the people who worked most closely with Saro-Wiwa were given the opportunity to speak for themselves, directly and in as unmediated a manner as was possible. Both of these people had so often had their version of Saro-Wiwa's story told on their behalf, that it was important for them to have the opportunity to speak for themselves in an unconstrained manner. The absence of intervention in the telling of their versions of Saro-Wiwa's story became a guiding principle for the production of the audio recordings. This allowed the contributors to maximize their imprint on the story, centrally guiding the subsequent editing process.

The key freedom involved in creating the audio archive, as opposed to working to the format, genre, and scheduling constraints of broadcast documentary or feature programming, was that it offered as much "space" as is required to tell the story in the fullest detail possible. While broadcast programs limit the on-air time allocated to a program, and so limit the amount of material recorded at source, this was not the case with an open-ended time allocation. Seven hours of audio were recorded with McCarron. This was free-ranging in the topics covered, from her Irish childhood, her education, her missionary work in Nigeria, the events that brought her to Saro-Wiwa, and all that passed subsequently. Hearing her story told in her own voice offers an insight into her personality and character that was not always as immediately conveyed in the written word. Moreover, hearing her voice firsthand, with the intimacy this creates in recounting events in Nigeria leading up to Saro-Wiwa's death, provokes a compelling intellectual and emotional awakening to the horror of the environmental abuse and destruction of Ogoni that she experienced firsthand.

Similarly with Dr. Owens Wiwa there was as much time available as needed to account for events in Ogoni and to tell the story of what had happened to his brother. Again, editorial intervention was minimized by recording the interviews as if they were being broadcast live. The interview with Owens Wiwa was recorded in a studio, and there were no "retakes" on any of the questions posed or answers offered. The interview as it exists in the archive is identical to that recorded in studio. This gave control of the final product, the archived version of the story, to Owens Wiwa, rather than to an outside editor at a later point in time. In this way, by avoiding the possibility of editing, the audio archives can offer a safe "home" to a story, a place where despite exclusion or misrepresentation in wider media, a story can be told and held with a minimum of editorial interference.

As to the mechanics of producing the audio archive, it is in essence a series of recorded interviews. Many were recorded on location. The two authors visited Rossport in Mayo with Sister Majella for the reinstatement of commemorative crosses for the Ogoni Nine at the Bellinanboy Shell terminal in November 2012. Others were recorded from the comfort of McCarron's home, or in a car when nowhere more conveniently quiet presented itself. The aim in deciding the location for interview recordings was to make sure the sound was as "clean as possible" to minimize distractions from the trajectory of the story itself. The interviews with Dr. Owens Wiwa were recorded "as live" in studio when he came to NUI Maynooth to launch his brother's book. The interviews are, on first encounter, deceptively simple. They seem to meander through the story as if it is being told for the first time. This impression belies the volume of research that underpinned the detailed understanding of the story that the producers had acquired, the work involved in formulating and reformulating questions, and the care and time taken in conducting the interview on the day.

The recordings with Owens Wiwa attempted to follow best practice for interviews. There was no discussion of his brother or the "story" prior to the recording, so that he did not feel he had already told the story and might perhaps gloss over details in the interview. The session started with easy warm-up questions, such as childhood memories of his brother. This allowed the interviewee to settle into the interview and to get a feel for the right pace and tone of questions. From there the questions emerged from the chronology of events in Ogoni, leading up to Saro-Wiwa's final detention. All the time, the interviewer needed to keep Owens Wiwa on the trail of the story while watching and reading how far he was able and willing to relive the detail of the destruction of Ogoni and in particular his brother's death.

As the events recounted became more brutal and savage, the questions got shorter and simpler, relating to specific places and violent incidents: What happened at Biara? What happened in Kaa? Tell me about Oloko? These are simple questions that drove the narrative and were, for Owens Wiwa, the key turning points of the story; they shaped the topics that were discussed in the interview and gave the archive a route through a detailed and complex story that was coherent and manageable for nonexpert listeners. Without thorough research and close listening, interviews don't always yield the kinds of key personal insights that Owens Wiwa so generously offered. Despite close research, it is not unusual for an interviewer to be surprised by answers; for instance, when questions don't reveal the kind of insider tragedy or intimacy that was expected. When asked about the last time he had seen his brother, he gave quite an everyday answer, as if there was nothing of sentimental significance for him in the last meeting with his brother. In that case the unexpected answer is a useful reminder not to impose too much meaning or significance on events before the interview, but to remain alert to the dialogic exchange and possibilities that arise in the live telling of a story.

The archive required work in the preproduction phase, to gather as much information as possible on the story of Owens Wiwa's and McCarron's relationships with Saro-Wiwa, and to formulate questions that allowed for broad and wide-ranging responses, while still carrying the story forward in a manner accessible to nonexperts. In production the recordings involved long sessions, so that the final archive would offer unlimited space to the contributor's testimony. In postproduction the editing was minimized, so that even apparently unrelated material was retained and valued as offering insights to McCarron's character and presence. Hopefully, the archive can become a place in which a story can be "laid to rest," where it can reside indefinitely. McCarron commented that the archive could act as an overall record of her life and what had happened to Ogoni and to Saro-Wiwa. To that end, it is important that the audio archive is publicly available and accessible.

Hosting the Audio Archive

In order to provide access to readers/users, the library decided to host the audio archive in SoundCloud via a link from the library website. This was an interim step in providing access while work is under way to develop the Digital Repository of Ireland, where the archive is planned to be stored in the future and in perpetuity. The Digital Repository of Ireland will be a national repository for social and cultural data, and will provide a central access point for data held by Irish institutions. The authors of this chapter were keen to launch the audio archive alongside the book of edited letters, which Owens Wiwa came to Ireland to launch in November 2013, and opted for Sound-Cloud as an interim, inexpensive solution.

SoundCloud is the world's leading audio platform for creating and sharing sound files. It was initially created for musicians to share recordings across the Internet, and later expanded into a full publishing tool. Individuals/groups can create a SoundCloud account and upload and share originally created sound files. While a limited amount of recording time is available free of charge, the scale of the Ken Saro-Wiwa Audio Archive necessitated an annual subscription to SoundCloud. This costs less than two hundred dollars per year and includes unlimited audio space. SoundCloud was seen as a good solution to making the audio archive available in a user-friendly way as quickly as possible. It is compatible with all major browsers and mobile devices and supports all audio file formats. Listener statistics give geographic location and most frequently played recordings. Users can post comments, like, repost, and share tracks and can embed tracks directly into web pages.

Each recording has approximately ten tags (keywords), increasing access possibilities during web searches. These tags were created by the authors. Some tags, such as the name of the person being recorded, the creators of the recordings (in all cases both authors), Kairos Communications, NUI Maynooth, Ken Saro-Wiwa, and Ogoni, are used as standard across all recordings (as of May 2014, there are fourteen individual recordings). Additional tags indicate the content and focus of the recordings.

SoundCloud allows for the inclusion of an image, effectively an album cover. The images used were primarily from the archive: letters, a cap that had belonged to Saro-Wiwa, a MOSOP flag, and photographs. On the front of the album, details such as the number of the recording, the title of the album, the NUI Maynooth logo, and image copyright details are included.

It was agreed from the outset with Sister Majella McCarron and Owens Wiwa that NUI Maynooth would hold copyright of the recordings and that requests to broadcast extracts from the audio archive would go to the library. The copyright of the images on the recording covers belongs to individual copyright holders, primarily, NUI Maynooth.

The University's legal representatives were briefed about the archive (as they had been about the book). They drafted a disclaimer for the website, which users must agree to before entering the audio archive.

The link to the Ken Saro-Wiwa Audio Archive on the NUI Maynooth library website is currently via the "Electronic Resources" link. In the future there may be more access points from the home page.

The archive is freely available worldwide via the Internet. The authors hope it will be a valuable resource in telling the story of Ken Saro-Wiwa and those connected with him, perhaps becoming a place of public engagement around Ken Saro-Wiwa's life and work.

Usage and Promotion of the Audio Archive

Between the launch on November 7, 2013, and May 2014, the audio archive has been played almost six hundred times. This however doesn't accurately reflect the listenership. While only fourteen hits are recorded from Nigeria, the University of Ibadan (where Ken Saro-Wiwa studied) requested permission to play the audio archive on their Community Radio Station. The university has approximately twenty thousand students, so potential listenership is very significant. It has also been broadcast on Newstalk 106, an Irish national radio station.

The audio archive and the edited letters have been widely promoted. International Human Rights Day on December 10, 2013, was marked with a talk by the two authors on the audio archive, and a visit to see the letters in the Special Collections area of the library. Groups of schoolchildren have visited the library to see the letters and to hear the story of Ken Saro-Wiwa.

A local public library requested a talk on Ken Saro-Wiwa, and a number of other lectures and presentations have also taken place. At lectures and presentations on the audio archive, the audiences never fail to be moved by the sound of Owens Wiwa's voice, reading Ken's poems "Ogoni! Ogoni!" or "For Sister Majella McCarron." While academics and activists have spoken about Ken Saro-Wiwa in their research, through their publications and in their teaching, it is in the timbre and accent of Owens Wiwa's voice that Ken Saro-Wiwa really comes to life.

CONCLUSION

The Ken Saro-Wiwa Audio Archive provides an opportunity for students and the public to engage meaningfully with a complex and controversial topic that may seem very removed.

There's an old saying that "the pictures are better on radio." In the case of the Ken Saro-Wiwa audio archive, that saying holds true. People listening to the recordings can construct mental images of the lives of the key protagonists in Ken Saro-Wiwa's story and understand better the roles that Sister Majella McCarron and his brother Owens played in his life. There are no actual pictures to distract the imagination, and so listeners can create their own landscape in an imagined Ogoni. But listeners don't just think in terms of pictures; audio allows the user to access the part of the mind that generates dreams, to conjure more than a three-dimensional picture of Ogoni. Audio allows the listener to smell, feel, and taste the world it creates. Listeners to the Ken Saro-Wiwa Audio Archive can smell the gas flares, taste the polluted water, and touch the oil-encrusted, infertile spoiled land. In so doing they can clearly understand why Ken Saro-Wiwa created the Movement for the Survival of the Ogoni People. The audio archive brings home the fact that it was, and is, the survival of the people at stake.

Beyond Ogoni, the audio archive helps the listener to understand other issues, too. In the immediacy of the first-person accounts and the intimacy of listening to another human voice, the passing of time collapses, the relevance and reality of events from decades ago become immediate. The audio archive, in this way, offers an insight into religious formation and convent life in 1950s Ireland. It gives an insider account of the thoughts and feelings of young missionaries traveling to Nigeria in the 1960s. Through Majella McCarron's and Owens Wiwa's recounting of their time with Ken Saro-Wiwa, particularly in the 1990s until his untimely death, the users are allowed to "see" Ken Saro-Wiwa, not just as an activist who paid the ultimate price for his beliefs but also as a friend and brother. Listening to the recordings, the users come to an understanding of the invisible ties that bind Sister Majella's work in Nigeria with her activism today against Shell in Erris,

County Mayo, in the West of Ireland. Somehow sound allows the listener to see very clearly the strong threads that connect the orator to the listener; the threads that also connect Ogoni to Ireland.

While recording that track of poetry for the archive, Owens Wiwa was asked if he would read from his brother's letters. He refused, explaining that he felt to do so would be inappropriate, as it would be to speak in his brother's voice. On reflection, the most poignant aspect of the audio archive is the silence that lies at the heart of it, the listener doesn't get to hear Ken's voice. Throughout his life, Ken fought for the rights of the Ogoni, and proclaimed that silence, in the face of their plight, would be treason. The stark fact remains, however, that Ken Saro-Wiwa was silenced. That silence is in evidence among the voices of his "Sister Majella" and his brother, Owens. It is a silence that offers testimony to the injustice and plight still suffered by Ogoni.

In a letter dated December 1, 1993 (NUI Maynooth Archive), Ken Saro-Wiwa urged Sister Majella McCarron: *"Keep putting your thoughts on paper. Who knows how we can use them in future. The Ogoni story will have to be told!"*

Creating the Ken Saro-Wiwa Audio Archive is, the authors hope, a way to ensure the Ogoni story is not forgotten.

REFERENCES

Corley, Í., H. Fallon, L. Cox. (2013). *Silence Would Be Treason: Last Writings of Ken Saro-Wiwa*. Dakar: Daraja/CODESRIA.
NUI Maynooth Ken Saro-Wiwa Archive PP/7/1.

Chapter Seven

York College Library's School Media Specialist

A New Library Model for Easing the Transition from High School to College

Christina Miller and John A. Drobnicki

INTRODUCTION

York College, a senior college in the City University of New York (CUNY) system, has a library faculty position that is unique within CUNY: a full-time school media specialist. This librarian (Christina Miller) is a member of the CUNY faculty union, works the same number of hours per week as the other York librarians, and must meet the same requirements for reappointment, tenure, and promotion; however, she divides her time between providing library services to the York College community and to the staff and students of the Queens High School for the Sciences at York College (QHSS) and the York Early College Academy (YECA), both of which are operated by the New York City Department of Education (DOE). Miller also occasionally provides information literacy sessions for classes from area public schools and students enrolled in York's College Now program.

Miller is York's state-certified school media specialist and a literacy specialist. She is a York College-CUNY graduate with a BA in economics and subsequently earned two masters degrees (an M.L.S. and an MS Ed Literacy, grades 5–12) at Queens College-CUNY. Miller has served as York Library's "High School Librarian" since the inception of QHSS in 2002, first as an adjunct (2002–2008) then as a full-time faculty member (2008–present). QHSS is located on the York College campus and is one of New York City's specialized high schools requiring top-tier performance on a citywide en-

91

trance exam. It is a small (400 students), academically competitive school. QHSS does not have its own library; the school shares the York College Library. QHSS students have local borrowing privileges at York Library and full access to the library's online resources, computers, and study rooms.

By her second semester at York Library, Miller began providing information literacy classes for QHSS students and professional development for teachers, and purchased materials for the library's collection to support the school's mission and curriculum. While the library needs of the QHSS community were Miller's first priority, she also provided reference assistance for York's college students.

In 2006, YECA was opened a short distance from the college's campus with 81 students in sixth grade. With a grade added each year, the school reached full capacity, 567 students in grades 6–12, in 2012. YECA is one of CUNY's twelve early college schools; students attend from grades 6–12 and can earn up to sixty college credits at York College by the time they graduate. From 2006–2010, YECA shared a building (and a library with a school media specialist) with the Catherine & Count Basie Middle School. In 2010 YECA moved to its current location, within walking distance of the college's campus, to a building it shares with a middle school; however, YECA does not have access to a library at its current site. Like QHSS students, YECA students have local borrowing privileges at York Library and access to the library's online resources, computers, and study rooms.

With QHSS's growth from one grade to four, the opening of YECA, and the increasing need to designate a point person in the library to liaise with K–12 populations, Miller was appointed a full-time faculty member in 2008 and began to provide information literacy classes for York College students; serve on library, college, and university committees; and liaise with academic departments. Miller then enrolled in Queens College-CUNY to earn her second masters.

BACKGROUND OF THE SCHOOL LIBRARIAN POSITION AT YORK

In 2001 it was announced that York College would have a high school on its campus commencing in September 2002, as would several other CUNY campuses. It was also made clear from the start that the students of the soon-to-be-established QHSS would *not* have their own school library or school librarian, but would use the York College Library. The announcement took York's faculty and staff by surprise, since they had not been asked to provide planning or input. Several issues were immediately raised by York's librarians, including:

1. The library was already understaffed, with only six full-time faculty members covering two reference desks. Adding additional responsibilities without increased staffing would be burdensome and short-change students and teachers.

2. In CUNY, librarians are members of the faculty and are evaluated for annual reappointment (as well as tenure and promotion) based on the same criteria as the classroom faculty; that is, teaching effectiveness, scholarship, and service. Would it be a violation of the faculty contract to have *college* librarians evaluated based on their teaching of, and reference interactions with, *high school students*? Would this constitute out-of-title work and a change in librarian faculty members' terms of employment? Would the college place a high school student in, for example, the classroom of a history professor without that professor's prior consent? If not, why were the library faculty being treated differently?

3. In order to be a librarian in a public high school in New York State, one had to be certified as a school media specialist (library), which required the completion of education courses, a specialized library science curriculum, and a practicum. None of the existing library faculty members at York would qualify for certification as New York State school media specialists, and had no training or expertise in providing library services to high school–age students. By making York College librarians responsible for the high school, was the New York City Department of Education depriving a member of the United Federation of Teachers (UFT) of a job?

4. As part of a four-year undergraduate school, the York College Library concentrated on collecting college-level materials to support the college's curriculum, as well as supporting the research needs of the faculty, which due to stagnant or reduced budgets over the years it had barely been able to maintain. Would the library be able to support the needs of high school students—albeit academically advanced—without an increase in funding? The library was already trying to cope with new college majors and programs, such as Communications Technology and Physician Assistant, with resultant increasing competition for scarce funds. Additionally, who would be responsible for collection development decisions?

5. Would the high school students have borrowing privileges, and if so, how would fines be enforced? (College students could be blocked from registering, but how would high school students be "forced" to pay fines?) How would the addition of high school students affect the library's electronic resource subscriptions? Should they be counted as

part of York's FTE? Would the library have to install filters on its computers to protect these minors from pornography and other online dangers?

(See the appendix to this chapter for how these issues were resolved.)

York's librarians brought these issues to the leadership of the Professional Staff Congress (PSC, the union for CUNY faculty and staff), both at the campus level and university-wide. Because of (among other things) the lack of consultation with York's faculty and the strain that the proposed high school would have on campus resources, including the library, the executive committee of York's PSC chapter passed a resolution that "this decision and its timetable be revoked and that the proper planning bodies be constituted to discuss the feasibility and implementation of a new high school on the York College campus." The Library Faculty Committee of the PSC's Delegate Assembly also raised concerns about the new high schools on CUNY campuses with PSC President Barbara Bowen and Vice President Steve London.

Whether the pressure from York's library faculty and the PSC impacted or not, the York administration ultimately agreed to make funds available for the library to hire an adjunct librarian responsible for working with the new high school. Three months after QHSS opened, Miller was hired by York to fill this position, especially because of her educational background and professional interests—she completed the school media course concentration at Queens College (CUNY) Graduate School of Library and Information Studies and was interested in fulfilling the requirements for New York State certification as a school media specialist. During her initial years in the position, Miller earned fifteen graduate education credits; participated in a 150-hour practicum at a local high school library; passed the New York State Teacher Certification exams, Language Arts & Sciences Test (LAST), and Assessment of Teaching Skills-Written (ATS-W); attended New York State–mandated workshops on Child Abuse Recognition & Reporting and School Violence Prevention & Intervention; and underwent a background check (and fingerprinting); and ultimately received provisional certification as a New York State school media specialist (library). After submitting evidence of the equivalent of two years of experience as a school librarian at QHSS, Miller received permanent certification in 2007. As QHSS grew, Miller's hours grew accordingly; this complied nicely with Title 8, Section 91.2, of New York Codes, Rules and Regulations for employment of school librarians: "[In] a secondary school with enrollment of more than 300 but not more than 500 pupils, a *certified* school media specialist shall devote at least one half of each school day to school library work" (Education 8 NYCRR, § 91.2; emphasis added).

As an adjunct, Miller was asked to be part of a planning committee for a second DOE school that would be affiliated with York: the York Early College Academy (YECA). When funding became available to add an additional full-time faculty line in the library, the then-chief librarian (Drobnicki) successfully argued for the creation of a line for a full-time, tenure-track school media specialist (the first position of its kind in CUNY), since the library served students from several DOE schools. A search was done, and York's president appointed the existing adjunct (Miller) as a full-time school librarian in 2008; she remains the only certified school media specialist in the CUNY system, although other CUNY librarians do liaison work with high school and/or middle school students. The Leonard Lief Library at Lehman College (CUNY) subsequently hired an adjunct librarian, who has a background in children's and young adult school librarianship, to work directly with the students of the high school on its campus (High School of American Studies—Lehman College), and the Brooklyn College Library has a designated librarian who oversees the library's outreach to high school students, including students enrolled in the STAR (Science Technology and Research) Early College High School program, Brooklyn College Academy, and College Now partnerships.

On September 1, 2005, CUNY and the DOE signed an agreement governing the compensation that CUNY would receive in exchange for letting the DOE operate eleven high schools on its campuses (including QHSS). The fee for providing librarians and books for the high schools would be based on the DOE's annual School Based Expenditure Report—in 2005, the figure was $60 per student. If a CUNY library did *not* grant full borrowing privileges to DOE high school students, the fee would be lowered to 83.3 percent of the amount. Since York granted full borrowing privileges to QHSS students, the library began to receive "high school funds" on an annual basis to purchase books and/or other materials, initially based on $60 multiplied by QHSS's enrollment (the amount has since risen as the amount in the School Based Expenditure Report has risen).

YORK LIBRARY'S SCHOOL MEDIA PROGRAM

Although QHSS first opened with only 100 students in ninth grade (the school reached full capacity in 2005, approximately 425 students), Miller created a mission statement, a vision, and strategic directions for York Library's School Media Program:

> Mission—To facilitate QHSS faculty and students' access and use of a wide variety of materials to meet their research needs.

Vision—The York College Library is a state-of-the-art facility staffed by a certified school library media specialist. The library serves as the information center for students and faculty of the Queens High School for the Sciences at York College. A dynamic partnership exists between the high school and the college; administrators, the school media specialist and teachers work toward common goals. They collaborate to ensure resources and programs are available to support the curriculum. Students are information literate, regularly visit the library and are comfortable using a wide variety of print and online materials for research and independent reading.

Strategies for growing the school media program will center on:

1. intra-institutional collaboration and cooperation (i.e., meet regularly with teachers and administrators);
2. curriculum planning (i.e., encourage teachers to share curricula, join the QHSS curriculum committee);
3. collection development (i.e., purchase materials to support the QHSS curricula);
4. instruction (provide group and individual instruction);
5. promotion of the library and its resources (i.e., publicize the library and its resources in the library and high school newsletters, on the library website, and through special programming, book displays, and exhibits);
6. networking (i.e., join committees and associations that focus on K–12 information literacy); and
7. evaluation of the program (maintain data for all aspects of the school media program).

Miller has become the point person in the library for QHSS administrators, teachers, and students, and also for York College's liaison to YECA, and she rarely passes up an opportunity to work with high school students. In order to sustain an active school media program, Miller recognized that she needed to develop good relationships with students, teachers, and administrators, and get involved in K–12 activities whenever the opportunity arose. Over the years Miller has engaged in myriad K–12 activities, including:

- providing information literacy sessions for an area public high school
- giving tours of the library to high school students participating in a regional science competition at York College
- judging high school science competitions
- teaching classes with York College professors during YECA students' three-week "Summer Immersion Program" during two summers at York
- participating in the New York Academy of Medicine Junior Fellows Program with QHSS students

- accompanying QHSS students and their teacher to author readings at the 92nd Street Y as part of its Literary Outreach Program.

At QHSS Miller was embedded in a journalism class and helped edit the school newspaper, *Synapse*; she also helped organize the school's annual three-day science poster exhibition in the library. In many professional development sessions and presentations at staff meetings provided for QHSS teachers, Miller highlighted new library resources or websites and encouraged teachers to integrate standards-based information literacy skills into their curricula. Miller wrote an article about the "American Association of School Librarians (AASL) Standards for the 21st Century Learner Lesson Plan Database" for the journal *The Charleston Advisor*, and gave two presentations (one to New York City DOE school librarians and one to QHSS teachers) promoting use of the database to integrate AASL Standards and the Common Core State Standards into a school's curriculum.

To publicize the library's school media program, Miller writes a column in the library's newsletter (now called *LibWire*) that highlights school media activities, including information literacy classes, collection development, class visits to the library, and special programs and projects that she participated in with high school students or that took place in the library over the previous year.

Miller provides approximately thirty classes each year for QHSS students and YECA students taking college courses at York. These consist of typical "one-shot" lessons and multisession units that take place in the library's computer lab, in a computer lab on campus, or in a QHSS smart classroom. Students also meet with Miller for research consultations, and seek assistance via e-mail. This past year, Miller provided a weekly library session for students taking the high school class "Writing the Research Paper" and was able to view and critique students' work in the class's dropbox.com space.

CUNY LIBRARIES' SERVICES TO K–12

In his book *Informed Transitions*, Kenneth J. Burhanna (2013a) notes the "impressive record of collaboration, engagement, and outreach demonstrated by librarians working to transition students across the educational continuum" (xi). Burhanna (2013b) defines the "transition movement" as "libraries and librarians collaborating across the educational continuum to prepare students for academic success" (6). Nowhere is this movement more exemplified than in the partnerships between K–12 schools and colleges. The introduction of high schools on college campuses, dual-enrollment schools, and college prep programs is based on the premise (and promising data) that students at both the college and high school level benefit (higher high school graduation and college retention rates, smoother transition to college, better prepared college students, etc.) if they are exposed to a college setting, receive college prep, or take college courses while they are in middle or secondary school (Barnett & Stamm, 2010; Berger, Adelman & Cole, 2010; Rosenbaum & Becker, 2011; Columbia University, 2012; Edmunds et al., 2010). As a result of these postsecondary opportunities, more academic librarians are interacting with middle and high school students, their teachers, and librarians (if they have one), giving all the parties an opportunity to articulate and anticipate the information literacy needs of students throughout a broader educational continuum than in the past. These collaborations and partnerships represent a national trend in which traditional boundaries between educational levels, institutions, disciplines, and academic and "everyday" learning are more fluid than in the past. (Miller and a library colleague, Dr. Anamika Megwalu, recently gave a presentation at a library conference about fostering students' transliteracy skills and helping them to apply their "everyday" learning to academic work.)

One of several factors Rosenbaum and Becker (2011) identified as contributing to the success of early college schools is the creation of "clear curricular pathways aligned with college-level coursework" (16). They quote CUNY early college administrator Cass Conrad who stated that "teachers [in early college programs] plan backwards from college, to make sure [students] know what they need to be successful in college-level classes" (16). Miller finds herself doing this "backward planning" when she designs information literacy sessions for high school students. From her teaching experience, interactions with college students at the reference desk, and work on committees that focused on information literacy, Miller is aware of the information literacy skills college students find difficult to master, and she emphasizes these skills in the instruction and reference assistance provided for high school students.

Miller was part of a CUNY/DOE Libraries working group that explored ways to ease the high school to college transition. The committee analyzed college assignments and syllabi to identify the information skills students would need to successfully complete the work; they explored ways (such as professional development workshops and online tool kits) K–12 teachers could align the skills in their assignments to the Common Core State Standards and college assignments. Although this committee was dissolved, at least two other groups in CUNY, the DOE/CUNY Library Collaborative and Graduate NYC!, are working on easing the high-school-to-college transition by connecting high school and college administrators, teachers, faculty, and librarians, and exploring ways to align curricula with information literacy standards and college expectations and increase incoming college students' preparedness to do college work.

Through CUNY's PreEducation/College Collaborative programs, each of CUNY's eleven senior colleges and six of its seven community colleges have a College Now program, a high school on its campus, or an affiliated early or middle college school. In addition, many CUNY colleges have formal and informal partnerships with K–12 schools or provide outreach to local K–12 schools on an ad hoc basis. Some of CUNY's affiliated early or middle college schools or high schools that share their campuses have their own libraries or share a library with another K–12 school, while others have neither a library nor are provided services by their affiliated CUNY library. An informal survey of CUNY libraries conducted by the authors in August 2012 showed that a majority of CUNY libraries provide services to K–12 populations. Of the ten (of eleven) CUNY senior college libraries and six (of seven) community college libraries that responded to the survey, nine offer borrowing privileges for K–12 populations; four provide remote access to the library's databases; ten offer information literacy classes for K–12 populations, and four offer interlibrary loans for K–12 populations. Of those colleges that provide information literacy sessions for K–12 populations, five have a designated high school liaison that provides the sessions.

THE FUTURE

A lot has changed in the twelve years since Miller created her vision for York Library's School Media Program. The physical library is no longer the "information center" for students and faculty of QHSS. Students now have access to the Internet, e-books, multivolume encyclopedias, and thousands of full-text journal articles, periodicals, and newspapers in their classrooms and from remote sites. The library's home page and the Internet have become the students' information center. Miller's role decries the concept that librarians may become obsolete—she is needed more than ever to help students navigate the information landscape and acquire information literacy skills for all their learning needs, to ensure that information skills are integrated throughout the high school curriculum, and to provide opportunities for students to develop their skills. York Library's school media position was an essential component of the collaboration between the college and high school, and critical in the development of a successful and expanding school media program at QHSS.

APPENDIX

The Library Faculty at York College were concerned about the following issues when it was announced that there would be a high school on campus:

1. The library was already understaffed, with only six full-time faculty members covering two reference desks. Adding additional responsibilities without increased staffing would be burdensome and short-change students and teachers.

   • Christina Miller was hired as an adjunct to be the liaison to the high school, which helped to alleviate the staffing issue.

2. In CUNY, librarians are members of the faculty and are evaluated for annual reappointment (as well as tenure and promotion) based on the same criteria as the classroom faculty; that is, teaching effectiveness, scholarship, and service. Would it be a violation of the faculty contract to have college librarians evaluated based on their teaching of, and reference interactions with, high school students? Would this constitute out-of-title work and a change in librarian faculty members' terms of employment? Would the college place a high school student in, for example, the classroom of a history professor without that professor's prior consent? If not, why were the library faculty being treated differently?

   • The library faculty did feel that they were not consulted when it was decided that the York College Library would be the library for the high school—but the hiring of Miller as the "high school librarian" (first as part-time and then as full-time) helped to smooth over that initial reluctance. Although all of the librarians assist anyone who comes to the reference desk, and it is not always apparent whether students are in high school or college, Christina Miller is the only librarian who teaches information literacy sessions and other workshops for QHSS and YECA (sometimes assisted by another librarian). And though every library faculty member is observed by a department colleague teaching an IL class as part of the contractually mandated annual evaluation process, Miller has always been observed teaching a class for York College students rather than high school students to assure she is held to the same standard as other library faculty.

3. In order to be a librarian in a public high school in New York State, one had to be certified as a school media specialist (library), which required completion of education courses, a specialized library science curriculum, and a practicum. None of the existing library faculty members at York qualified for certification as a New York State school media specialist, or had training or expertise in providing library services to high school–age students. By making York College

librarians responsible for the high school, was the New York City Department of Education depriving a member of the United Federation of Teachers of a job?

- Although state certification as a school media specialist was not required to be a library faculty member at York College, it was one of the preferred qualifications in the advertisement for the full-time job that was secured by Miller. The New York City DOE often does not comply with Section 91.2 of New York Codes, Rules and Regulations for employment of school librarians, and it did in fact request a variance "to provide equivalent library services in alternative ways"; this deflected any potential issues around the question of union solidarity.

4. As part of a four-year undergraduate school, the York College Library concentrated on collecting college-level materials to support the college's curriculum, as well as the research needs of the faculty, which due to stagnant or reduced budgets over the years it had barely been able to maintain. Would the library be able to support the needs of high school students—albeit academically advanced—without an increase in funding? The library was already trying to cope with new college majors and programs, such as Communications Technology and Physician Assistant, with resultant increasing competition for scarce funds. Additionally, who would be responsible for collection development decisions?

   - The library had several years of poor budgets prior to the opening of the high school, but the Office of Academic Affairs made funds available to acquire books suitable for high school students. And, as mentioned above, the university and the Department of Education reached an agreement in 2005 that provided for funding of the libraries that served affiliated high schools. This funding has been very advantageous, since the materials that have been purchased are also utilized by college students.

5. Would the high school students have borrowing privileges, and if so, how would fines be enforced? (College students could be blocked from registering, but how would high school students be "forced" to pay fines?) How would the addition of high school students affect the library's electronic resource subscriptions? Should they be counted as part of York's FTE? Would the Library have to install filters on its computers to protect these minors from pornography and other online dangers?

- The library has sought the cooperation of the high school principal when there have been instances of unpaid fines or lost books, and it has not been an issue. Because their school is off campus, YECA students who seek borrowing privileges must have their parents or guardians sign a letter stating that they will be responsible for any fines or lost materials. The University IT policy explicitly prohibits the installation of software that filters based on content, so that has also not been an issue. The high school enrollment is so small that it has not affected the cost of any of the library's electronic subscriptions, since an additional 400–500 FTE would not push the library up into a more expensive category. Something unforeseen was the switch to a network log-in system for York College students for PCs that excludes QHSS students because they are not in York's "Active Directory." The solution thus far has been to provide QHSS students with an unsecured, generic account that they all share. As the library moves to a reservation system that is linked to York College students' individual network log-ins, the generic shared account may present problems, and the library is working with York's IT Department to provide individual accounts for QHSS students.

REFERENCES

Barnett, Elisabeth and Liesa Stamm. (2010). *Dual Enrollment: A Strategy for Educational Advancement of All Students*. Washington, D.C.: Blackboard Institute. http://www. blackboardinstitute.com/pdf/bbinstitute_dualenrollment.pdf

Berger, Andrea, Nancy Adelman, and Susan Cole. (2010). "The Early College High School Initiative: An Overview of Five Evaluation Years." *Peabody Journal of Education* 85, no. 3: 333–47. doi:10.1080/0161956X.2010.491697.

Burhanna, Kenneth J. (2013a). Introduction to *Informed Transitions: Libraries Supporting the High School to College Transition*, edited by Kenneth J. Burhanna, xi–xiii. Santa Barbara, CA: Libraries Unlimited.

———. (2013b). "The Transition Movement: From Blueprint to Construction Zone." In *Informed Transitions: Libraries Supporting the High School to College Transition*, edited by Kenneth J. Burhanna, 3–22. Santa Barbara, CA: Libraries Unlimited.

Columbia University, Community College Research Center. (2012). "What We Know About Dual Enrollment. Research Overview." Community College Research Center, Columbia University (February): 1–7. http://ccrc.tc.columbia.edu/Publication.asp?UID=1054.

Edmunds, Julie A., Lawrence Bernstein, Elizabeth Glennie, John Wilse, Nina Arshavsky, Faith Unlu, Deborah Bartz, Todd Silberman, W. David Scales, and Andrew Dallas. (2010). "Preparing Students for College: The Implementation and Impact of the Early College High School Model." *Peabody Journal of Education* 85:348–64. doi:10.1080/0161956X.

Miller, Christina. (2013). "The American Association of School Librarians (AASL) Standards for the 21st Century Learner Lesson Plan Database." *The Charleston Advisor* 15, no. 2: 5–10. doi:10.5260/chara.15.2.5.

Rosenbaum, James E., and Kelly Iwanaga Becker. (2011). "The Early College Challenge: Navigating Disadvantaged Students' Transition to College." *American Educator* 35, no. 3: 14–39. http://www.aft.org/pdfs/americaneducator/fall2011/Rosenbaum.pdf.

Chapter Eight

Unleashing the Power of the iPad

Michelle Currier and Michael Magilligan

INTRODUCTION/INSTITUTIONAL
CLIMATE AND OPPORTUNITY

Commencing throughout the 2010–2011 academic year, librarians at SUNY Canton, a small technical college in the New York State public higher education system, began the initial phase of a concerted and systematic effort to develop initiatives aimed at transforming their traditional academic library in ways designed to increase student awareness of and engagement with the library and its services, and heighten the student experience within the building. A recent building renovation project, the addition of tutoring labs, and an Information Services Help Desk had helped to significantly increase traffic flow in the library building, but use of librarians, library services, and resources remained limited. SUNY Canton had invested in reinvigorating the spaces and furnishings in the library, and students began to arrive; however, Canton librarians were seeing themselves as stewards of a building, caretakers of space, with responsibility for unlocking doors in the morning, locking doors at night, concerned with behavior management and environmental control—but little in the way of a librarian's professional training and skills seemed required to manage the day-to-day operations of the library. In general, the teaching faculty did not spend enormous amounts of time collaborating with librarians on pedagogical concerns, nor did they request assistance incorporating information literacy outcomes into their class assignments. In fact, although one-shot library instruction sessions were scheduled occasionally in the library instruction classroom in the library, faculty did not frequent the building often other than to visit the café. Students rarely engaged with the librarians either, in part because they were generally unaware of who the librarians were, and in part because the long-held perceptions of the building and the library staff were rather dismal. Clearly, a new approach was needed.

During this time at SUNY Canton, many exciting and forward-looking transformations had been realized, including the institution's transition from a two-year associate's degree and certificate–granting institution to a bachelor's degree–granting institution; new construction on a convocation, athletic, and recreation center and a new residence hall that were nearing completion; and a spike in enrollment in general, and growth in online programs specifically. This had all changed the face of the institution considerably. The library was poised to capitalize on all of this momentum, and took advantage of the new energy on campus to begin a transition of its own that exceeded the bounds of its aesthetic one. The building renovation and the changing culture and climate on campus were the springboard, and were for all intents and purposes external to the core library mission, vision, and purpose. A reinvention of self, a rebranding of the library mission, vision, and purpose, with the librarians and services placed centrally, was about to begin.

Seeking Funding

Although many small and incremental changes were made during the 2010–2011 academic year, including expansion of programs, events, and a host of outreach efforts, and the inception of an awareness campaign aimed at educating the SUNY Canton library user population on services, programs, collections, resources, staff, and more, all initial efforts remained on a small scale due to a limited or nonexistent budget to support additional or larger scale efforts.

After completing an environmental scan of campus-based issues that might lend themselves to a corresponding innovative solution to complement the library's own reinvention, Canton librarians determined that rising textbook costs and a dearth of innovative and emerging technologies on campus were primary issues with which the university was contending and to which the library could vigorously respond. Although already managing a relatively high-use textbook reserve program, the decision to attempt a project that would combine both the introduction of emerging technology (a small collection of iPads) and alternatives to traditional, high-priced print textbooks (a small collection of high demand electronic textbooks available via Kindle app on the circulating iPads) would be undertaken. The lack of availability for direct institutional support, either through the technology fee or library budget, forced Canton librarians to seek external funding for the project.

Two institutional grant-funding opportunities arose during the 2010–2011 academic year, which Canton librarians pursued in support of their projects. The first, called the Student Computing Access Program (SCAP), a fund previously administered by SUNY and awarded on local campuses, offered competitive grants to faculty and staff in support of teaching and learning technology innovations for program areas, departments, labs, learning centers, or student support areas, for student use that would potentially improve student learning and engagement, academic success, or otherwise improve student outcomes through the use of technology. Librarians submitted a grant proposal for this program entitled "Introducing Emerging Technology in Support of Library Services: Teaching and Learning with Apple iPads," aimed at introducing iPads in the library primarily as e-reader technology and as a means of introducing electronic textbooks into the already-existing reserve textbook collection. Although these two aims were identified in the proposal as priority areas for project outcomes, it was specifically noted (and would be borne out in subsequent years) that the infusion of Apple iPad technology into library services would provide significant additional uses and potential benefits to students, faculty, and the teaching and learning enterprise at SUNY Canton (see appendix I below for the uses identified in the 2010 SCAP grant proposal).

The second grant opportunity came in the spring of 2011, on the heels of librarians receiving award notification of the SCAP funds. The Carl D. Perkins Grant program, administered on campus, provided competitive grant opportunities to support the vocational and technical education programs available through SUNY Canton. Librarians wrote a grant in partnership with the TRiO Support Services office, the details of which tackled the rising and often exorbitant costs of textbooks, coupled with the publishing practice of "updating" and producing new editions regularly, which the librarians argued had created financial and academic hardship for postsecondary students on college campuses everywhere. In an attempt to combat this ongoing issue, Southworth Library cited its existing program consisting of a selection of high cost/high demand textbooks, a significant portion of which were donated by generous faculty members, but which required regular updating to be truly effective and meet the ongoing and continuous student demand. In addition, the proposal indicated an intention to provide access to digital copies of textbooks to be made available via the collection of iPads that the library had recently received grant funding to purchase, as well as via a collection of netbook computers available in the TRiO offices. In addition to expanding the availability and number of items in the collection, the Perkins Grant would simultaneously broaden access to electronic textbooks that might have the secondary benefit of providing a robust and enriching media experience as a result of the inevitable exposure to and use of the interactive web-based features that accompany the electronic textbook. Students would not only be offered expanded access to required course materials and texts through the iPad but would also be utilizing cutting edge, modern technology relevant to and supportive of their chosen curricula in technical and applied program areas.

Implementation

To the librarians' great delight, both grant proposals were approved with full funding requested, resulting in the availability of five iPads added to the reserve collection, and seventeen high demand electronic textbooks added to the library's Amazon account and accessible via the Kindle app loaded onto each of the circulating iPads. The librarians made plans to introduce these innovations during the first full month of the new academic term in the fall of 2011, with a large scale event and awareness campaign promoting the project. Tying in various campus departments with programs taking place in the library, including Health Services, Diversity Affairs, and with collaborations and donations from Campus Dining Services, the month of September in 2011 became Apple Month. In addition to all of the events and outreach efforts aimed at promoting the new technology with an "apple" theme, the librarians had spent time and effort proposing to their dean that she allow funding of five iPads for staff use, with the creation of a new, more relevant public service point on the second floor (see appendix II below for the proposal sent to the dean).

Following submission of the proposal by the Library Department chair, the dean of the division under which the library was presently situated approved the requisition of five iPads for staff use to drive innovation in the mobile environment. The librarians commenced the 2011–2012 academic year equipped with a circulating collection of iPads for student use, dedicated iPads for faculty librarian use to aid in the provision of mobile reference and patron support services, and a small collection of electronic textbooks with which to supplement the high demand reserve collection. The librarians were excited about the developments with respect to their initiatives, and the support they had received in terms of both financial backing and unmitigated encouragement from their leadership, to begin a project they hoped would breathe new life into the library and reshape campus and student perceptions of the library and its librarians as cutting edge, student-centered, and most importantly, relevant. As the SCAP proposal requesting funding for the initial five devices articulated, the uses for the devices could not adequately be envisioned or detailed upon commencement of the program. The librarians would soon come to conclude that the portable possibilities were nearly limitless.

Digital Possibilities

Although Canton's iPad program was modest in scope at the outset, with only five iPads in circulation to commence the 2011–2012 academic year, librarians soon realized that the frontier was practically limitless. The devices themselves were so new, the implications for delivery of library services were yet to be considered, much less implemented. Circulation of the iPads, limited during the first year to students only (since the devices were funded by the Student Computing Access Program) numbered 660 for the entire year. SUNY Canton's student population is small, with a total FTE hovering around three thousand, but only roughly half of those are residential students who would have physical access to the devices, so 660 circulations was more than satisfactory for program inception. Use of the electronic textbooks was also modest. One of the more exciting developments to come in the 2011–2012 academic year was the utilization of the iPad as a tool to enable more efficient reference and public service transactions with patrons. For the first time, librarians were being seen as tech savvy, connected, and responsive, in a manner that met the needs of the patron, both in time and place.

The 2012–2013 academic year, however, saw increased usage of the iPads. With the ability to budget for additional devices, the collection increased to ten; and promotion and marketing of the devices continued through a variety of channels. With the addition of new teaching faculty, and some creative and energetic new librarians on the library team, the possibilities began to take shape.

The 2012–2013 academic year saw general circulations rise to 861, which was both positive and encouraging. Even more so, however, was the development of an innovative team of librarians working together to drive innovations in library service with new programming and events developed around mobile apps and iPad use, and fantastic teaching faculty/librarian relationships that developed, which resulted in collaborations and coteaching sessions in multiple course sections over the course of the academic year. The program's modest start was beginning to evolve in ways never originally conceived.

INNOVATIONS IN LIBRARY SERVICE

One of the most essential and defining functions of any library is in providing reference services. Traditionally, this transaction is reserved for a predetermined service point(s) within the physical library building. The technological advances in ways librarians communicate have opened up alternative methods of reference that transcend the traditional model of a librarian sitting at a reference desk waiting to be approached by a patron seeking an answer to their question. Some of the newer trends in "virtual librarianship" include conducting the reference interview via online chat, over e-mail, and even by text messaging. In blending old-world librarianship with digital-age technology, the iPad has allowed SUNY Canton librarians to redefine the reference interview by expanding the role of the librarian, creating a deeper well of information offered, and making the patron more accessible and easier to approach.

Handheld technology like the iPad has enabled the reference librarian to not only be approachable but to be mobile. No longer chained to the reference desk, the librarian is now allowed the freedom to roam and become a more visible presence within the building. The freedom to roam allows for a deeper reference transaction that opens up opportunity to instruct an individualized information-literacy session on the spot. With an iPad in hand, the librarian can accompany a patron to show them how to find information, and not just provide directions or instructions on where to go to find such information. By being able to roam, the librarian's focus can shift to actively engaging patrons at any point in the building and at any moment. This form of active reference not only increases the librarian's profile but also breaks down patron's apprehensions in asking for help. This new model has been adopted by both academic and public libraries; and SUNY Canton made the digital shift beginning with Apple Month in 2011.

In making the decision to include roaming reference as part of public service hours, Canton librarians have all reported far more student engagement as opposed to normal stationary reference desk duties. By actively seeking out students to meet their needs, Canton librarians reported not only increases in reference transactions but also a deeper understanding of the needs of its student population. Significantly, in student satisfaction surveys in the years following the introduction of iPad-enabled reference service, students have overwhelmingly responded that the relationships and people in the library building are by far the most valuable part of their student experience in the library; undoubtedly, the "connections" have been aided to some extent by this new mode of operation. In essence, this form of roaming reference allows for librarians to have a far better pulse on the information needs of their patrons by actively engaging with and soliciting feedback from them in truly dynamic transactions. Utilizing handheld technology also allows for librarians to gauge the digital literacy skills of their patrons, and provides an instant opportunity to instruct patrons on how to sharpen these skills. This form of reference is far more proactive, and might even be considered "preventive librarianship." The proactive approach informs librarians of developing trends in the populations they serve, which they can then use in determining the best methods and practices in responding to patron needs. Users also come to see their librarian as a cool and technology-savvy, approachable information professional and not just the stodgy keep-it-quiet librarian stereotype. This form of reference requires that the librarian also see him- or herself as an educator, actively seeking out opportunities to instruct, not just as a last resort if a patron gets in over his head. This level of interaction challenges both the librarian and patron to redefine the librarian's role, and highlights the library as being not only a hard copy holding location but as a center for learning and incorporating digital literacy skills into everyday research.

Canton librarians have found that one of the strongest opportunities for incorporating iPad technology into the academic framework is in the field of digital humanities. This field of scholarship embraces the use of digital mediums to capture, preserve, and publish information from the multidisciplinary social sciences and traditional humanities disciplines. Canton librarians were in an enviable position of jump-starting their iPad program with digital humanities partnerships, as there was a concurrent establishment of digital humanities initiatives from the English/Humanities Department. This fortuitous timing opened the door for cross-collaborations among the library and the teaching-faculty colleagues that not only established an iPad presence in the classroom but also allowed the library to move its iPad program into new and innovative arenas.

In establishing coteaching opportunities, Canton librarians first had to reach out to faculty to "pitch" the idea that they could instruct more than just bibliographic instruction sessions. The traditional library model for instructing information literacy often views digital literacy as simple web surfing and database searching for academic articles. While successfully being able to navigate the vast number of databases for relevant academic articles is teaching successful research skills, is it imparting to students real-world digital information skills? One of the main perspectives of Canton librarians at this juncture was to stress the importance of teaching nontraditional digital literacy skills, such as iPad applications. As some faculty members might be unfamiliar with iPads, it was an important first hurdle to overcome the misconceptions that iPads would not have much pedagogical value. In contrast, Canton librarians were emphatic that in this digital age teaching a student to create and publish digital content is every bit as important, and quite possibly an even more practical skill, than many learned in the traditional classroom.

Numerous faculty members were enthusiastic and receptive to opening up their classroom to digital projects; and one of the first and best representations of what Canton librarians were striving for was in an original digital poetry project undertaken with an English professor.

To celebrate National Poetry Month, Canton librarians collaborated with the professor to tailor a project that would tie in the theme of poetry with their course syllabus. The concept was to have a librarian teach two class sessions on the iPad applications Garageband (musicmaking application) and iMovie (moviemaking application). After acquiring these base digital skills, students were then asked to write their own original poetry and use an iPad to put these poems to either music or movies that, again, would be their own original content. To highlight this project, the involved librarian then created a YouTube page to host the video poetry projects, a SoundCloud page to host the audio poetry projects, and a podcast of the audio projects for dissemination on National Poetry Day. These three digital showcases were hosted on the library website, and the library used displays and e-mails throughout campus to raise awareness of this project. The response to this collaboration was overwhelming in its enthusiasm, and was a solid first step in learning the proper use and marketing of iPad technology in raising the profile of the library as the center for digital learning on campus.

One of the corollary benefits of this project was not only the increased faculty buy-in with the library and its services but also the elevated levels of student engagement. In essence, the professor was able to supply the students, if the library would supply the technology and instruction on how to employ it. After the classroom digital literacy instruction sessions, students then had to make a private consulting appointment with the librarian (at the library) to set them up with an iPad, to troubleshoot any questions they might have, and to instruct them on how to publish digital content to the aforementioned digital distribution platforms. Although more of the onus was on the librarian to produce this project, the benefits that were realized from its completion were invaluable. Some of these outcomes include:

- With the individual reference consultation sessions, reference statistics and iPad circulation numbers were greatly increased for the data collection period.
- General awareness of the library's iPad circulating collection increased.
- Librarians were seen by students and faculty alike as digital content specialists who were committed to working with them.
- The digital platforms for publishing a student's original work showed tangible evidence of the value of iPad digital literacy for faculty and college administration.
- The iPad classroom initiatives were proven to be a viable and fruitful collaboration that could now be used for future grants to increase the program.

The original digital poetry project is just one example of how iPad technology can be used in the classroom as a meaningful method to engage and instruct students. There are countless apps that can be used in this fashion if one has a willing faculty to work with. With a focus on creative thinking, the possibilities to incorporate this technology transcend all disciplines and can be used from Accounting to Zoology. Figure 8.1 shows Allan Carrington's

Wheel of Pedagogy 2.0, based on Bloom's Taxonomy, which illustrates iPad applications and their uses in academia. (See the very colorful original at Carrington, 2013.)

Continuing to build on their growing iPad successes, Canton librarians soon found that an additional, and extremely effective, use of iPads was in their potential as part of complementing their mobile reference services and providing more engaging programming. While many academic libraries, particularly when compared to public libraries, do not focus heavily on programming, SUNY Canton has thrived on a student-focused approach that considers patron engagement a main priority; and in recent years, and with the Southworth Library reinvention project under way, programming has become a large component of their student-engagement activity. Viewed as

Figure 8.1. Allan Carrington's Wheel of Pedagogy 2.0.

the cultural, artistic, and scholarly cornerstone of the campus, as the library has committed to envisioning and delivering unique and innovative programming, it has inspired its campus colleagues to follow the lead. With this spirit in mind, Canton librarians blazed a path with iPads as a means of accessing a digital layer of information that has allowed for a deeper user experience with its research services as well as its programming and events activities.

Using handheld technology to access Quick Response (QR) codes has become a common and accepted practice within the field of librarianship. QR codes are barcodes that, once scanned with the proper app on a handheld device, delivers digital content to that device. This content is in the form of a URL for a website that is then displayed to the user scanning the code. Creation of these codes is free and easily done on a variety of public websites, and their use allows for any number of possibilities. SUNY Canton employs QR codes in the stacks to deliver the specific database pages and secondary source materials of the subject areas where the code is displayed. Having the database pages easily accessible also coincides with the mobile reference program, so that the librarian is now free to help patrons find books and instruct them on digital research that coincides with that subject all in one stop. Original content can also be created using LibGuides to customize the digital content one would want the patron to receive.

With respect to library programming, any website, self-created or public, can be used to enhance the experience and add an element of digital content for education and showmanship purposes. Building upon QR codes are apps that feature augmented reality (AR) technology, which has been used by Canton librarians within programming to great effect.

AR technology allows for "augmenting reality" by adding a layer of digital content on the handheld device that overlays with a real-world object. Librarians at Canton have used an app known as Aurasma to create original videos that are played after scanning a predetermined photo. Similar to QR codes, the barcode scanned has now been replaced by a photo, and the website displayed is replaced with a video. For example, at a Love Your Library Day program, Canton librarians created a virtual tour of the library that used photos of staff as triggers that, when scanned with the Aurasma app, would then play a video of that staff member introducing herself and discussing the area of the building that she was highlighting. Event participants were given iPads from the circulation desk to accompany them on their "tour," and sent on their way to explore the library with device in hand. Not only was this tour wildly successful on program day, but following this and other AR initiatives, Canton librarians began to receive consultation requests from various academic departments and student organizations on how to effectively use this technology in their own department and organization/group efforts. These requests reflect how Canton librarians are not only effectively raising the visibility and scope of library service but also redefining the role of librarian as a digital content specialist. These programs also have allowed for Canton to effectively promote and market its innovative ideas through scholarship and positive campus public relations.

Regarding scholarship, Canton librarians have been active in presenting iPad initiatives at library and higher-education conferences. In such conference presentations, Canton librarians discussed the digital initiatives and then allowed attendees to create digital content on iPads in a true workshop-style presentation. The use of AR is not in widespread use in libraries, so when shown the ease of use and range of ideas that this technology allows for, presentation attendees and fellow librarians were quick to respond with enthusiasm. Attendees were also instructed on how to create videos on iMovie and how these videos are quickly published, and can be used as part of any number of outreach and marketing campaigns. Following some of the presentations, given the buzz created by their work, Canton librarians were featured on a spot during the nightly news on the local ABC affiliate station. Highlighting Canton's full infusion of iPad technology, this news feature illustrated Canton's commitment to be on the forefront of digital innovation.

In response to the rising popularity of the newly developing iPad program at SUNY Canton, and the extensive campus-based and local media coverage the library's use of the iPads had garnered, Canton librarians began to receive additional inquiries from teaching faculty about possible collaborations in the classroom. A significant number of faculty requests were specifically related to the number of iPads available, in the hopes that the library could arrange to acquire a "classroom set," since the library's collection was still limited to ten devices and was prioritized for student circulation. Given the library's budget, and the many priorities to which its budget was already tied, the possibility of acquiring a classroom set of iPads without additional external funding was impossible. But Canton librarians were determined to respond proactively to the faculty interest, and leverage the media coverage and continued enthusiasm about the program in an effort to move it forward.

In the summer of 2013, Canton librarians submitted a third grant application entitled "Developing a Mobile Library Instruction Program with iPads," requesting funding through the Northern New York Library Network Technology Services Improvement Grant to support the acquisition of this classroom set. The grant request was funded in full, with a number of faculty already on board for coteaching sessions to start the 2013–2014 academic year, and many others to follow in the spring. The cornerstone of this program is the self-contained mobile cart that houses, charges, and allows for configuring twenty-five iPads. With this cart in hand, Canton librarians are free to bring iPads into the classroom and use handheld technology as a means of instructing any academic discipline. Setting up consultations with faculty and tailoring digital content lessons is the new model for Canton librarians, and one that could be replicated at any academic library. Canton's mobile iPad classroom allows for unparalleled creative collaborations between faculty and the library, redefining and expanding the role of the librarian in an academic library.

ASSESSING THE PROGRAM

Recognizing that the program is still in its infancy, it has been useful to gauge its successes with respect to its limited rollout within the framework of its expected continuing utility and support on the Canton campus, and the overall ability of the program to effect the changes that were noted in some of the original proposals, that is, changing the perceptions and the reputations of the library and its librarians on campus. Of note in this regard is the fact that the program was never billed as a "pilot," so that if in its first or second years it could be evaluated within a window of success indicators, and abandoned if criteria for success within that window were not met. It was from its inception a solid, if small and limited, program provided the full support of the library department planned for continued commitment. The program's primary aim, of course, being to effect a change in the way the library did business and the way the librarians engaged with students, faculty, staff, and the campus at large in a way that heightened awareness of the librarians' tech-centric, student-focused, digital content expertise. As such, librarians felt free to experiment with novel ways to support the institution's academic endeavors with iPads, and felt supported to drive innovation in new directions. The iPads and iPad technology are inherently infused into library business presently, and for all intents and purposes the library's image, its use by and engagement with the campus, and the overall impact it has on the institution's academic, cultural, and social endeavors have improved immeasurably. If for no other reason than that, if measured only by popular opinion and reputation enhancement, this program would be considered successful.

That is not to say that "hard numbers" have not been collected and analyzed and that continuing efforts to refine data collection with respect to the iPad program are not still on the horizon. Of course they have and they are. Circulation statistics for iPad use have been tracked since inception of the program, and broken down by borrower type, faculty/staff versus student use. Comparisons have been made in circulation of iPads across years, and factors have been identified that have potentially increased or decreased circulation. Further, efforts with respect to outreach, promotion, and education of users with regard to services relating to the iPad are refined or revised for coming years based on the numbers that have indeed been collected.

While circulation of devices is easy to track with standard library management system circulation software, it is more difficult to assess what users are doing with the devices when they use an iPad, what applications are being launched, if e-reader technology is used, and how they are engaging with or perhaps even creating content, since the devices are not networked and users do not log into them in order to use them. So, pulse surveys, satisfaction surveys, and other tools have been developed and deployed throughout these early stages of the iPad program to gauge overall level of interest in the devices, in particular apps, and satisfaction with iPad technology and the user experience relating thereto. Overall response has been positive, and preliminary data suggest that the small collection of circulating iPads is used primarily as a means of exploring emerging and unfamiliar technologies, and experimenting with the device as a novelty when it is used individually. As with many other factors relating to iPad use, user experience is expected to continue to evolve as the iPad program continues to evolve on Canton's campus; and with the iPad Mobile Classroom Instruction program, the sophistication of responses and user expertise relating to the devices is bound to be elevated as that aspect of the program continues to take shape and users respond to these kinds of assessment questions.

The iPad Mobile Classroom Instruction program is already beginning to provide some new and interesting data. One of the more recent assessment tools employed is the iPad Instruction Evaluation Survey, which the librarian for Digital Technologies and Learning administers post-session whenever he teaches an iPad instruction session. This survey form asks the student to not only assess the librarian's performance but also gauge their digital literacy skills. Students are asked if they feel that due to the digital-literacy session, they now have a better understanding of digital skills and what they felt was the most important component of the information taught. They are also asked what suggestions they might have to make these sessions more engaging from a student's point of view as well. When submitted, the form automatically goes to the library assessment team via e-mail where the results are then reviewed.

One of the more striking outcomes of this assessment process is how closely student needs are to the projected goals of the mobile library program. Overwhelmingly, students report that gaining digital skills utilizing the iPad and educational applications is something that is not only engaging to them but is also a literacy that many students feel they do not currently possess. While many are quick to assume that students in the digital age come equipped with digital skills because of the predominance of social media, in reality social media is a very narrow scope of what digital literacy encompasses. Assessment efforts through this survey confirmed that most students did not have much exposure to working with apps or iPads and that this program was indeed filling a void in instructing vital digital information skills that the students wanted to see not only continued but expanded.

Since the iPad Mobile Classroom program is a new evolution of the iPad program as of this most recent academic year, the numbers are still in their infancy. Preliminary data for a single semester of instruction responses are indicated in figure 8.2, which shows the distribution of responses to one question in the post-session iPad Mobile Classroom Instruction Evaluation: "How comfortable with/knowledgeable of iPads and educational applications/digital content do you feel you are now?" The graph shows student users' self-assessment of their own learning with respect to the acquisition of skills relating to iPad use that are commonly taught in the introductory sessions with the iPad mobile cart.

Librarians developed this assessment tool, along with other frameworks for the iPad Mobile Classroom Instruction program, to outline the parameters for use of the program by faculty, and to make it the most successful experience with respect to anticipated teaching and learning outcomes on the part of both the librarian and the teaching faculty member. The end goal: to move the program successfully into the future.

MOVING THE PROGRAM INTO THE FUTURE

In moving the iPad mobile classroom into the future, Canton librarians first had to establish the policies that would govern its use. One of the first discussions the librarians had was how to ensure librarians figured into the equation when the cart was requested for use, considering that many teaching

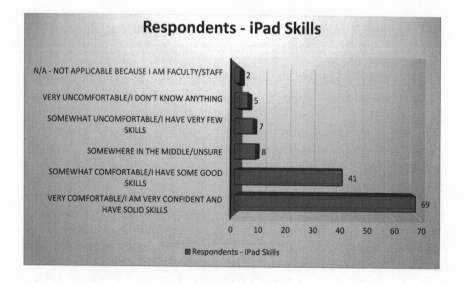

Figure 8.2. Responses to query concerning comfort with iPad skills.

faculty might express interest in exploring the iPad technology without recognizing the need for digital-content-specialist guidance. The first policy established was that the mobile cart, when requested, comes with a librarian who offers digital content expertise in crafting and coteaching lessons with the faculty member. The librarian's role in the coteaching scenario is to cover use of the iPads, basic device skills, and then more specific skills relating to the app or apps used to achieve the learning outcomes as codetermined by the librarian and the teaching faculty member; not to be sitting on the sidelines after pushing the cart into the classroom.

The second consideration was the method that a faculty member would be able to request the mobile cart session, and the remaining policies were drafted with consideration to the iPad being returned to the cart without any form of adjustments or deletions made to the content held on each device.

It was decided that the procedure for requesting the cart would be by submitting a digital request form. This form was drafted and placed on the library home page for faculty to submit with preliminary information on the nature of their request. This information includes: how many sessions requested, when and where the sessions are located, course name, particular apps needed, and a description of the classroom activity the faculty member is seeking. It should be noted that on the page where the request form is located, iPad Mobile Classroom Instruction policies and procedures are prominently displayed for making the request, and it is clear when submitting this form that the faculty member needs to consult with the librarian for Digital Technologies and Learning to again ensure that this is indeed a collaborative venture between librarian and faculty member. This page also has an app purchase request that allows for faculty or students to request an app for purchase that would enhance student learning. As apps are the driving force behind the iPad collaborations, the library is always actively seeking collection development input from the community in shaping the learning outcomes for students.

While the initial year of the iPad Mobile Classroom Instruction program has seen some successes, it is clear based on preliminary responses that additional activity and plans for future academic years are forthcoming and that the program will be expanding a great deal. The key for continued success with the iPad Mobile Classroom Instruction program is for librarians to establish collaborations not only with individual faculty but with academic departments as a whole. In promoting its availability, Canton librarians made presentations at faculty assemblies and at department meetings to offer this library service and illustrate its value. Early indicators of the success of this word-of-mouth campaign came when librarians were promptly invited to department meetings without soliciting invitations. This clearly demonstrated a raised awareness of the program, and more importantly, there was desire on the part of the faculty to incorporate it into their classroom.

It has become clear, on a number of levels, that librarians need to be proactive and utilize a combination of their networking skills and determination in implementing their vision for iPad innovation. Having an idea and "pitching" it to faculty was an extremely important first step in establishing an iPad presence in the classroom, and often one faculty member would see this service being used by a colleague and then would submit requests to incorporate the program into their classroom as well. Once brought to their attention, many faculty members are often prompt and willing partners. As is often the case, success begets success, and in the implementation of the iPad Mobile Classroom Instruction program, this has certainly proven true.

RESULTS AND CONCLUSIONS

In drawing conclusions from Canton's iPad initiatives, some results are unmistakable. Most notable is the shifting nature of what is considered digital literacy and how the library needs to respond to this changing landscape. Real-world digital literacy skills, including using educational apps, need to gain legitimacy and should be taught as academic tools. It is perhaps not enough to offer emerging technologies as a means of exploration and individual enlightenment. Rather, academic libraries should perhaps consider their instructional role as primary, and incorporate digital literacy initiatives and the instructional opportunities relating thereto into their missions in order to best meet the needs of the populations they serve.

Additionally, it can certainly be argued that initiating a small but evolving iPad program at SUNY Canton provided a level and type of legitimacy and "digital content expertise" that improved the library and the librarians' reputations on their campus, particularly as being contributors to the scholarly and academic mission of their small college of technology in ways they had not previously accomplished.

From initial startup to successful implementation, Canton's iPad program can be viewed as a possible new model for libraries in higher education, with emphasis on how to unleash the portable possibilities that iPads and digital innovations offer.

APPENDIX I

Additional Uses

The iPads in the library have potentially dozens of other uses besides supporting our textbook reserve collection. What we hope to see following the introduction of iPads in the library:

- Students will gravitate toward the iPad as new, interesting, and desirable technology, and the library will be recognized as the place where students can come to familiarize themselves with and "try out" cutting edge innovations.
- Faculty will gravitate toward the iPad as well, and may develop an interest in adding content to their course lectures that is enabled through classroom use of the device.
- Librarians will be able to use the iPad to effect more positive reference-service interactions. A traditional laptop is simply too bulky and heavy to carry and use easily while one is mobile. Roving reference (reference available on other parts of the campus) would be dramatically improved through use of the iPad, as would mobile reference that takes place in the library building itself.
- iPads could be used for quick-access catalog searching at the circulation desk or reference desk for patron use. The current use of the library catalog requires a substantial wait time for logging on to a computer, accessing the Internet, and navigating to Canton's web page then on to its library website and finally to SLEUTH, the library catalog. iPads could be readily accessible for this purpose, which would aid in customer satisfaction, customer/patron retention, and increased use of library services.
- Apps for the Southworth Library catalog as well as for the institution itself could be developed and made freely available, which would increase convenience and ease of access to these resources for students and patrons (both on and off campus), but would also manifest itself in improved methods and modalities of communication between the campus community and its students, stakeholders, customers, etc.
- iPads would constantly drive innovation in the library and in teaching and learning. Making this technology available will create additional uses for the device beyond that which can be detailed or envisioned at this time (Currier, 2010, pp. 2–3).

APPENDIX II

Proposal #2—"Handheld Librarianship and Relevant Service Points"

In an environment that is often hectic, where services and resources are layered on top of one another, we feel that it is essential that we provide library services that are both highly visible and highly relevant to students' needs. We discussed what we perceived to be two rather glaring deficiencies in the setup of services and service points in the current configuration of library space.

First, the reference desk on the first floor does not generate the amount of patronage that it should, and we would like to make reference services more readily available and more likely to be utilized. The major issue we identified with the reference desk is its location. Given the current configuration, patrons tend to go to the circulation desk for answers to all of their questions, whether for directional, informational, or reference purposes. The reference desk seems to get swallowed up by the circulation desk, and the librarian who mans the reference desk point of service disappears with it. Additionally, when students need assistance finding books or navigating resources on the second floor, the reference desk librarian is confined to that one rather inconvenient spot.

Second, we think it is a glaring deficiency that we do not have staff coverage of the second floor—where the majority of the library patrons are—for most of the day. We need to build relationships with students and be present *where they are*. So we propose the following:

We would like to consider removing the reference desk from the first floor and creating a point of service upstairs. Creating the point of service upstairs would be as simple as placing a desk, similar to one of the high desks we have near the front doors, in a conspicuous location with each staff member equipped with a laptop and an iPad so that we can be mobile upstairs with our reference services. We would locate ourselves at this point of service during our scheduled reference hours.

Benefits:

- Increased visibility of library staff
- Increased use of reference services
- Library staff will become familiar with emerging and mobile technologies, particularly in the provision of reference services
- We will be building relationships between library staff and student patrons
- Librarians will be extending themselves professionally, and creatively addressing the needs of our student population in an increasingly mobile environment (Currier, 2011, pp. 2–3)

REFERENCES

Carrington, Allan. (2013). "The Pedagogy Wheel." *In Support of Excellence* Website and Blog. http://www.unity.net.au/allansportfolio/edublog/?p=324. Creative Commons Licensed.

Currier, Michelle. (2010). "Introducing Emerging Technology in Support of Library Services: Teaching and Learning with Apple iPads." SCAP Proposal Submission.

Currier, Michelle. (2011). "Library Proposals." Library Proposals Submitted to Dean.

Chapter Nine

Training Library Staff with Badges and Gamification

Cyndi Harbeson and Scott Rice

INTRODUCTION

Digital badges and gamification are increasingly being used in the business world to motivate employees, and in academia as a pedagogical tool. At the Carol Grotnes Belk Library and Information Commons at Appalachian State University, the authors employed the use of digital badges and gamification to reinvigorate a technology training program. The goal of the library's badge training program was to establish a means of providing continuous technology training to all library personnel in a manner that was sustainable, encourage ongoing participation, and meet the myriad technology training needs of a diverse staff. The project involved creating a number of digital badges, a means of displaying those badges, a set of requirements for each badge, a reward system for attaining the badges, and a team of badge experts to monitor the process. By gamifying the technology training program, the authors hoped to increase the levels of motivation and engagement of the staff. The badge training program also establishes a means of measuring the progress made by individual staff members and the staff as a whole in becoming more technologically knowledgeable. With the increased focus of assessment on the campus, as with other colleges and universities, this last step was especially important.

Appalachian State University is one of sixteen universities in the University of North Carolina system. With approximately seventeen thousand students and more than 150 undergraduate and graduate majors, Appalachian State University combines the best attributes of a small liberal arts college with those of a large research university. The university's core academic missions of teaching, scholarship, and service are strongly supported by the Carol Grotnes Belk Library and Information Commons, whose own mission is to assist those who pursue knowledge.

As an information commons with more public computer workstations (over 350 desktops and laptops) than anywhere else on campus, Belk Library is on the forefront of technology on campus. Because of the library's role in providing access to a wide range of technologies on campus, it is essential that all of the library's staff be able to address the technology needs of students. Belk Library has a staff of approximately thirty-five faculty librarians and fifty staff members, which means that providing everyone with the wide range of technology training they need is a significant challenge. While staff need to be able to respond to students' technology support needs, they also need technology training in order to be more effective in their own work. Given these challenges, a badge training program became the perfect solution for developing ongoing technology training for a variety of skill levels and interests. Through the use of gamification, the library's training program became more than a requirement for job performance, it became a fun way to gain additional knowledge and skills.

GAMIFICATION

Gamification is "the use of game design elements in non-game contexts" (Deterding, 2011). Game design elements include such aspects of games as competition, rewarding incremental achievements, providing meaningful choices, increasing levels of difficulty, scaffolding of learning, and display of status and achievements, among others. When these elements are lifted from games and placed in a nongame context, they can create engagement, increase motivation, promote learning, and encourage problem solving (Kapp, 2012). Gamification is already in use by many private companies and nonprofit and educational organizations such as the Corporation for Public Broadcasting, EDUCAUSE, Samsung, Warner Brothers, Seton Hall University, and the University of Illinois at Urbana-Champaign. Game design elements are currently being used for such diverse purposes as training, marketing, and customer engagement, among others.

It is becoming increasingly common to see elements of gamification used at colleges and universities, in part because of the way it provides a more interactive learning experience. Training programs incorporate gamification because it provides the intrinsic motivation necessary to encourage and sustain participation. Because motivation is a key concept of game play, developing training programs incorporating gamification can be particularly sustainable and successful. Intrinsic motivation is defined by Karl Kapp as occurring "when a person undertakes an activity for its own sake, for the enjoyment it provides, the learning it permits, or the feeling of accomplishment it evokes" (Kapp, 2012, p. 52). Because the library encourages staff to participate in staff development, but does not generally require participation, it was especially important for library staff to be intrinsically motivated to participate.

Gamification provides this intrinsic motivation by drawing upon some of the instructional design principles developed by Mark Lepper, a researcher at Stanford University. Lepper proposes four principles that provide learners with intrinsic motivation: control, challenge, curiosity, and contextualization. According to these principles, a successful training program allows participants as much control over their learning as possible, continually challenges them through multiple goals and increasing levels of difficulty, inspires a sense of curiosity, and contextualizes the activities to highlight their functionality (Kapp, 2012, pp. 57–58). These principles already exist in most games, which is why developing training programs based on games can be so successful.

LITERATURE REVIEW

Businesses and corporations have embraced badge training programs more readily than universities and libraries. In *The Gamification of Learning and Instruction: Game-based Methods and Strategies for Training and Education*, Karl Kapp states that "a number of organizations are using gamification to train workers, educate students, solve problems, and generate new ideas and concepts. These organizations range from business schools to software companies to pharmaceutical companies to government organizations, and beyond. In almost every industry it is possible to find an example of the gamification of learning, innovation, and problem solving" (Kapp, 2012, p. 19). More recently, the impact of gamification in academia is beginning to appear with greater frequency in the literature. The New Media Consortium's *Horizon Report: 2013 Higher Education Edition*, which provides information about the impact of key emerging technologies on education, lists a time-to-adoption of two to three years for games and gamification (Johnson et al., 2013). According to the *Horizon Report* "educational game-play has proven to increase soft skills in learners, such as critical thinking, creative problem-solving, and teamwork. This idea is the basis of the relationship between games and education" (Johnson et al., 2013, p. 21). Gamification in the classroom is being considered with more seriousness as scholars begin to look at the pedagogical implications of these new trends.

Much of the current literature discusses the overall impact of gamification and badges on learning. In her article, "Digital Badges," Katie Ash examines the use of digital badges in educational settings. Among the advantages is "the ability to create learning pathways where none previously existed" (Ash, 2012, p. 25). Similarly, Veronica Diaz finds that "in a higher education setting, digital badges are symbols that represent discrete academic achievements or valued skills not represented by course outcomes or a degree" (Diaz, 2013). Diaz notes that badges are a way to motivate students while also validating skills and life experiences as a part of student learning (Diaz, 2013).

In *Gamification by Design*, Gabe Zichermann and Christopher Cunningham discuss the use of badges in games. Badges "encourage social promotion" and "mark the completion of goals and the steady progress of play within the system" (Zichermann & Cunningham, 2011, p. 55). This book focuses extensively on design concepts, but also delves into some of the theory that lies behind successful gamification efforts. For Zichermann and Cunningham, the relative success of gamification results from the level of engagement the user builds with the service or program. Considerations such as recency, frequency, duration, virality, and ratings can determine the level of engagement for a particular game (Zichermann & Cunningham, 2011, p. xvi). Building games that are both engaging and motivating is a key concept for Zichermann and Cunningham; one that is an essential part of any training program.

The importance of engagement is echoed elsewhere in the literature. In her article for *American Libraries*, Meredith Farkas argues "Research has shown that elements of game play, such as fantasy, competition, quests, and visible achievements, can motivate people and make learning more immersive. Organizations both within and outside of education have begun to use gamification to meet learning and engagement goals" (Farkas, 2014, p. 26). In order for game-based learning to be effective, Farkas cautions, there is often a need to rethink how instructional content is delivered. Because game-based design requires "visible and incremental acknowledgement of achievements," digital badges are an ideal element to include in training programs and information literacy learning modules.

Just as gamification is becoming more common in academic settings, libraries are also embracing these concepts of game-based learning by using it in programming and instruction. In *Public Services Quarterly*, columnist Melissa Mallon compiles reviews of gamification programs initiated by academic libraries around the country (Mallon, 2013). Current gamification programs include a plagiarism game called "Goblin Threat" developed by Mary Broussard and Jessica Urich at Lycoming College; "Head Hunt," a game to facilitate student orientation at the Ohio State University Libraries; and an information literacy instruction game called "Quarantined: Axl Wise and the Information Outbreak" developed by Bee Gallegos, Tammy Allgood, and Karen Grondin at Arizona State University (Mallon, 2013, pp. 217–20). The University of Central Florida also used game-based learning concepts as part of their information literacy instruction program, where students earn digital badges for successfully completing different modules (Farkas, 2014, p. 26). In her column for *Library Journal*, Liz Danforth also wrote about gamification in libraries and referenced projects such as BiblioBouts (bibliobouts.org) as a game-based learning resource focusing on improving students' information literacy skills. While Danforth recognizes that "there is a world of promise for libraries and other institutions supporting meaningful and valuable intellectual endeavors through well-designed gamifications, she also cautions librarians that "rewards-based extrinsic motivators—e.g., badges, achievement points, top ranks on leaderboards—are neither as sustainable nor as powerful as intrinsic motivators" (Danforth, 2011, p. 84). Gamification programs must be planned and carefully implemented, but opportunities abound for libraries to take advantage of this new trend in learning.

PREVIOUS TRAINING PROGRAMS

For many years, the Belk Library has had a Training and Development Committee that provides training and professional development opportunities. Historically, the focus of the committee has been on providing much-needed technology training for all library personnel. One of the earliest training efforts for the committee was an implementation of the popular 23 Things program. This program presented a different technology concept every week, with links to resources and a requirement that each participant learn something about the technology (such as wikis, YouTube, or blogs), and then create a blog post with their reflections on the possible uses of the technology in the library. The program was voluntary, and each week a participant completed the activities gave them a chance to win one of a number of prizes awarded at the end of the program. Less than 25 percent of library staff participated in this program, and no one completed all twenty-three topics.

This program was followed by a series of technology seminars titled "Teaching Tech 2.0," in which staff were invited to participate in workshops designed to teach specific technology skills necessary for their work. In order to encourage participation, the committee included incentives such as winning tickets to a summer series of cultural events, an iPad, or a Kindle Fire. The programs were each carefully designed in order to take into account the different needs and skill levels of the staff, and efforts were made to provide workshops at different times to accommodate staff schedules. With 23 Things, many of the components were self-directed and offered online, so that individuals could work at their own pace within the constraints of their schedules. Despite the best efforts of the committee, all of these programs suffered from similar drawbacks. Of primary concern for the committee was the issue of flagging interest from staff. In most cases, these programs were designed to be implemented over the course of the academic year, and participation waned within a few months of the program kickoffs. The authors also found that the way in which the library incentivized the training programs was generally unsuccessful. There was one large prize distributed at the end of the program through a drawing in which individuals entered through their participation in the trainings. The incentives failed to motivate staff to participate because there was a general feeling that the prizes were too unobtainable and, in some cases, undesirable. Staff also had the perception that these technology topics did not coincide with necessary job skills.

During the Teaching Tech 2.0 program, the committee gathered feedback from the staff through the use of surveys after every workshop. The goal was to develop a technology training program that more closely met the needs of library personnel while also encouraging greater levels of participation. As the Teaching Tech 2.0 program drew to a close, the committee analyzed the results of the surveys in order to begin developing a new direction for providing the library with technology training opportunities. The responses to the surveys indicated that there was a wide spectrum of technology needs. The next training program needed to address a range of skill levels, a wide variety of topics, and needed to more closely address the skills and knowledge required to perform job responsibilities. Developing a training program based on digital badges and gamification was the answer for Belk Library, because it incorporated all of these various needs in one program while providing the motivation necessary to ensure staff participation.

PROJECT OVERVIEW

The Training and Development Committee began developing the library's Badge Training Program in the Spring of 2013. The program is based on a system of badges with specific requirements to earn each badge. Library staff are able to compete with each other for badges, and be rewarded for achieving a certain number of level of badges. The badges increase in difficulty depending on the technology area selected, with expert-level badges requiring the learning and skills gained by earning beginner-level badges. Staff are allowed to select the technology areas that they think will be most rewarding, both personally and professionally. Badge earners appear on a leaderboard that lists the staff members who have earned the most badges. The leaderboard helps to encourage friendly competition among the staff as individuals compete for the top spot on the board. Earned badges are displayed on a badge tree and can also be uploaded to the Mozilla Backpack, which allows individuals to share the badges they earned in a variety of ways.

Using the survey responses, the Committee determined the technology areas in which the majority of staff indicated a need for further training. The authors designed a badge tree that divided the badges offered into two main technology areas: Web Applications and Desktop Applications. In order to not overwhelm the staff, the beginning number of badges offered was limited. There was a total of twenty badges in the Web Applications branch and a total of twelve badges in the Desktop Applications branch, for a total of thirty-two badges that could be achieved initially. Displaying the badges in this tree form allows the badges to have hierarchical levels to allow for increasing levels of difficulty for certain applications. For instance, there are three separate badges that can be earned for Microsoft Word. Each badge represents different aspects of the program, with the higher-level badge requiring more specialized knowledge. The badge tree also allows staff members to easily choose what badges they want to earn and shows them their progress toward completing different branches.

For each badge, there is a list of requirements necessary to complete in order to earn the badge as well as a link to resources that will assist in meeting the badge requirements. Before selecting a badge, staff members can look through the various requirements and decide whether they want to pursue the badge. By listing the requirements up front, staff members are better able to gauge which badges would be most helpful in developing skills to enhance job performance. In order to earn a badge, a staff member completes the requirements using the available resources and then notifies the person responsible for developing and maintaining that badge, known as a badge expert.

The Badge Training Program is entirely self-directed. Library personnel must decide which badges to earn and take it upon themselves to gather that information and develop the necessary skills. They are free to use the information offered, find their own information resources, consult with badge experts, or do whatever else they feel is necessary to learn the skill. When they have completed the list of tasks, they submit the final product or products to the badge expert, and that person determines if the requirements have been met and, if so, grants the staff member the badge. The badge is then automatically displayed on the staff member's web page and on the leaderboard. While the program requires staff members to be self-motivated to complete the assignments, it also has the flexibility to work with everyone's schedule and allows the individual to choose from a wide variety of technology training modules. Metabadges are also given based upon the acquisition of other badges. For instance, earning all the badges for Microsoft Excel, Word, and PowerPoint, will earn the metabadge "Office Champ." Once an individual completes an entire branch of the badge tree, they are then given the opportunity to become a badge expert and assist others with achieving the same technology skills they just acquired.

Badge experts are responsible for developing and maintaining the badges in their areas of expertise. They are an information resource for other staff members wishing to learn that particular technology or for staff who are simply needing consultation while working with that particular technology in their everyday work. For example, a staff member having difficulty with performing a needed task in Microsoft Excel, like creating a graph, could quickly look up the badge experts in Excel and ask one of them how to do it. Badge experts will also be asked to verify that someone has done the needed work to earn a particular badge in that area, and be responsible for making any needed adjustments to the number and type of badges or the required tasks for badges in their area. Having a team of badge experts assists with the overall sustainability of the Badge Training Program, because the management of the badges is spread out among a variety of individuals in different departments. The responsibility for creating and maintaining badges does not rest solely on a single individual or even on the Training and Development Committee as a whole. Once staff members complete a branch of the badge tree, they will then have the opportunity to become badge experts themselves.

While one of the main benefits of the Badge Training Program is the intrinsic motivation it provides, the program also provides extrinsic motivation in the form of incentives. For each badge earned, the staff member also accumulates a set number of points. These points can then be redeemed for various prizes as part of a tiered system. Easier badges to attain have a lower points value. Likewise, the most difficult badges to earn have a higher corresponding points value. There are five tiers of prizes, with each tier worth a different number of points. Individuals can redeem points at any time once they have earned the sufficient number of points. In this way, staff are motivated to work toward the prizes that are most appealing to them.

To provide a reward system for achievement of badges, an internal grant was written to provide funding for the rewards. It was decided to offer smaller initial incentives with requirements that increase with the number of badges achieved. The authors developed six tiers with each tier requiring a greater number of points in order to redeem the prize (see table 9.1).

Providing different levels of prizes serves the purpose of keeping staff members motivated to continue earning badges in order to get better incentives. It also keeps staff from hitting the point at which they believe themselves finished with technology training, as this should be considered an ongoing process. Also, it increases the sustainability of the program, as providing funding for smaller incentives is generally easier to maintain than one large reward, and all staff feel like they can earn something through their participation.

Table 9.1.   Tiered System for Redeeming Prizes

Tier	Points Needed	Prize
Tier I	5 points	$5 Bookstore Gift Card
Tier II	10 points	Tablet Carrying Case
Tier III	20 points	$25 Amazon Gift Card
Tier IV	40 points	Sony Headphones
Tier V	60 points	$75 Amazon Gift Card
Tier VI	80 points	Amazon Kindle Paperwhite

Technical Requirements

The initial requirements for a system to provide badging included:

- a system to track badge and metabadge achievements for 100+ individuals
- display of a "badge map" so all badges and their interrelations can be seen at once
- display of a leaderboard
- a points/prizes system to award prizes for progress in the system
- method for exporting badges to Open Backpack
- quizzing/file submission system

In order to meet the requirements, several existing systems were evaluated, including Credly, Purdue Passport, and others. It was determined that none of these systems provided all of the necessary functionality for the badges program, so a homegrown system was programmed with the use of PHP, jQuery, and a MySQL database. The Open Backpack functionality was provided by adapting Badge-It Gadget Lite, a small set of PHP scripts that interface with Open Backpack and upload badge information to it. The quizzes and file submission were added in by adapting the open-source software Wassail from the University of Alberta. This software was intended to be used for information literacy assessment but was repurposed to provide quizzing capability for showing that a staff member has mastered the skills necessary for a particular badge. The software also includes file submission capability, so if a badge expert deems that earning a badge requires the completion of a finished product, the badge earner can turn it in using the software. For example, the badge expert for the Microsoft Word badges might determine that to prove first level of mastery, a potential badge earner might need to create a file, populate it with text, and add in some basic formatting commands. The file would then be submitted to show that the badge earner had fulfilled the requirements for the badge.

Finally, partway through the development of the badge program, the campus made the decision to subscribe to the Lynda.com e-learning suite, which provided a great deal of resources that badge experts could draw upon to provide information on specific badge skills and to prove fulfillment of badge requirements. Tutorials in Lynda.com could be identified for approximately 50 percent of the badges to significantly reduce the development time needed for badges.

LESSONS LEARNED

The most important lessons learned thus far are that securing the cooperation of upper management in the library is crucial to success, and investments in time and preparation on the front end interface save a lot of retrenchment later. When the committee began development of the Badge Training Program, initial efforts involved presentations to the library administration and to the coordinators of each department in order to gather buy-in. In the case of Belk Library, upper management was very supportive of the overall project, and the authors were able to develop the infrastructure for the program as well as recruit badge experts from throughout the library. As unexpected usability issues with the website resulted in a number of delays with getting the program started, enthusiasm for the program began to wane. Garnering continued support for the Badge Training Program as the authors worked out these issues of usability proved to be a challenge. In retrospect, testing the website and workflows early and often would have helped to smooth out these issues and result in a more timely launch of the program.

The most time-intensive areas in developing the badging program included developing the online components of the program and developing the requirements and resources for earning each badge. The use of the Lynda.com website drastically reduced the amount of time needed to develop these components as suitable e-learning courses could be identified for many badges, providing both the resources for learning the badge skills and the means for proving the acquisition of those skills. Initially, badge experts began creating the requirements for each badge from scratch, but it quickly became apparent that this idea was far too time-consuming and in many cases unnecessary. Once Appalachian State University subscribed to the Lynda.com website, the authors were able to make use of these resources, which saved the committee time and also ensured a level of consistency among the varied badges.

ASSESSMENT

The Training and Development Committee's plans for assessment include measuring the amount of participation among staff as compared to previous training programs. The leaderboard incorporated into the Badge Training Program to display who has earned the most badges also doubles as a means to gather usage statistics. The committee hopes to both increase the percentage of staff that take part in the program as well as increase the number of technologies that are mastered by participants. Additionally, as with the library's previous training programs, the committee intends to develop and disseminate surveys in order to gather user feedback. These surveys will allow the committee to not only improve the user interface and design but will also assist the committee in determining which areas to expand in the program.

Before the committee officially launched the Badge Training Program, the authors asked for volunteers to form a focus group to provide feedback on the system. The focus group consisted of five staff members from four library departments who were not badge experts and had not previously seen the website that houses all the elements of the Badge Training Program. This group met once for about an hour and explored the user interface. They provided suggestions, criticisms, and general comments about the site, such as including instructions for how to login to the university's subscription to the Lynda.com website on the main page, that allowed the authors to make necessary improvements before launching the site to the entire library.

FUTURE DIRECTIONS

The library's Badge Training Program is based on providing opportunities for staff to receive needed instruction in technology, but there are many other ways the program could be expanded. Possible future additions to the badging program include expanding training opportunities beyond technology-related applications, implementing the training program with the library's student workers, and creating an orientation program for new hires. Because of the versatility of the program itself, badges can be created to support almost any type of training or professional development opportunity, and the library's team of badge experts have the autonomy to respond to training needs by developing new badges. Expansion of the Badge Training Program beyond technology training opportunities is only a matter of time.

The extensibility of the system is one of its strongest points, as new technology areas and badges can be continually added. In addition, hard technology skills need not be the only achievements recognized by badges. So-called soft-skills, such as customer service, or reference interviewing can be included as badges. Other behaviors that need to be encouraged can be rewarded with badges as well. The first staff member to find a new technology or online resource could have a "First!" badge attached to it, which encourages exploration.

In this way, the badge training program can easily be expanded to encompass other areas of staff development. The committee's plan is to branch out to incorporate training on safety, customer service, and core competencies. The program could also include cross-functional training to increase collaboration among library departments. Developing additional training opportunities is a relatively seamless process in this program model, which is a major benefit of using digital badges for training. Once additional areas are determined, there are relatively few steps to complete before implementation. For instance, to add safety training to the program, the authors would create a set of badges representing different types of training (emergency preparedness, first aid, etc.), create a list of requirements for each badge, designate badge experts, and then add a Safety branch to the badge tree. Other training modules can be designed and implemented just as easily.

Another possible direction for the Badge Training Program is incorporating student workers into the matrix. The library is one of the largest employers of students on campus, employing over 150 students each year, and uses students in nearly every department. Students work in the mail room, at the Circulation and Reference Desks, in Bibliographic Services, Technology Services, and Special Collections. They also perform such varied tasks as shelving, shelf reading, scanning, checking in/out items, assisting patrons, and processing items of every format. These student workers require a wide range of skills and abilities to excel in these positions. In most cases, the library trains for maximum flexibility among students in order to get the most utility out of their hours. For instance, a student might be trained to check in and out materials at the Circulation Desk, to provide a front-line triage for low-level reference and directional questions at the Reference Desk, and also be asked to do shelving. Each of these tasks require a fairly distinct set of skills, and with so many students to track it is difficult to keep up with what training each student has received. A badging system would keep track of the training each student receives and also indicate the areas in which he or she can work. Students would then be able to be plugged in where assistance is needed, with some assurance that the tasks required will be accomplished well.

Providing consistent and thorough orientations for new hires is essential to every organization, and Belk Library is no exception. While the library has developed orientation checklists to provide this consistency, a badge tree could be an easier way to accommodate the different tasks that are required of any new hire. This badge tree could delineate the skills, knowledge, people to meet, and paperwork and tasks a new hire would need to accomplish.

As the new hire completes each task, the personnel manager could award badges to fill out the tree. This not only gives structure to the process of orienting a new hire but allows the new hire to prioritize the many tasks and knowledge areas required to get up to speed in a new job. This also makes it possible for the new person to know that they are done with orientation and need not wonder what information they may be missing.

Though not necessarily related to staff training, it is important to realize that badging and gamification have implications for information literacy as well. A badging system could provide a list of the skills and knowledge necessary, for instance, to be considered information literate at the First Year Seminar level, or information literate in their major, or for an overall level of competence achieved at the undergraduate level. If the library were to tie in its efforts with the General Education program on campus, certain badges, such as using a Citation Management System or passing an information literacy test could be made a part of graduation requirements.

CONCLUSION

A program designed around the use of digital badges and incorporating elements of gamification is an innovative way to provide consistent, comprehensive training for library staff. Providing opportunities for library personnel to receive training in current and emerging technologies is an essential form of professional development. Technology training is particularly conducive to the use of digital badges, because the very completion of the program encourages staff members to explore technologies. Digital badges, in turn, are a way to provide motivation, encourage participation, and ensure the sustainability of a library training program. While technical expertise and a knowledge of programming are certainly useful when developing this type of program, it is not essential. There are online open-source systems that will support digital badges, and the list is growing.

In the case of Belk Library, a badge training program was the solution to the challenge of providing multiple levels of technology training for a variety of different applications. Staff members with varied interests are all able to explore a wide range of potential badges and choose the ones that are most relevant to their job duties. Supervisors are able to ascertain the level of expertise their employees have with regard to different technologies, and can also encourage staff members to learn about particular technologies. This type of professional development will ensure that library personnel will maintain a basic knowledge of certain technologies while continuing to expand their skills.

The library still has a long way to go until the authors' vision for the Badge Training Program is fully realized. Early setbacks in the interface design stages delayed the launch of the digital badges site. The authors do not yet know the full impact this new training program will have on the library as a whole or in what ways the program will develop; however, the Training and Development Committee developed the Badge Training Program with a firm foundation in the overall benefits of using gamification elements in staff training and development. Early interest from badge experts in particular, and from other staff members in general, indicate the potential this training program has for increased engagement with technology throughout the library.

Librarians and library staff must possess basic technological skills and, in many cases, become technologically savvy in order to respond to the needs of library users. Because technology changes so rapidly, it is an area in which continued training is particularly vital. Establishing a training program based on digital badges and including elements of game design is a means to easily connect staff with opportunities to expand their technology skills. In the authors' experience, it is also a way to provide training that is self-directed and encourages widespread participation. The extensibility of the badge system also allows for expansion in a number of different areas, makes possible a flexible approach to future technological advances, and provides a method to develop the future direction of the library with regard to technology as well as assess its progress.

REFERENCES

Ash, K. (2012). "Digital Badges." *Digital Directions*, 24–30.

Danforth, L. (2011). "Gamification and Libraries." *Library Journal* 136, no. 3: 84.

Deterding, S. (2011). "Situated Motivational Affordances of Game Elements: A Conceptual Model." CHI 2011, May 7–12, 2011. Vancouver, BC, Canada.

Diaz, V. (2013). "Digital Badges for Professional Development." *EDUCAUSE Review Online*. http://www.educause.edu/ero/article/digital-badges-professional-development.

Farkas, M. (2014). "Just a Game? Library Gamification Encourages Engagement and Learning." *American Libraries* 45, no. 1: 26.

Johnson, L., S. Adams Becker, M. Cummins, V. Estrada, A. Freeman, and H. Ludgate. (2013). *NMC Horizon Report: 2013 Higher Education Edition*. Austin, TX: The New Media Consortium.

Kapp, K. M. (2012). *The Gamification of Learning and Instruction: Game-based Methods and Strategies for Training and Education*. San Francisco, CA: Pfeiffer.

Mallon, M. (2013). "Gaming and Gamification." *Public Services Quarterly* 9, no. 3: 210–21.

Zichermann, G., and C. Cunningham. (2011). *Gamification by Design: Implementing Game Mechanics in Web and Mobile Apps*. Sebastopol, CA: O'Reilly Media.

Chapter Ten

Gamification and Librarianship

A New DART-Europe Ready to Roll

Diana Parlic, Adam Sofronijevic, and
Mladen Cudanov

THE STORY OF GAMIFICATION

The story of gamification is as old as humankind. One could say that *Homo sapiens* is inherently also *Homo ludens*. One of the first uses of the game approach related to business goes back to 1912 when the manufacturer of Cracker Jack started adding a toy to the box of popcorn. Such an approach has given a game character and feeling to the product. In the 1964 movie *Mary Poppins* the song "A Spoonful of Sugar" explained how "in every job that must be done, there is an element of fun" and stated that "you find the fun and snap, the job's a game" (Fitz-Walter, 2013).

There are many other fine historical examples that connect games and business, but it is rather difficult to pinpoint the exact date of origin of the term *gamification*. Many consider the year 2002 as the starting year, and Nick Pelling the first person who used this term for the purpose of describing his workplace (Pelling, 2011). In the late 2000s, the term *gamification* found its place into everyday communication (http://en.wikipedia.org/wiki/Nick_Pelling).

There has been much research aimed at determining the role of fun in all the experiences that users will remember. Recently, many application designers started to incorporate video game elements directly into their work. Typical examples were Chore Wars and Bunchball, appearing in 2007. Chore Wars is an application that included game elements to make housework easier and more fun. This application represents all family members as online characters and gives them awards for housework finished and registered via the website chorewars.com. Also, Bunchball was organized to provide gamified business solutions to organizations and companies (http://www.bunchball.com/about).

Jane McGonigal is one of the many influential authors important for defining the gamification concept. She is a world-famous game designer, and author of the book *Reality Is Broken: Why Games Make Us Better and How They Can Change the World.* She is also well known for her talks on game elements such as "The Game That Can Give You 10 Extra Years of Life" (McGonigal, 2012a).

In 2011 one of the world's leading IT companies, Gartner, started the development of gamification, and Gabe Zichermann discussed gamification development in his books and research (Zichermann, 2011). Twenty-five million dollars was invested in gamification in 2011, and it was predicted that half the organizations that want to innovate their processes will decide to include game elements by 2015 (Gamification).

INTRODUCING GAMIFICATION

The concept of gamification is not a new one. The Olympic Games were an example of how people praised games and the participation in them, because they knew they would compete and be awarded publicly. "Happy hour" is also an approach that is used by businesses to motivate people. A typical example is encouraging customers to buy cookies or rolls in the last working hours by lowering prices (Aichholzer, 2012).

The main idea of gamification is the use of game elements and techniques in business processes. Gamification is basically about learning from games and applying this new knowledge in a business environment. There are many definitions of gamification but no such definition that is universally agreed upon. The one that is very often cited states that gamification is an approach that uses game elements and techniques in a context that does not have any similarities with games (Werbach & Hunter, 2012).

Game Elements

For the purpose of a clear understanding of the gamification concept, it is important to be familiar with games and game elements, as well as their characteristics and function. The main game elements are (Gray, Brown, & Macanufo, 2010):

- Goal of the game—shows us what is expected of the participants to achieve.

- Game area—is the area outside the real world in which the participants will play a game.
- Game borders—refers to any kind of limits; for example, time limits, space limits, etc.
- Game rules—gives an explanation of how the participants will play a game.
- Objects—helps to keep up with the game in progress and the results during the game.

The Pyramid of Elements is a framework for the gamification concept, and it describes the three-level system that organizes and connects the game elements (https://class.coursera.org/gamification-002/lecture/41) (see appendix I below).

The SAPS Award System concept is based on four elements that represent awards, and they all have influence on the leaderboard status. Elements are rated according to the influence they have on players (Zichermann & Cunningham, 2011).

1. Status—is the position of one player compared to other players and refers to a group of people or a team. This award can function in the real world, but also in a virtual environment. The most commonly used mechanisms that belong to status as an element of SAPS are badges, levels, and leaderboards.
2. Access—implies that a defined group of players will have early access to particular activities or information, as an award for a level passed or something similar. This type of award is not in monetary form or any tangible form, but confers the feeling of personal satisfaction to players and a high reputation among other players.
3. Power—this element represents power as a type of award. A typical example for this type of award is assigning the role of forum moderator to the player who has passed a defined number of levels or participated in some activities. Just having the power of the moderator's role will be enough for the player to perform this role for free and to enjoy it. Many forums give similar types of power; a good example is the forum of the popular video game World of Warcraft.
4. Stuff—given that the list of elements of the SAPS reward system is composed by rank, the last element on the list is one that players want the least. This does not mean that it should be completely ignored, because there is always a group of players who want this award. If you have a small reward that you can offer to your players, and that is exactly what they want, then this element of the SAPS reward system

is the one that will be the most effective. For example, there is no need to offer a player the status and title "King of Ice Cream," if what he or she wants is simply an ice cream.

Authors Dan Hunter and Kevin Werbach propose a six-step process for successful implementation of gamification practice in an organization (https://class.coursera.org/gamification-2012-001/lecture/54):

1. Define business goals
2. Describe target behaviors
3. Describe players
4. Define loop activities
5. Don't forget fun
6. Implementation of an appropriate tool

Johan Huizinga, an early twentieth-century thinker, presented his theory of the *magic circle*. The magic circle is actually a special place in the real or virtual world. Within the borders of this realm the players reject the rules that are applicable to the rest of the world and accept and behave according to the rules of the game. The game has its own rules, its objectives and obstacles, and when the players are within the borders of the magic circle, they obey these rules willingly, and attempt to behave in accordance with them. One could say these rules are applicable to a gamified business. The company creates its own game circle and sets specific goals. Players aim to realize these goals, not because they had been forced to, but because they are voluntarily becoming a part of the gamified system. This process is very difficult to implement successfully and entails great responsibility, but, on the other hand, brings a number of benefits for both sides (Werbach & Hunter, 2012). Games usually have a very powerful influence on people. Sometimes this influence is so powerful that people even forget that the time spent on the game is just for fun and entertainment. Also, the game, as a basis of gamification, makes people think in a different way, and through this approach teaches lessons from a completely different area, which does not have anything in common with games.

Many authors have devoted their attention to fun as a feeling, and one definition provided by Nicole Lazzaro, president and founder of XeoDesign Inc., distinguishes between different kinds of fun that can be achieved (Lazzaro):

- "Easy" fun—hanging out with friends and having fun, an everyday and common kind of fun.
- "Hard" fun—includes some accomplishment, achievement, reaching a goal, or recognition.

- Fun aimed at people—a kind of fun that can be realized through teamwork and in contact with other people.
- "Serious" fun—involves creating a sense of fun while performing different activities that are in some way important to the person who performs them, regardless of whether the environment views them in the same way.

The important issue for many who practice gamification is creating a solution that promotes a sense of happiness in human beings. Most often, this problem can be analyzed by means of positive psychology. Positive psychology, developed by Martin Seligman and Mihaly Csikszentmihalyi, is based on the analysis of causes that make people happy and successful, and help them to prosper (Seligman & Csikszentmihalyi, 2000). Psychologist Jane McGonigal has defined the concept, which she calls Perma—the name composed of the initial letters of the elements it consists of (McGonigal, 2012). These are:

1. Positive emotions
2. Engagement
3. Relationships
4. Meaning
5. Achievement

McGonigal believes that these elements are the key for achieving a sense of happiness and fulfillment, a sense of self-satisfaction.

One of the creators of the theory of positive psychology, Mihaly Csikszentmihalyi, presented some interesting findings related to the game and a sense of happiness that is created when people participate in games. He believes that games can cause two main extreme states: anxiety and boredom (Csikszentmihalyi, 2004). Situations in which people participate in some very easy games, games that do not require specific skills, abilities, and knowledge, produce a sense of boredom. There are no ups and downs, there are no obstacles, no unsolvable quests in the game, and people are not interested in playing. Another extreme situation is the one involving a game that is too difficult. A too difficult game may be a game that requires skills, abilities, and knowledge above average, a game in which the obstacles do not allow a player to progress. Such games cause anxiety and a feeling of dissatisfaction. Achieving a sense of happiness is somewhere between the two extreme states. The ideal situation is one in which a player never finds it too easy nor too difficult to play.

Understanding the players, their behavior and characteristics, is an important process for the implementation of gamification. The aim is not just to know what players are searching for in games but also to know as much as possible about them in general. In this regard, the participants in the game are mostly defined by two types of characteristics. They are demographic characteristics and behavioral characteristics. For business functions such as marketing, this is the initial introductory phase to define segments and classify people according to their characteristics in these segments.

One approach, represented by Richard Bartle, allows for four basic types of game participants (Bartle, 1996). Four basic types of players in Bartle's classification are:

- Killers—their aim and satisfaction is not only to win, but they want to fight and feel as though they did something important by squashing their competitors.
- Achievers—they see success in an achievement or recognition of achievement, in something that will motivate them and lead to the goal.
- Socializers—are the players who find that the most important thing in the game is the contact with other players: they enjoy interacting with them and encouraging communication.
- Explorers—as the name implies like to research. They want to explore the territory of the game, all the opportunities that exist in the game, always experiencing something new and exciting in the game.

It is important to emphasize that not all players fit just one of these categories. A player usually has in him- or herself the characteristics of each type of player. It is often the case that a player changes his or her behavior over a certain time period, or that for a particular period of time behaves, for example, as a researcher and then alters his or her behavior several times. Knowing the players and their personal characteristics is important because such knowledge may indicate how the players will react in different stages of the game and what it is that motivates them (Wei & Finkel).

SUCCESSFUL AND UNSUCCESSFUL EXAMPLES OF GAMIFICATION IMPLEMENTATION

There are many successful cases of implementing gamification, but also many that are not. The Microsoft translation project, the Windows 7 language game, is tied to the use of elements of the game that refers to the internal application of gamification. Microsoft is a large and successful company that operates in many countries, and its main software product at the time of its gamification implementation—Windows 7—also had to be adjusted to a number of countries in which this system was used. For Microsoft employees, this was an extensive but not overly interesting job—to test a new operating system in the languages of those countries. In this situation, Microsoft introduced game elements, and in every country, in their own language, employees tested Windows 7 and provided their input for the system and thus participated in a gamified system that provided virtual rewards and badges for those that performed the best. This encouraged all employees to perform better at their jobs and make a better "localized" Windows. Leaderboards were also introduced, and all employees were able to monitor their results as to where their localized Windows was ranked on the list. This internal implementation of gamification has produced the following results: 4,500 participants, more than 500,000 dialogue windows viewed, about 7,000 errors reported, and just as many repairs were made (Nicholson, 2012).

Disney also tried to introduce gamification in their Disneyland hotel complex in California. This is an example of unsuccessful implementation of gamification. The target group included all employees in the laundry service in the hotel complex. In fact, there was a huge monitor in the laundry room that presented all employees with information about their work performance, so that each employee was able to see his or her results, but also the results of other employees. Those performance indicators informed employees about how quickly they fulfill their tasks, and the whole concept was based on the list of leaders. The idea was to encourage employees to work more efficiently. This approach had an opposite effect from the one they had expected. Unnecessary competitiveness was created, and employees were pushed to skip even their toilet breaks just in order to finish as much work as they could. On the other hand, those employees who were ranked poorly were under pressure because they constantly feared losing their jobs.

DART PORTAL

The DART portal is a leading portal that integrates master's theses and doctoral dissertations from 541 universities and 27 European countries. The number of papers is increasing daily, and as of May 2014 was close to 430,000. The DART portal was created as a partnership of research libraries and library consortiums working together in order to provide unified access to European master's theses and doctoral dissertations. The partnership includes national libraries, consortiums, and research institutions, and they all contribute in some way to the development of DART. This portal is supported by the League of European Research Libraries (LIBER) (fr. *Ligue des Bibliothèques Européennes de Recherche*), and it is also a European partner of the Networked Digital Library of Theses and Dissertations (NDLTD) (http://www.DART-europe.eu/About/info.php).

DART was created in 2005 as a project planned to be completed in eighteen months. Its basic resources have been obtained solely through partnerships and collaboration. The project had several goals:

- Creating an open-access portal that enables free search of doctoral dissertations and master's theses at the European level.
- Creating a platform that will be the base and will support those institutions that do not have their own local repository.
- Defining the base that will help in counseling and will provide basic guidance and advice concerning the whole process of writing a paper.
- Create a service for presenting digital theses and dissertations.
- Defining a business model that will have the potential for long-term sustainability and will provide additional services, such as support for checking copyrights and preventing counterfeiting works and copyright infringement.

Since 2007, DART has entered its second phase of development. The partnership is now an ongoing program that provides support for research, management, and use of theses and dissertations from a single point of entry—the DART portal. Users are transferred to institutional repositories in order to retrieve the full text of theses and dissertations.

The portal functions as a single common point for researchers, as well as for publishers from Europe in the field of master's theses and doctoral dissertations (Moyle, 2008). The crucial aspect of DART is that all theses and dissertations available through it are in the open-access (OA) publishing model. DART is partnering with universities in order to ensure that as many master's theses and doctoral dissertations from all over Europe as possible are to be found at this one Internet point. This means that the DART portal still does not provide an opportunity for individuals to post their works directly, but the communication channel is exclusively through the universities.

The basic functions provided by the DART portal as of May 2014 are:

- Search
- Content download from partner repositories
- Sending feedback

The search function can be used by entering keywords, and as a result the user gets a list of all master's theses and doctoral dissertations containing the defined search words in the title of the paper, abstract, or in the keywords. It is also possible to browse by predefined tools that group all papers by several criteria. One can browse papers by university, by collection, or by country of origin. Content download is provided by partner repositories, and the DART portal moves traffic to partner sites providing both an efficient service for users and satisfaction for partners. Sending feedback is enabled by providing a comment field for users. All suggestions and comments regarding the operation of the portal can be sent via this field. By providing timely and accurate responses, the DART portal gives its users the feeling that they are at the center of the service improvement effort.

Based on these functions, it is possible to define the user groups. These are:

1. Authors of master's theses and doctoral dissertations. If they are in the process of writing their papers, they may be interested in all papers relevant to their work that can be found through the portal.

2. Authors of master's theses or doctoral dissertations who have completed their paper, defended it, and it can now be found through the portal in one of the partners' repositories. This group of users may be interested in monitoring the use of their paper, that is, how many times it has been downloaded by other users.

3. Professors of higher education institutions who are related to master's theses and doctoral dissertations. They also may use the portal in two ways. They may be interested in monitoring the interest of the academic community in the papers that have been completed under their supervision, but also they may be interested in all the other papers and use the portal for information retrieval. In the process of mentoring, this may be helpful in directing a student's work toward novel findings presented in the papers of others.

4. Universities, as institutions, are often DART portal users, and they use it to monitor the interest of the wider academic community in papers produced at their institution.

5. Industry or profit organizations may be interested in all aspects of materials that can be found through the portal. It is always of interest to find out about new research, but it is also essential to follow the general trends of scientific interest and level of achievements in certain fields.

6. Librarians, like the above-mentioned groups, may also have an interest in the DART portal. The most common use of the portal, as far as librarians are concerned, is as an information retrieval tool used by librarians or considered important in the field of user education. But it can also be a source of materials that is used for the purpose of personal development and lifelong education. Also, librarians can perform specific scientometric calculations on behalf of universities and individual researchers based on the information available through the portal.

General Proposition for Improving the Functionality of the DART Portal

DART currently operates as a portal, but its functionality can be improved. This could be achieved by the enrichment of already existing functions. The portal users could be engaged through various activities that will make them relate more closely to the portal.

The first step in this process is to engage all potential authors of a thesis and dissertation and turn them into users of the portal at an early stage of their research. This approach offers much more opportunities than the existing one, where authors find out about the portal only after their thesis or dissertation has been uploaded by their respective institution. Another existing possibility is that authors use the DART portal as an information retrieval tool during their research. In order to engage authors and make their workflow more related to the portal, a proposition can be put forth to make a personalization of the portal that should lead to the creation of a community of users around the DART content and functions.

To personalize the portal is to create technical possibilities for each user to have his or her own space within DART. A username and password will protect this space and ensure long-term preservation of all the activities and materials gathered here by the user. In addition, this will allow DART to evaluate and award user activities and thus create possibilities for the gamification of the user experiences related to DART.

The personalization of the portal would enable the creation of a community of users around the content and functions of DART. This activity would be most effectively carried out by the creation of a DART forum. The forum would be a place to gather all the users of DART and allow them to actually help each other in the process of writing a paper by providing expert advice, suggestions, and links to useful topics or literature sources.

User accounts should contain the user's personal information, his or her previous education, professional orientation and professional activities, area of research interest and information on the time frame regarding the user's formal educational process, and the stage of the research he or she has reached. Other specific information may be very helpful, such as recommendations from the users who have already finished their research and the writing of the paper regarding their experiences in a specific field or institution. Such information will be helpful for the creation of topics and grouping of threads in the DART forum. An important option regarding user privacy is to provide the possibility for users to choose whether they want their account to be public (accessible to everyone) or private (with functionalities that allow for just certain users or user groups to access the profile).

Each author in the research process and in the process of writing his or her paper goes through several stages. At the beginning, the authors may not be sure of the exact area of research and the subject of their paper, and the only thing that many of the authors know is their general area of scientific interest. In this phase the forum, which fosters user interaction, may be very helpful. A well-organized forum could be used as a specific interactive information retrieval tool, allowing for efficient user orientation in regard to the research field, area of interest, or progress of one's research. Authors that do have a specific research topic and field of interest may use the new DART forum functions for the exchange of experiences and ideas, and for serendipitous encounters with other young researchers.

Finally, a group of users that will also find the new DART functionalities useful are alumni who may help other authors still in the process of writing a paper and share their experiences with them.

University professors and librarians of academic libraries could also be distinguished as two separate user groups of DART. Both of these groups may contribute with their experience and knowledge to the development of papers by commenting and sharing their opinions via the DART forum.

The most important mechanism that needs to be fostered through the implementation of gamification is the cooperation within the community. Community building will be enabled by personalization of user experiences and enhanced functions through unique usernames and forum functions that will allow different users to communicate and collaborate over long periods of time.

One important consequence of the possibilities of long-term collaboration and communication within the DART community is joint work on theses and dissertations. Joint authorship of texts has been theoretically considered, and nowadays it has matured enough that such a possibility must be considered as a reality if both motivation and technical support exist (Casati, Fausti, & Maurizio, 2007) (Hall, 2009).

Gamification Elements for the Proposed DART Improvement

Before a detailed proposition of the game elements aiming to improve DART functionality is presented, it is important to answer the basic question of why such techniques can be effective for achieving this aim.

First of all, it is important to know how to define, within the scope of practice of gamification, the sorts of elements and the overall process that will be implemented in the framework of enhancing DART functionality. According to the presented theory, gamification practice can be described as internal, external, and one that aims at behavior change. For the purpose of improving DART functions, the proposition presented here will focus on the external and behavior change use of gamification. The external use is defined by a goal or goals aimed at external users, customers, and consumers. In the case of DART, external stakeholders are those external subjects with whom DART wants to foster stronger relationships and a stronger connection to the DART service. At the same time, the proposition presented here aims at achieving a certain change in the general behavior of large user groups such as master's and doctoral students, professors involved with mentoring of theses and dissertations, university administration, and librarians. Based on this, the authors conclude that the practice of gamification proposed in relation to the DART portal also aims at the behavior change.

The overall goal of the proposition of gamification of the DART portal is to improve its functionality. This can be subdivided into specific aims, and these are defined as follows. The first is to increase the overall use of DART within the existing framework of functions. The second is to increase the use of DART within the proposed framework of improved functions. Both of these can be measured by the number of users, number of downloads achieved at partner repositories from users coming from the DART portal, and by the value of the DART brand within the academic communities of Europe and beyond. The proposition also aims at increased collaboration between users, higher levels of user engagement, and a higher level of interactivity in writing the paper. Also an increase in the number of institutions involved as DART partners, along with the number of papers submitted to DART.

For these purposes the SMART goals as defined in Doran (1981) will be used. SMART objectives should be:

- Specific—this feature means that it is much more efficient to have a single goal, but one that is mostly broadly defined. When defining specific goals, it is useful to answer questions such as what DART wants to achieve and why, who was involved in achieving the goals, in what place and what are the requirements to achieve this goal?
- Measurable—a characteristic of measurable goals is also very important, because it points to a specific criterion to measure the achievement of goals and progress on the path toward it. If the goal is not measurable, the team will have no way of knowing how to progress toward its achievement and what actions should be taken.
- Achievable—when defining goals, the process will help to define the ways in which they can be achieved. For this reason, it is important that targets are not set so that they are very easy to achieve, but neither are they impossible to reach.
- Relevant—refers to the selection of the target that is consistent with the business and for which the company really cares.

- Timed—the importance of the characteristics of each goal is that DART determines an exact date for achieving the goal. Also, time-bound goals help the team to focus on core activities, their implementation, and the achievement of objectives within the required timeline.

Before the elements of practice of gamification for each selected user group are defined, it is important to take a holistic look at the process activities involved. This means having a clear picture of the activities carried out by each user group and to place these activities in a virtual loop of gamification. The very beginning of this may be defined as activities of authors who are just starting with the development of their master's thesis or doctoral dissertation. Their primary motivation is to complete their work in the most efficient way; so in the initial phase, their activities would be most likely directed to downloading papers, research activities, and participation in forums on threads that are about the basic issues regarding the research process. This group of authors will be most likely to evaluate the forum post by others and rank the usefulness of contribution of others to the community. Another group involves authors that have already finished their papers. They will be in a position to contribute more to the forum, but also to evaluate posts and threads created by others. The next target group of users of DART and the DART forum are professors supervising the research and master's and doctoral processes. Their focus will be on the students they are mentoring and perhaps on other students in the same field or from the same institution. They can contribute important materials to the community, and also their evaluation should be ranked as more valuable. In this order, the groups of users are moving up the gamification loop by achieving points and rewards and thus reaching certain levels and statuses that confer academic prestige.

Due to the volume and complexity of the processes proposed as improvements to DART, the proposition is focused on elements of the gamification practice for three user groups: authors, professors, and universities.

The Framework for Gamification Implementation into the DART Portal

One can say that gamification is about adding additional layers of motivation to an existing business framework. If such a proposition is accepted, motivators driving the activities of participants in a gamified DART portal may be discussed. In general, the main idea behind the gamification of the DART portal is to add another facet to academic entities. Such a facet—a personalized, gamified DART portal—will provide opportunities for networking, collaboration, and the presentation of academic results and achievements. So the general motivator for all academic entities involved (institutions, individual researchers, professors, etc.) will be strong enough if momentum around the

proposed DART portal takes off, motivation around these entities is successful in the new environment, and opportunities are available to use the portal
for expressing scientific achievements.

In line with the six-step gamification process described previously, the
relevant steps are defined as follows:

1. Defining the business goals

   - *Higher utilization of the DART portal*—that is, an increase in the
     number of DART visitors, as well as the number of users who will
     visit the portal again. These indicators will provide the information
     if participants have achieved the set objective through quantitative
     data, including the number of visitors, the number of pages visited,
     and the total number of downloaded theses and dissertations. In the
     framework of the concept of SMART goals, this is defined through
     concrete expected results. This means that the goal is defined by
     increasing the number of visitors to the portal by 30 percent within
     six months after the introduction of gamification. This implies that
     DART has the functionality of monitoring visits in order to com-
     pare the current number of visitors to the portal after a defined
     period with a new number. The planned retention time on the portal
     in the same period of time should also increase by 25 percent.
   - *A higher level of user engagement on the portal*—which comes as
     the logical continuation of the previously achieved goal. Primarily
     this refers to the creation of a community of DART users through a
     series of defined activities. The goal is to create a user community
     around the DART content. This will be enabled by opening a user
     account in order to improve functionality, and its use will be driven
     by the number of proposed elements of gamification. As part of the
     evaluation, certain quantitative indicators will be monitored that
     can clearly show the extent to which the objectives have been
     achieved. The number of created user accounts on the portal is one
     of the indicators that will show the authors how this functionality is
     effective at creating a community and the possible interest of target
     groups. The expected number of created user accounts in the first
     six months should amount to fifteen thousand. There is also the
     number of active accounts, which is appropriate for monitoring the
     activities of users, and also to eliminate the situation when a user
     has opened an account but then stopped visiting DART. The ex-
     pected number of active accounts is expected to be five thousand
     for the same time period of six months. It is also suitable to monitor
     how many user accounts have left more than fifteen comments on
     the forum on a monthly basis. According to the Pareto principle, 80

percent of the results come from 20 percent of users (Koch, 2004). Based on this principle, the expected number of very active accounts is one thousand. In general, important indicators are also the number of comments left on the forum by all user groups, the number of open threads, and the number of documents posted by users. An increase in the number of master's theses and doctoral dissertations that can be found through the portal after the introduction of gamification is also expected. The aim for this goal is set at 15 percent in the first six months.

- *A larger number of the involved institutions*—these institutions are, as already mentioned, DART's main partners. They do not have activities on the portal themselves, but rather perform analysis, track statistics, and make decisions based on the data gathered. The evaluation for the increase in participation of institutions and their collaboration with DART is planned through indicators that tell us about the number of universities present at DART, as well as the number of master's theses and doctoral dissertations from the respective universities. The expected result of the introduction of gamification leads to an increase in the number of universities present on DART to 10 percent in the first six months.
- *Increase in collaboration among users*—this activity is planned primarily through the introduction of new functionalities on DART, that is, the introduction of creating accounts and forum. These two functionalities will be defined separately for each target group through gamification elements that would help encourage users to participate in these activities. The plan is to increase collaboration among users by sharing experiences, opinions, advice, and material assistance.
- *Increasing interactivity during development of works*—the final goal is related to the process of improving the forms of cooperation among the users on the portal, where attention is primarily directed at the target group of authors.

2. Description of target behaviors—this element of the framework for gamification implementation refers to the description of behavior that the authors expect as a result for user groups. Within the framework of the existing functionality, the authors' goal is a greater number of views regarding master's theses and doctoral dissertations on the portal. In the framework of the enhanced portal or the gamified portal, the expected behavior of user groups is influenced by the possibility of creating user accounts, as well as the use of the forum, and is directed at users who cooperate in preparing a doctoral dissertation. The expected behavior includes activities in which users comment on content

proposals from other users and exchange suggestions for the literature lists and the proposed research methods. The idea is to encourage all users of the portal to share reviews, opinions and advice, and the experience they have gained, in order to encourage closer communication and a higher level of interaction.

3. Description of future players—they can be generally classified into four groups. They include authors in the process of writing a master's thesis or doctoral dissertation, then authors who have defended their thesis or dissertation, professors, and finally universities as a specific user group. All future players will express the behavior of researchers and will be directed toward research (pushing the limits) or will act as achievers (seeking success through achievements, merit, or recognition of success).

4. Defining the activities of the loops—the basic activity is the scale of progress of users through the proposed gamification loop. Users will be active through forum discussions, interactivity with other users, and evaluation of their activities by other users. They will be awarded points for these activities and progress toward achieving higher levels in the DART virtual hierarchy. They will be also awarded points for achievements in real life such as defending a doctoral dissertation or publishing a paper in a peer-reviewed journal. In a combination of virtual world activities relating to the DART portal and real-life activities relating to academic activities of users, the status of users will be defined in regard to the DART community. Hopefully this status will become a specific indicator of academic excellence, pushing the use of DART even further.

5. Do not forget the aspect of fun—in gamification practice an important concept that must be realized is the focus on fun. It is important, with constant twists and surprises, to maintain uncertainty and not to allow portal users to find themselves in one of the two extreme states: the state of boredom or anxiety. When the current functionality of the DART portal is addressed, the creation of a sense of fun could be related to awards that may be given to the users after a random number of downloaded papers or page views on DART. Given that the current functionality does not have the option of opening a user account, the rewards would be granted according to the IP address. The proposed improvement of the portal would allow for the possibility of this same award and consequently the surprise factor, as well as additional activities that would foster a sense of fun. For the user in this scenario, awards will be given out according to the user account activity.

6. The use of appropriate tools—will be explained in detail in the following part of the text.

Gamification Elements Targeting DART Users

There are several gamification elements that will reward certain actions of users. These will be described in some detail for the group of authors just starting their research and for those users who have already defended their thesis or dissertation. These are illustrative enough to include gamification elements targeting other user groups. The elements targeting authors starting their research are:

1. Rating the DART user profile. This element of gamification aims to motivate users of this group to put more work into filling out their profile. Suitable elements to accompany this action would be a graphical representation of profile details—in the form of columns or circles that are colored according to percentage. The rating of the user profile would be consistent with the availability of formal information, such as updating information on the current year of study, and practical experience or research papers that have been published. The rating will also contain a part that relates directly to the research work of the user, and progress toward the doctorate. Each phase of development of the author in regard to their DART status and level will be related to specific criteria that must be met in order to move to the next level. Moreover, each of these levels will include their name, and each user will have a specific title according to the information on progress toward completion of their research work. Here the authors will use the implementation of the gamification mechanisms. They are: achievement—the author tends to aim for or to achieve a 100 percent filled-out user profile; epic significance—because the author is moving toward a significant goal, and that is completing their work where the filled-out profile is just one of the activities; level—seen by filling out the user profile, users move from one level to another; status—users will move from a lower to higher level but with defined titles that will be related to their DART status.

2. Rating activities on the forum. This means that besides the information related to their profile, other activities will also be considered for awarding points and for moving through the gamification loop. The number of comment threads would not give the authors relevant criteria for user activities, so additional information regarding the quality of these activities is needed. All users will be able to rank the comments and threads of other users, giving a certain rank to each of these, which then relate to points for a user posting a thread or comment.

The activities also have to be defined for the group of authors who have already completed their master's thesis or doctoral dissertation. These activities are:

1. Rating the DART user profile. This activity is similar to the one planned for the first group of authors. Here the users will have additional motivation to fill out their profile with data relating to their defended thesis or dissertation, giving more reliable and detailed metadata on these documents than those found at institutional repositories.
2. Encouraging authors to communicate within the forum. This activity is about the authors with experience in preparing a dissertation or thesis being encouraged to share their experiences and advice with other users of the portal. It would be useful also to have threads defined on the forum by area of scientific interest, so that user orientation is more efficient. This group of users can realize benefits from frequent and quality communication as leading to an increased number of downloads of a particular master's thesis or doctoral dissertation, which is of course the primary goal of any author.
3. Listing of leaders. This is a list of all users of the DART portal ranked according to their points achieved through DART-related activities and real-life activities reported in their user profiles. It is important for the motivation of users not to present the full list, since most users will not go to the very top of the list and may become discouraged as a result; instead, users can be presented with their relative position within their field of study or relative to other users from their university or in regard to their advancement on the list.

Regarding the user group of professors, the gamification elements are fairly the same. One has to bear in mind certain specifics regarding the design of the point-awarding system that have to include awarding a different number of points for activities to those who have already achieved certain academic prestige in real life. Advancement through the gamification loop for this user group needs to be faster and reflect their achievements in the real world, but also to retain certain subtle distinctions regarding DART-related activities in order to motivate users from this group to engage in them.

Universities as specific users of DART are to be considered also in the analysis of gamification elements. Universities are very much interested in the overall success of their members, both professors and students. DART will therefore be providing representations of the status achieved by individual users, but also of the collective success of members of the same institution. One important consideration is the affiliation of each user that will be a part of the DART user profile. Since this is the only information that can tie the user to his or her institution, special points will have to be awarded for filling out this information. Overall success of a university will be calculated on the basis of success of individual professors and students, and then suitable representation will be provided. Electronic badges appropriate for a university site will be one such representation, and several others, both physical and virtual, will be provided.

CONCLUSION

The DART portal is very important for the scientific and research community of Europe. It provides access to a crucial body of scientific communication—defended theses and dissertations of European universities. The DART portal is functioning very well at the moment, covering most European countries, with hundreds of partnering institutions and hundreds of thousands of theses and dissertations offered to users. A proposition for gamification of the DART portal builds on this strong ground and adds flavor to scientific and research processes related to DART. Such a proposition may be evaluated by the rate of achievement of defined business goals, such as an increased number of DART users or theses provided, as described in the section "The Framework for Gamification Implementation into the DART Portal." This evaluation has to take into account the time frame of networking effects and the time needed for these effects to translate to defined business goals.

By broadening the functionalities of DART and by transforming it from a portal into an online community, the proposal points the way for making DART a central focal point for the master and doctoral research community of Europe. By careful implementation of gamification elements, such a virtual community can thrive and grow fast, relating the identity and status of individual researchers and institutions in the virtual world with these important characteristics in the real world.

APPENDIX I: THE PYRAMID OF ELEMENTS

1. Dynamics—are the structures characterized by patterns that reflect experiences in games. The following elements are key for dynamics:

   • Limits—are objects that exist in every game. Space limits, for example, in games offer the participants the possibility of making meaningful choices and solving interesting problems. Limits are considered as one of the most important elements in games, so game designers should always plan them in detail.

- Emotions—as it is well known, every game may arouse different types of feelings: happiness, success, satisfaction, but sadness or disappointment as well. Emotions encourage players to move forward, to participate in games, and to spend time playing games, so this aspect is very important to every game.
- Story—is a factor that makes a game a unified whole, the story connects all parts of a game. If the game does not make sense, gamification will not be properly implemented and will not yield the expected results.
- Progression—represents the player's understanding that he or she will be able to progress, to change his or her current position in regard to the game story. It is a concept that usually presents moving through levels or a defined scale by collecting points or solving problems.
- Relationships—are relationships between team players, but also between rivals or competitors.

2. Mechanics—are defined as processes or elements that make the game move forward and keep players interested in participating in games:

- Challenges—exist in games through the definition of players' aims.
- Chance—means that the result in a game is not always solely the consequence of a player's actions, but rather includes accidental circumstances.
- Competition and cooperation—elements that are opposite, they are encouragement for players to cooperate for achieving an aim, or to fight for it against competing players.
- Feedback—gives information about the current player's position and provides them with an opportunity to consider and decide on future steps.
- Acquiring resources—is the process of attaining different kinds of resources in the game, allowing players to keep participating in games.
- Awards—include any kind of benefits awarded in the game as recognition for achieving something, for moving through levels, etc.
- Transactions—refers to every purchase or sale between players.
- Win definitions—define what is considered as a win in the game.

3. Components—include typical examples of dynamics and mechanics, which are very often used in gamification:

- Achievements—refer to attaining awards or moving through a game's levels.

- Avatars—are virtual representations, usually 2-D pictures, of every player in the game.
- Badges—are graphic representations of achievements a player has made in the game.
- Boss fights—are typically difficult tasks that need to be achieved in order to move up to the next level of the game.
- Collection—refers to a collection of defined goods, resources, virtual "stuff" in the game.
- Content unlocking—refers to previous set tasks or actions that the players should complete to unlock the next content or level.
- Presents—have an impact on the time period that players spend playing games. The way that games can make people have fun and be happy just because they are awarded is very important.
- Leaderboards—are a typical element of every game and very often are used in gamification. It is based on the status or level that every player has on the leaderboard, according to the number of points or any other criteria.
- Levels and points—levels are parts of a game, and all the players playing a game move from one level to another and thus progress in the game by earning points, and points are awarded according to the success of the players in playing the game.
- Social influence—a very important type of influence, and it means that the players can observe what their friends do in games through social networking or participating in the same game.
- Teams—are groups of players who participate in a game together as a team.

REFERENCES

Aichholzer M. (2012). *Introducing Gamification*. Accessed May 12, 2014. http://markenregisseur.at/gamification-short-intro/.

Bartle, R. (1996). "Hearts, Clubs, Diamonds, Spades: Players Who Suit MUDs. *Journal of MUD Research* 1, no. 1: 19.

Casati, F., G. Fausti, and M. Maurizio. (2007). "Liquid Publications: Scientific Publications meet the Web." Accessed May 28, 2014. http://eprints.biblio.unitn.it/1313/.

Csikszentmihalyi, M. (2004). "Flow, the Secret to Happiness," *Ted Talks*. Accessed May 8, 2014. http://www.ted.com/talks/mihaly_csikszentmihalyi_on_flow.

Doran, G. T. (1981). "There's a S.M.A.R.T. Way to Write Management's Goals and Objectives." *Management Review* 70, no. 11: 35–36.

Fitz-Walter Z. (2013). "A brief history of gamification." Accessed May 12, 2014. http://zefcan.com/2013/01/a-brief-history-of-gamification/.

Gamification. "Learn about Gamification, History of Gamification." Accessed May 10, 2014. http://gamification21.wordpress.com/content/2-history-of-gamification/.

Gray, D., S. Brown, and J. Macanufo. (2010). *Gamestorming, A Playbook for Innovators, Rulebreakers and Changemakers*. Sebastopol, CA: O'Reilly.

Hall, G. (2009). *Fluid Notes on Liquid Books*, in: (eds.) Luke, T. W., and J. Hunsinger, *Putting Knowledge to Work and Letting Information Play*. Springer, 22-36.

Koch, R. (2004). *Living the 80/20 Way: Work Less, Worry Less, Succeed More, Enjoy More.* Yarmouth, ME: Nicholas Brealey Publishing.

Lazzaro, N. "Why We Play Games: Four Keys to More Emotions without Story." Accessed May 7, 2014. http://www.xeodesign.com/xeodesign_whyweplaygames.pdf.

McGonigal, J. (2012). *Reality Is Broken: Why Games Makes Us Better and How They Can Change the World.* New York: Penguin Press.

McGonigal J. (2012a). "The Game That Can Give You 10 Extra Years of Life," *Ted Talks.* Accessed May 8, 2014. http://www.ted.com/talks/jane_mcgonigal_the_game_that_can_give_you_10_extra_years_of_life.html?.

Meyer, P. (2003). *Attitude Is Everything: If You Want to Succeed Above and Beyond.* Waco, TX: Meyer Resource Group.

Moyle, M. (2008). "Improving Access to European E-theses: The DART-Europe Programme." Igitur, Utrecht Publishing & Archiving Services.

Mumford, M. (2012). *Handbook of Organizational Creativity.* San Diego: Academic Press.

Nicholson, S. (2012). "A User-Centered Theoretical Framework for Meaningful Gamification." Accessed May 16, 2014. http://d-nb.info/1020022604/34#page=39, http://www.quilageo.com/wp-content/uploads/2013/07/Framework-for-Meaningful-Gamifications.pdf.

Pelling N. (2011). "The (short) prehistory of 'Gamification.' " Accessed May 16, 2014. http://nanodome.wordpress.com/2011/08/09/the-short-prehistory-of-gamification/.

Seligman, M. E., and M. Csikszentmihalyi. (2000). "Positive Psychology: An Introduction." *American Psychological Association* 55, no. 1: 5.

Wei, K., and D. Finkel. "Gamers and the Games They Play." Worcester Polytechnic Institute. Accessed May 12, 2014. http://www.wpi.edu/Pubs/E-project/Available/E-project-050409-135413/unrestricted/MQP_Report_Final_Edited.pdf.

Werbach, K., and D. Hunter. (2012). *For the Win.* Philadelphia: Wharton Digital Press.

Zichermann, G. (2011). "Gamification Corporation: The Leading Source for Gamification News & Info—About Gabe Zichermann." Accessed May 10, 2014. http://www.gamification.co/gabe-zichermann/.

Zichermann, G., and C. Cunningham. (2011). *Gamification by Design.* Sebastopol, CA: O'Reilly.

Chapter Eleven

Creating Connective Library Spaces

A Librarian/Student Collaboration Model

Alexander Watkins and Rebecca Kuglitsch

Libraries struggle to be relevant spaces that attract students, yet are more than simple study halls. The library as a connective space is one solution. This idea is not just about providing study space or collections space or even their juxtaposition, but about coming up with innovative ways to harness their proximity. In this chapter, the authors will discuss how to begin developing such spaces by working with student design teams. This library wanted to develop spaces that foster both intentional and informal learning and are grounded in strong disciplinary identities for the sciences and the arts. The authors argue that this connection with students strengthened the vision for the spaces, made it easier to argue for changes, as well as provided benefits to the student participants. In this project, the library particularly hoped to harness the synergy between science, technology, engineering, mathematics (STEM), and art and design (which, when combined with STEM, is known as STEAM) to develop spaces that promote an atmosphere of creativity. In both fields, creativity often occurs when the scientist or artist draws a new connection, when a striking pairing of two previously unrelated ideas suddenly comes together. Connecting users to the library's resources will facilitate informal learning activities: discovery, exploration, and self-directed research.

These spaces will support this connection-drawing, both within and between each space. They are high-traffic, central spaces, occupying two broad symmetrical hallways that flank the central entrance of the main library. They are the main paths into the building for all entrants and funnel students deeper into the library regardless of their subjects of interest. For this reason, they are especially important, since in addition to inspiring students in their respective discipline, the spaces can highlight these two strong areas of the university for any current or prospective student, providing opportunities for informal learning. This initial division, too, can be used to informally enrich the education of science and art students by showing the strong connections between two disciplines often rhetorically positioned as opposites.

But how can the library achieve these connections? The answer was to forge more connections by working with a service learning project in a well-established technical writing course at the University of Colorado Boulder (CU). Students in this class form design teams to help local institutions solve problems. The class attracts students with backgrounds ranging from the hard sciences to human sciences to design. With budget and time constraints familiar to many libraries, and with a core principle of supporting student learning, leveraging this existing service-learning program was a perfect solution to the library's needs. Moreover, working with a student design team provided user-generated ideas that are a better fit for student needs than librarian-generated ideas. The authors suggest that other libraries redesigning their spaces will find working with a student design team useful—but also that working with the library was beneficial to the students. Hopefully, this experience may inspire other libraries to develop their own rich, intentional learning spaces in collaboration with the ultimate users of these spaces: students.

LITERATURE REVIEW

The project of developing intentional learning spaces that provide a place for students and visitors to engage with the sciences and arts draws from work in several fields. The literature on library spaces and on spaces that enhance informal learning in the disciplines informed the authors' approach to and goals for the redesigned spaces. The literature of service learning in libraries and service learning as authentic learning inspired the connection to a technical writing class as a means to jump-start the redesign.

There is extensive literature on intentional and informal learning in library, education, and subject specific fields. The redesign of the Art and the Science Commons brought together ideas about intentional space design in libraries with ideas about informal learning in both art and science disciplines. Libraries have generally defined intentional learning as the studying and group activities that take place in the library. On the other hand, both the art and the science fields use informal learning to discuss free-choice activities that generally take place entirely outside of the academic context. What the library hoped to do was expand the intentional learning taking place in library spaces to include the kind of informal subject and content learning that have become so important to science and art education.

There is a major question in library science literature about how librarians can design library spaces that encourage learning and how the success of new design projects can be assessed. Scott Bennett has worked toward a methodology of creating library spaces designed for learning (2003; 2009; 2011). He attempts to assess how well libraries are facilitating "intentional learning" wherein students take responsibility for high-level skills, develop personally meaningful goals that include but also go beyond their own schoolwork, and then self-assess their own learning (Bennett, 2011, p. 766). He identifies twelve activities that can measure some degree of intentional learning from the National Survey on Student Engagement ("NSSE Home," n.d.); however, NSSE's questions focus mostly on studying behavior, making it difficult to assess whether students are simply doing schoolwork, or if they are truly engaging in intentional learning. Using assessment methods can also help align library informal learning with campus priorities for learning (Lippincott & Duckett, 2013). Harrop and Turpin studied students' learning preferences and how those preferences translated into space selection, once again focusing on studying and activities that center around course work. They suggest developing a diversity of spaces that cater to the multitude of studying preferences (2013).

Learning activities are not just limited to studying or even necessarily related to the academic experience. They can include the kind of enrichment experiences that many people choose to engage in all the time; in this regard, informal learning can also be referred to as free-choice or everyday learning. There has been recent research and broad recognition especially in the sciences about the importance of informal learning. This movement has most importantly been catalyzed by the Learning Science in Informal Environments (LSIE) report, which argues that much of Americans' science learning comes from these nonschool activities (Bell, Lewenstein, Shouse, & Feder, 2009; Falk & Dierking, 2010; Semmel, 2010). It is the engagement and fun of hobbies like amateur astronomy, places like science museums, or activities like visits to national parks, that make these informal learning activities so effective, even in some cases more productive than formal education (Falk & Dierking, 2010). Much of this research has focused on museum environments. According to the IMLS response to the LSIE report, libraries have been inadequately studied for this kind of informal learning (Semmel, 2010).

Likewise in the arts, formal and informal learning have long been interrelated, due to the generally acknowledged enrichment potential of art museums, cultural activities, and performances. There is a robust discourse around the educational potential of these informal learning spaces (Knutson, Crowley, Russell, & Steiner, 2011; Simpson, 2011; Unrath & Luehrman, 2009; Werth, 2010). Knutson et al. approach art education as an ecology that includes both formal and informal settings (2011). Each environment has unique affordances that can promote learning—for example, resources like art objects or studio space—and they argue that this diversity is especially important to arts education (Knutson et al., 2011, p. 311). The question then is: How can librarians ensure that the library is part of a diverse learning landscape?

Libraries strive not only to be locations for studying and group work, but to become part of the informal learning ecosystems of both the arts and the sciences. Libraries have not yet been a major part of the conversation about informal learning in these disciplines, which often focuses on museums: art, natural history, and science. There is value in a diversity of venues for informal learning, however, and libraries should leverage their unique affordances, such as resources for deep self-directed inquiry to create informal learning environments. For example, a student's interest might be piqued at a science or art museum (or perhaps, by a library display or serendipitous browsing); the library's in-depth research resources can support their further exploration.

While the libraries at CU recognize and value informal learning, it is difficult to establish such spaces, given the constraints of budget and lack of time that plague most libraries. One solution is working with classes that have service learning components. The potential of a partnership between the library and service learning has been sparingly but enthusiastically explored in the literature. It has often been used as a tool for achieving results the library might otherwise be unable to attain due to financial and staff constraints. Students can undertake projects that would simply be unfeasible for the library. For example, Northern Kentucky University was able to partner with marketing research classes and obtain good qualitative and quantitative research that would otherwise have been difficult to afford (Chesnut, 2011). Similarly, Cal State San Marcos worked with business students to develop a cohesive marketing plan as well (Meulemans & Fiegen, 2006). Cornell University's web team worked with student programmers to develop a mobile site and iPhone app. These tools were recognized as important services, but ones that would require specialized skills and excessive staff time to develop; working with students allowed the university to meet the needs of users without monopolizing staff time (Connolly, Cosgrave, & Krkoska, 2010). In all of these cases, service learning allowed the library to develop programs and tools they could not otherwise provide.

Service learning partnerships can not only provide an opportunity to develop projects but also allow libraries to better access user experiences and opinions. Unlike librarian-led assessment, service learning projects typically are performed by the library's users themselves. Brown-Sica notes that working with students "can provide data interpretation from a student's point of view that can aid in making evidence-based decisions," based on her experiences working with classes in architecture, human factors engineering, and civil engineering to develop plans redesigning the Auraria Library (2013, p.

276). Librarians at Eastern Washington University harnessed student expertise on the student experience in a similar way, by working with a technical communications course to promote RefWorks and assess its use (Meyer & Miller, 2008). The extremely positive results of their case study suggest that the user perspective of the technical communications students made their outreach particularly effective. Harnessing a service learning class provides libraries with authentic insights into their users' needs and experiences that librarians so often seek and so rarely find.

But while it is clear that libraries can benefit from service learning partnerships and related activities, what do students gain from service learning in the library? The pedagogical literature suggests that they can gain much. Service learning in particular provides a space to situate learning; this situated context in particular enhances retention and transfer (Booth, 2011, p. 40). Moreover, it offers an opportunity for authentic, engaged learning (King, 2004, p. 122). Authentic learning is defined by Herrington, Reeves, and Oliver as a constructivist approach rooted in situated learning and legitimate peripheral participation (2014, p. 402). In other words, authentic learning provides students with a real context and situation in which to exercise their skills as individuals learning to do something. Indeed, learning by doing is an approach most instructors support as highly effective, and is frequently cited as an approach that students prefer (Lombardi, 2007, p. 1). It gives students a way to take part in legitimate peripheral participation—learning to do something in an expert atmosphere. A classic example is Lave & Wenger's differentiation of learning physics in high school, where the community of practice is learning to become an adult who has graduated high school, versus learning physics in graduate school, where one learns to be a physicist (1991, p. 99). This participation makes authentic learning particularly effective and is an essential part of service learning. Lombardi writes, "Students should know what it feels like for actual stakeholders beyond the classroom to hold them accountable for their work products" (2007, p. 9). Accountability from actual stakeholders was a key part of the redesign team, and this real, meaningful context for service learning supports engagement and learning. Ultimately, the authors believe that the redevelopment of the Science and Art Commons maximizes learning not only for the eventual users of the space but also for the students who helped develop it.

DESIGNING THE SCIENCE COMMONS

There were several reasons to enhance the science areas at Norlin Library. First, while there are strong science branch libraries at CU, the main library is the flagship library on campus, and maintaining a presence in that space is a key to showing that science belongs with the humanities and social sciences as a part of the liberal education. The science areas are also adjacent to high-traffic areas on a campus with a seating shortage, making it particularly important to develop the area into a usable workspace. Finally, the space is on the main campus tours, making it ideal as a showcase for CU's scientific innovation. As universities like CU become increasingly tuition dependent, it becomes increasingly important to clearly reinforce the strengths of the university.

At the initiation of the project, the space clearly did not fulfill any of these goals. It was oddly shaped and awkwardly laid out, with a lot of wasted space and little identity. Although the words "Science Alcove Gallery" were visible, and the science reference collection and print periodicals were available, they barely served to identify the space. Printers placed by the entry doors disrupted the flow of traffic, and large tracts of empty space were underutilized, providing little encouragement to study, work, or relax.

Librarians drafted a problem statement and identified the main goals for the space: to develop an appealing, usable space with a clear science identity that would support informal learning. After reviewing this, the student design team met with a small team of librarians interested in the science space. The group discussed goals for the space, problems the library had already identified, library constraints and capacities, and other projects that could serve as inspiration. With this background, the design team began to conduct further local research. They surveyed both students using the science space and tour group leaders that routinely led groups through the space in order to pinpoint stakeholder priorities. Using the survey information, the design team developed a basic plan for the space, and presented an oral report of their findings to the small group. This gave the library a chance to check in at a midpoint, request adjustments and further information, and check in to see if their suggestions were roughly viable. For example, students initially presented one single redesign plan. The library requested a tiered system of suggestions so that any changes could be more gradually implemented, a structure better suited to the library's budgetary constraints. After this meeting, students refined their plan and developed a final report. In the final report, students recommended, roughly in order of priority:

- more study seating,
- lounge areas,
- student and faculty research displays,
- better layout,
- more artwork and more appealing décor,
- and potential development of interactive displays.

While budget constraints precluded implementing all of these suggestions, the tiered recommendations made it easy to prioritize and then implement relatively inexpensive solutions. The report was received in May; by the end of the summer, the science area was recarpeted; printers were relocated to avoid blocking traffic; an unused room's walls were demolished, leaving space to install couches and a lounge area; and the area was repainted. Without the student report, these relatively inexpensive but high-impact changes would have been difficult to accomplish. This initial round of improvements left the area a pleasant, usable, but not distinctive space. Reducing the most overt issues with the space left the library free to focus on improving the space's identity over the following school year.

In order to identify the space as one focusing on science, librarians worked to find displays that highlighted the interplay between the library and the intellectual work of the university's scientists. A display of student work in the Science Commons was a relatively quick way to identify the space. One of the science librarians worked with another writing and rhetoric class where undergraduate students wrote academic scientific papers and paired them with a poster designed to communicate the scientific argument visually and accessibly. Excerpts of the papers and citations to the works they relied on are displayed in the Science Commons with the posters, highlighting the library's online resources as foundations for very concrete student work. Another display is in development, this one contextualizing the life and writings of a well-known biologist who worked at CU.

Displays like these are good starting points, even as the library is working to establish long-term relationships with other units on campus that might furnish other meaningful displays in the future. The student report provided several possibilities for future collaboration, such as working with the campus's museum studies program or art faculty who explore connections between science and art. The library is also exploring grant possibilities for innovative displays and considering further ways to make the space comfortable but identifiable. Without student input, it would have been very difficult to jump-start the low-effort, high-impact changes that allowed the library to focus on these larger questions.

DESIGNING THE ART COMMONS

The goal for the art area was to transform a high-traffic hallway that was simply book storage into one that could connect users to resources in order to encourage informal learning and real engagement with the library's collections. The area had several problems: a lack of aesthetic appeal for an area supposedly about art, a confusing and inaccessible layout, and it hid materials like art magazines that would be popular. The librarians hoped to reveal resources and collections by making the space more inviting, accessible, and logically organized. They aimed to add more student space in order to encourage users to spend time exploring the rich art collection.

After the success of the Science Commons' work with a student design team, the authors decided to work with the class again for a redesign of the arts section. The students were given the primary goals of:

- increasing and improving student study spaces,
- creating an attractive corridor,
- advertising library materials,
- and maintaining collections space and ensuring a logical stacks flow.

While the librarians wanted to add more student space, the library could not just be a study hall. Instead it needed to connect students to the things that make a library: vital physical collections, digital assets, and expert faculty librarians. These are the unique resources that can enable free-choice enrichment for informal learning. This was especially important as the collection is not just used by scholars seeking to write research papers but also by aspiring artists and architects looking for inspiration.

The student design team met several times with the Art & Architecture Librarian, discussing his hopes for the space, the problems the library had already identified, and some of the project constraints. The team surveyed users of the space to find out what new features they desired and what they were most dissatisfied with. The students gave a presentation on their ideas, while the librarians gave feedback that was incorporated into the final design consultation.

The student team came up with a two-phase recommendation. The idea that came through most strongly was that the Art Commons should have a unique identity; that it should be clear that the user is in the part of the library dedicated to creativity, design, and aesthetics. They proposed several plans that would give the commons a coherent identity and connect users and library resources:

- displays of architecture models and student artwork along the long hallway wall,
- magazine displays around a lounge seating area,
- turning shelves to 45-degree angles to improve flow and to create a distinctive look,
- new creative group study areas with whiteboard walls,
- a quiet study area with better lighting, closer to the windows, and with more power outlets.

The student report was immensely helpful because they had the time and dedication to really think about the space and to survey users. Because of this they were able to come up with creative ideas about creating an identity for the space. Having this data to back up suggested changes made it easier to advocate for improvements. As a result of this advocacy, a lounge with magazine displays is being implemented, and plans have been drawn up for further changes when funding becomes available.

INFORMAL LEARNING IN THE ART AND SCIENCE COMMONS

The authors envision two complementary spaces for art and science, designed for informal learning, that could bracket the wide spread of the library's educational mission. By pairing these two disciplines, the broad spectrum of knowledge contained within the library is symbolized, with the College of Arts & Sciences, the largest college of the university. Mirroring art and science initially positions them as opposite poles, but somewhat paradoxically can also serve to bring them closer together. Through a shared atmosphere of creativity, these spaces can highlight the similarities between the disciplines. While creativity is commonly acknowledged as a foundation of the arts, it is less explicitly seen as a key to the sciences. The similarities can be seen in the language used to describe a piece of art and a good scientific idea: an experiment is elegant, an observation is beautiful, a graphed curve is graceful. This suggests that science and art are not so far apart, that creativity and experimentation go hand in hand, and that STEM is really STEAM. Working with the student design team brought the library closer to achieving this goal. For example, the student team suggested that the science librarians work with faculty and students in the Art Department and in the Technology, Arts and Media program to obtain artworks for the space that relate to and explore the sciences.

A major goal of each space is to connect users with the library, revealing the library's vital role in the research process by advertising the collections to the many patrons that use the library's major through-ways. The redesigns aim to create spaces where users interact with the unique resources and services of the library. Librarians strive to seamlessly supply users with resources, yet success in providing easy access can obscure the library's role in research. The Ithaka Report suggests that faculty in general, and faculty in the sciences in particular, view the library primarily as a buyer of content (Housewright, Schonfeld & Wulfson, 2013, p. 66). This understanding of the library and the library's role in education is painfully limited, eliding many of the services libraries offer. The student suggestions to aesthetically display the art magazines or develop data visualizations of CU-based research reveal the library's resources as existing within a flow of print to digital, as do some of the simple displays already implemented. All of these displays emphasize the library's key role as a place for the creation of new knowledge.

As well as highlighting the role of the library, one of the most important goals for these redesigned spaces was that they promote both intentional and informal learning. The library wanted the spaces to foster studying, collaborations, and other course-focused work. But the spaces should also be hubs for the kind of informal learning that is so important in arts and science education, locations that leverage library resources to provide free-choice opportunities to engage and dive deeply into these subjects. The Science Commons can increase general scientific literacy by making science visible, accessible, and simply fun to students regardless of their major. Only about 30 percent of Americans take college-level sciences courses (Falk & Dierking, 2010, p. 486). Yet if the goal of the university is to produce well-educated and well-rounded students, enticing nonscience students into understanding science is especially important. Moreover, by bringing together resources from across the sciences, the space can also promote interdisciplinary research in the sciences, which is becoming increasingly important. The art commons can leverage its unique resources to provide a place to explore the arts through structured research but also through casual reading, browsing, and serendipitous discovery. This is an exploration different from but complementary to that of museums or art studio spaces. The library can be a key niche in the ecosystem of informal learning, and can help produce students who value multiple ways of knowing and exploring their world.

SERVICE LEARNING IN THE REDESIGN PROCESS

CU is lucky to have a robust educational infrastructure for collaborative opportunities. To develop these spaces, librarians worked with students in an upper division technical communication and design course to develop the plans. Writing 3035, a technical writing course in the College of Arts & Sciences' Program for Writing and Rhetoric, focuses on client projects. In the class, students work on a project for a campus or community client over the semester and present them with a final design product. The library has well-established relationships with the faculty members who teach the class, so librarians were readily able to work with them. It is likely that librarians at many universities have similar service learning or experiential learning courses available to them, and the authors encourage them to seek these opportunities out for several reasons beyond the library's needs for innovative, student-generated ideas.

The collaborative partnership between this class and the library benefits students and aligns with the goal of supporting authentic learning across the university. Service learning projects like this class and the redesign project quite clearly fit most of the criteria for such learning. With the goal of supporting student learning on campus, it made sense to work with such a course, which so strongly supports learning in a context that reflects a real situation and authentic assessment. Likewise, the emphasis on multidisciplinary approaches and accountability to multiple stakeholders is a perfect fit with the ideals of authentic learning (Lombardi, 2007). The students were accountable to the library, as their client, but also to one another as team members and the user population for whom they were designing. They had to investigate whether the library's goals matched the actual needs of the users of the spaces, and communicate if they did not. They had to balance the needs of students with the realities of a tight library budget. Students on the redesign teams not only learned about technical communication, both formal and informal, but practiced it. They were not designers, but they learned to participate in a design community. This learning is situated in a natural and authentic context—and one that allows them to have a visible impact on a community they participate in. The client projects are not mere facsimiles of a real situation, but allow students to work with a real need and offer real solutions that they could, in some cases, see put into place immediately. It is clear that supporting classes like this is part of the library's mission.

Beyond this, service learning involving the library and this project in particular also improved students' understanding of what the library has to offer. The intensely situated learning meant that students on library design teams could not help but learn more about the library. Students who participated in the redesigns mentioned their surprise at the array of services and materials the library provides. While each redesign team was only a small group, that group learned about the library's purposes, goals, and user-focused mission. A challenge for libraries is demonstrating to students that they are more than simply a place for finding books. The students' work to meet the goals for the space helped expand their perspectives on what the library provides. This newfound knowledge will likely be shared with their peers, and these peer-to-peer communications are particularly effective.

CONCLUSION

Based on this experience, the authors argue that service learning programs are a mutually beneficial model for librarian/student collaboration. The library gained invaluable insight and ideas for redesigns, while the students had a meaningful project that also exposed them to the goals, ideals, and services of the library. Through working with student design groups the library was able to contribute to students' authentic learning experiences. By leveraging students in service learning classes, the librarians were able to obtain a user perspective on implementing connective library spaces.

These projects supported the goal of creating spaces that would bring users and resources together to enable and promote informal learning behaviors: curiosity, discovery, and exploration. These spaces will help place the library into the ecosystem of informal learning in science and art by allowing for the discovery of new interests through interactions with collections, exhibits, librarians, and peers. The library plays a unique role in informal learning, which the new designs will enhance by connecting learners to resources for in-depth, self-directed learning through research.

The spaces are meant to make multiple connections, between librarians and students, between students and resources, and between disciplines. Especially important to these spaces was the pairing of science and art; bridging these areas suggests the creativity inherent in science and the rigor necessary for art. These two subjects can encompass the breadth of the library's resources, and place both as central to a liberal education in the twenty-first century.

The twenty-first-century library is a connective space, one that inspires as well as informs. It will take experimentation and initiative to achieve this vision, but this process can be sustainably carried out through collaboration with service learning programs. Such a library has an integral role to play in students' intentional and informal learning, a role that is absolutely vital.

REFERENCES

Bell, P., B. Lewenstein, A. W. Shouse, and M. A. Feder. (2009). *Learning Science in Informal Environments: People, Places, and Pursuits*. Washington, D.C.: National Academies Press.

Bennett, S. (2009). "Libraries and Learning: A History of Paradigm Change." *portal: Libraries and the Academy* 9, no. 2: 181–97. doi:10.1353/pla.0.0049.

Bennett, S. (2011). "Learning Behaviors and Learning Spaces." *portal: Libraries and the Academy* 11, no. 3: 765–89. doi:10.1353/pla.2011.0033.

Bennett, S., and Council on Library and Information Resources. (2003). *Libraries Designed for Learning*. Washington, D.C: Council on Library and Information Resources.

Booth, C. (2011). *Reflective Teaching, Effective Learning: Instructional Literacy for Library Educators*. Chicago: American Library Association.

Brown-Sica, M. (2013). "Using Academic Courses to Generate Data for Use in Evidence-Based Library Planning." *The Journal of Academic Librarianship* 39, no. 3: 275–87. doi:10.1016/j.acalib.2013.01.001.

Chesnut, M. T. (2011). "Recession-Friendly Library Market Research: Service Learning with Benefits." *Journal of Library Innovation* 2, no. 1: 61–71.

Connolly, M., T. Cosgrave, and B. B. Krkoska. (2010). "Mobilizing the Library's Web Presence and Services: A Student-Library Collaboration to Create the Library's Mobile Site and iPhone Application." *The Reference Librarian* 52, no. 1–2: 27–35. doi:10.1080/02763877.2011.520109.

Falk, J. H., and L. D. Dierking. (2010). "The 95 Percent Solution." *American Scientist* 98, no. 6: 486. doi:10.1511/2010.87.486.

Harrop, D., and B. Turpin. (2013). "A Study Exploring Learners' Informal Learning Space Behaviors, Attitudes, and Preferences." *New Review of Academic Librarianship* 19, no. 1: 58–77. doi:10.1080/13614533.2013.740961.

Herrington, J., T. C. Reeves, and R. Oliver. (2014). "Authentic Learning Environments." In J. M. Spector, M. D. Merrill, J. Elen, and M. J. Bishop (Eds.), *Handbook of Research on Educational Communications and Technology*. New York: Springer New York.

Housewright, R., R. C. Schonfeld, and K. Wulfson. (2013). *Ithaka S+R US Faculty Survey 2012* (pp. 1–79).

King, J. T. (2004). "Service-Learning as a Site for Critical Pedagogy: A Case of Collaboration, Caring, and Defamiliarization across Borders." *Journal of Experiential Education* 26, no. 3: 121–37. doi:10.1177/105382590402600304.

Knutson, K., K. Crowley, J. L. Russell, and M. A. Steiner. (2011). "Approaching Art Education as an Ecology: Exploring the Role of Museums." *Studies in Art Education: A Journal of Issues and Research in Art Education* 52, no. 4: 310–22.

Lave, J., and E. Wenger. (1991). *Situated Learning: Legitimate Peripheral Participation*. New York: Cambridge University Press.

Lippincott, J., and K. Duckett. (2013). "Library Space Assessment: Focus on Learning." *Research Library Issues* 284: 12–21.

Lombardi, M. M. (2007). "Authentic Learning for the 21st Century: An Overview." *Educause Learning Initiative* 1 (2007): 1–12.

Meulemans, Y. N., and A. M. Fiegen. (2006). "Using Business Student Consultants to Benchmark and Develop a Library Marketing Plan." *Journal of Business & Finance Librarianship* 11, no. 3: 19–31. doi:10.1300/J109v11n03_03.

Meyer, N. J., and I. R. Miller. (2008). "The Library as Service-Learning Partner: A Win–Win Collaboration with Students and Faculty." *College & Undergraduate Libraries* 15, no. 4: 399–413. doi:10.1080/10691310802554879.

"NSSE Home." (n.d.). Accessed April 8, 2014. http://nsse.iub.edu/.

Semmel, M. L. (2010). "The LSIE Report and IMLS: Supporting Learning in the Informal Environments of Museums and Libraries." *Curator: The Museum Journal* 53, no. 2: 155–62. doi:10.1111/j.2151-6952.2010.00016.x.

Simpson, R. (2011). "Informal Learning and the Voluntary Arts." *Adults Learning* 22, no. 10: 16–17.

Unrath, K., and M. Luehrman. (2009). "Bringing Children to Art—Bringing Art to Children." *Art Education* 62, no. 1: 41–47.

Werth, L. (2010). "Beyond the Art Lesson: Free-Choice Learning Centers." *Arts & Activities* 148, no. 4: 22–53.

Chapter Twelve

Merging Web 2.0 and Social Media into Information Literacy Instruction

Rachel Wexelbaum and Plamen Miltenoff

INTRODUCTION

Colleges and universities regard academic librarians as information literacy "experts." The advancement of Web 2.0 and social media have altered student information-seeking behaviors, their research process, and what they consider credible sources. While Web 2.0 and social media usage have become ubiquitous among undergraduate students, most do not use these tools as effectively as they should, nor are they aware of how to locate or evaluate information received through these tools. Academic librarians have begun to integrate Web 2.0 and social media in their library instruction, teaching students how to use and evaluate social media for research and real-world problem solving.

DEFINITIONS

Information Literacy

Academic librarians have used the term "information literacy" since the 1970s. Its original definition, "techniques and skills for utilizing the wide range of information tools as well as primary sources in molding information solutions to [the user's] problems" (Zurkowski, 1974, p. 6), has evolved into "a set of abilities requiring individuals to 'recognize when information is needed and have the ability to locate, evaluate, and use effectively the needed information'" (Association of College & Research Libraries, 2014). Librarians and educators have come to accept websites, search engines, and social media as information sources and research tools equivalent to traditional print reference materials, and have adjusted their information literacy standards to reflect the role of Web 2.0 and social media in the research process (Association of College & Research Libraries, 2014; International Society for Technology in Education, 2007). Information professionals coined the term *transliteracy* (Ipri, 2010) then *metaliteracy* (Mackey & Jacobson, 2011, p. 70) to encompass the critical-thinking, composition, and collaborative skills necessary to produce and share information—as well as locate and interpret it—in the digital world.

> "The ability to read, write and interact across a range of platforms, tools, and media from signing and orality through handwriting, print, TV, radio and films, to digital social networks." (Sue Thomas, Transliteracies Project Group, 2005)
>
> "Information literacy is the metaliteracy for a digital age because it provides the higher order thinking to engage with multiple document types through various media formats in collaborative environments." (Mackey & Jacobson, 2011, p. 70)

Some librarians also identify five "social media literacies":

- Attention
- Participation
- Collaboration
- Network awareness
- Critical consumption (Rheingold, 2010, p. 17)

For the purposes of this book chapter, the authors will use the umbrella term *information literacy* when speaking about media and digital literacy, as well as transliteracy and metaliteracy.

Web 2.0

In 1999, Darcy DiNucci first coined the terms *Web 1.0* and *Web 2.0* (DiNucci, 1999). While Web 1.0 is limited to static HTML web pages, Web 2.0 "will be understood not as screenfuls of text and graphics but as a transport mechanism, the ether through which interactivity happens" (DiNucci, 1999, p. 32). DiNucci saw the future—that high-speed wireless Internet and mobile devices would lead to a myriad of apps for communication, collaboration, and entertainment. Without Web 2.0, the social media explosion could not take place.

Social Media

America Online (AOL) executives coined the term *social media* in the late 1990s. According to the executives, "AOL was this mashup of technology and communications and media itself . . . [providing] places where [the users] can be entertained, communicate, and participate in a social environment" (Bercovici, 2010). Once social media became more sophisticated and began to meet the academic needs of students and faculty, academics would define social media as "a collection of internet websites, services, and practices that support collaboration, community building, participation, and sharing" (Junco, Heiberger & Loken, 2010, p. 119).

ATTITUDES TOWARD SOCIAL MEDIA IN EDUCATION

In his book *New New Media*, Levinson identifies five characteristics of twenty-first-century social media that distinguish them from older forms of print and electronic media:

- Every Consumer Is a Producer
- You Get What You Don't Pay For
- Competitive and Mutually Catalytic
- More than Search Engines and E-mail
- Ultimately Beyond the User's Control (Levinson, 2013, p. 3–4)

At first, the unpredictable unmonitored nature of social media made K–12 and college educators wary of using these resources in the classroom. While some K–12 teachers are teaching students how to use collaborative online tools, such as Google Drive, and depend more on course management systems, the majority of teacher development programs still do not provide instruction on how to use social media for educational purposes, even though this is the milieu of current and future K–12 students (Kirschner & Wopereis, 2013, pp. 88–89). Most college and university faculty also lack experience, training, and motivation to use Web 2.0 and social media in the classroom (Martinez-Alemán, 2014, pp. 15–16); those faculty teaching hybrid or online classes are much more likely to employ Web 2.0 and social media for teaching, and will ask their students to collaborate and create content using those tools with or without support (Seaman & Tinti-Kane, 2013, pp. 14–16).

To this day, some faculty do not encourage students to text and multitask with different apps or devices, as studies have shown that continuous interruption from texting, chatting, tweeting, pinning, etc., may lead to "attention deficit" and reduced academic performance in traditional academic environments (Paul, Baker & Cochran, 2012, pp. 2,122–23). Faculty also remain wary of the credibility and validity of information made freely available online through Web 2.0 and social media, as well as student temptation to plagiarize from the Internet (Martinez-Alemán, 2014, p. 16; Seaman & Tinti-Kane, 2013, p. 16).

Wikipedia in particular shook the traditional definitions of "authority" and "peer review" (Wexelbaum, 2012). At the same time, students were more likely to use social media than their teachers, and more likely to use resources such as blogs and Wikipedia for research (McGough & Salomon, 2013, p. 284; Kim, Sin, & Tsai, 2014, p. 173). Because students are often fooled by web design and visual cues as to what may be credible online information in Wikipedia and other resources (Connaway & Randall, 2013, p. 44; Lim, 2013, p. 406), librarians often led the way in teaching students (as well as faculty) how to locate credible information from social media sources, how to create copyright-compliant content through social media, and how to use social media for group projects, presentations, and other collaborative problem-solving efforts (Rheingold, 2010, p. 17).

Social media classes and programs in higher education are typically oriented toward mass communications or marketing—two professions where undergraduates must learn practical social media applications for their careers. Students interested in entering the publishing industry and public relations also learn how to use social media for advertising. These programs do not focus on using social media for academic purposes. While academic librarians do regularly teach undergraduates about blogs, wikis, and information management tools, advancement of information literacy skills through employment and analysis of social media is a new frontier.

HOW MILLENNIALS AND GENERATION Z USE WEB 2.0 AND SOCIAL MEDIA

Today, the majority of incoming college and university students belong to two different generations: "the Millennial generation" (also known as Generation Y, born roughly between the early 1980s and early 2000s) and the younger Generation Z (born approximately between the early to late 1990s and the present day). Described as "digital natives," both generations were born with computers, Internet, and instant access to information. Generation Z, born with smartphones and other mobile technologies, is even more "wired" than their Millennial predecessors, often using multiple technologies and apps at one time, and most likely to multitask on their devices (Bershidsky, 2014; Margaryan, Littlejohn & Vojt, 2011, p. 431; Paul, Baker, & Cochran, 2012, p. 2,117). While both generations like to text, Generation Z is most likely to communicate in images (also known as "emoticons" and "emojis") in place of words (sparks & honey, n.d., slide 35). Generations Y and Z are attending college classes right now, or will be in a few years, and higher education struggles to fully understand their psychological development, educational needs, and learning styles.

Older generations have the misconception that Millennials and Generation Z are tech-savvy, social media masters (Kirschner & Wopereis, 2013; Martinez-Alemán, 2014, p. 14). This is what higher education authorities believe about Millennials and Generation Z in terms of their Web 2.0 and social media skills and their classroom expectations:

> Fluency in multiple media, valuing each for the types of communication, activities, experiences and expressions it empowers; learning based on collectively seeking, sieving, and synthesizing experiences rather than individually locating and absorbing information from a single best source; active learning based on experience that includes frequent opportunities for reflection, expression through non-linear associated webs of representations rather than linear stories, and co-design of learning experiences personalized to individual needs and preferences. (Margaryan, Littlejohn, & Vojt, 2011, p. 429)

As these generations learned how to use computers and mobile technologies at earlier ages than digital immigrants, they are often critical of K–12 and college faculty use of YouTube videos and other passive forms of social media usage in the classroom (Mao, 2014, p. 220), and desire more input on the design of their online learning experiences (Mao, 2014, p. 220; Margaryan, Littlejohn, & Vojt, 2011, p. 429). At the same time, only a small minority of Generations Y and Z report receiving formal instruction in the use of Web 2.0 and social media tools (McGough & Salomon, 2013, p. 284). Students do not always know how to select appropriate collaborative Web 2.0 tools for group projects, even if they are taking an online class (Margaryan, Littlejohn, & Vojt, 2011, p. 437), often lack awareness of where to go for help to learn more about Web 2.0 and social media on their campuses (McGough & Salomon, 2013, p. 284), and do not know how to conduct effective research through their social media channels, let alone Google (Connaway & Randall, 2013, p. 44; McGough & Salomon, 2013, p. 284; Kim, Sin, & Tsai, 2014, p. 174; Lim, p. 406; Margaryan, Littlejohn, & Vojt, 2011, p. 431). In fact, Generations Y and Z are more likely to use social media to ask parents or peers for help locating and evaluating information, rather than search for and evaluate social media content independently (Connaway & Randall, 2013, p. 43; Lim, 2013, p. 406; McGough & Salomon, 2013, p. 283).

Social media allow people from around the world to communicate with each other and form online communities. While they have the ability to meet and learn about people from other cultures, religions, and racial backgrounds this way, the majority of Generations Y and Z use social media primarily to communicate with family, friends, and classmates within the United States

(Bolton, Parasuraman, Hoefnagels et al., 2013, p. 249), focusing on small, local networks to acquire information considered "of value" (Connaway & Randall, 2013, p. 43; McGough & Salomon, 2013, p. 283; Sohn, 2014, p. 149). The lower their socioeconomic status and education level, the more likely undergraduates will lack connections to the "information elite" who would introduce them to active creation of Web 2.0 and social media content (van Dijk, 2013, p. 109). This is especially the case for female students and minorities (Margaryan, Littlejohn, & Vojt, 2011, p. 431; van Dijk, 2013, p. 109). It is said that 85 percent of Internet and social media users lack these ties to the "information elite," thus making them less likely to contribute to Wikipedia, maintain blogs, or use social media to solve real-world problems (van Dijk, 2013, p. 109).

Generation Z, even more so than their Millennial predecessors, are hyper-aware of Internet privacy and security issues (Alter, 2014; PewResearch Internet Project, 2013). Females are more likely than males to use social media for two-way communication and posting and sharing photos, and tend to have more "friends" than males (Kim, Sin, & Tsai, 2014, p. 172; PewResearch Internet Project, 2013); for these reasons they are less likely to use their real names, or provide all of their personal information in social media profiles than males (Alter, 2014; PewResearch Internet Project, 2013). Because they do not want to be "watched" by parents or certain friends who share the same social media channels, and do not want their chats made public, Generation Z is abandoning Facebook in favor of media such as Blink, BurnNote, Skim, SnapChat, and Whisper, which do not save chat dialog (Alter, 2014). They also may be hesitant to create new social media accounts for academic purposes for fear of people finding them, or what they post, through Google.

The fear of discovery may have an effect on online student content creation. Unless one counts personal photos shared with friends and family, most students do not actually use Web 2.0 and social media for independent content creation (PewResearch Internet Project, 2013). In fact, the majority of these young people are passive consumers of branded social media content (Bolton, Parasuraman, Hoefnagels et al., 2013, p. 248; Kim, Sin, & Tsai, 2014, p. 174; Margaryan, Littlejohn, & Vojt, 2011, p. 431). While Generation Z is more confident about posting their opinions online than their predecessors, most people in these generations do not feel confident enough in their knowledge base to contribute to Wikipedia or create original multimedia (Kim, Sin, & Tsai, 2014, p. 174; Margaryan, Littlejohn, & Vojt, 2011, p. 431).

Millennials and Generation Z of both genders say that they use social media to follow news (Gangadharbatla, Bright, & Logan, 2014; Kim, Sin, & Tsai, 2014, p. 174; PewResearch Internet Project, "Social Media Fact Sheet," 2014). "News" through social media can appear in the form of blog posts shared through Facebook, personal posts or tweets, or links to actual news articles. Depending on what social media users choose to follow, their news sources will not only have a bias toward the users' personal beliefs and opinions, but they may also be inaccurate news sources to begin with. For this reason, while Generations Y and Z prefer accessing social media channels for up-to-date news, they still believe that traditionally published newspapers are the most credible, objective source of information (Gangadharbatla, Bright, & Logan, 2014, p. 59). Due to the massive amounts of posts or tweets that people follow in their feeds, most people skim the headlines of news stories published through social media, often not seeking the details or questioning the validity of the information (Connaway & Randall, 2013, pp. 43–44; Lim, 2013, p. 406). If their social media only reflects one point of view of current events, and all of their "friends" share news from that same perspective, the younger generations will believe that it must be right and will not search for alternate viewpoints (Connaway & Randall, 2013, pp. 43–44).

Undergraduates are more likely to use Wikipedia and online magazines as a source of background information than any other information resource, while graduate students will seek out blogs in their disciplines (Kim, Sin, & Tsai, 2014, p. 172). Studies have shown that undergraduates have a difficult time identifying credible information in results retrieved from Google searches, as they often are "fooled" by heuristic cues such as table of contents and lists of references, as well as clean web design (Lim, 2013, p. 406). They will also refer to infographics for statistical information, regardless of who posted the infographic or whether or not the information is cited, because the charts and data look "official." Faculty and peers have equal influence on whether or not undergraduates will perceive information located online as credible or not (Lim, 2013, p. 414; Sohn, 2014, p. 149). For this reason, it is not uncommon for Wikipedia-using undergraduates to swear that traditional encyclopedias are more authoritative and credible than Wikipedia entries, even if they compare two entries on the same topic side by side and find the entry from Wikipedia to be more comprehensive and accurate.

In short, although Generations Y and Z may have more familiarity with Web 2.0 and social media tools than their professors, most lack the expertise to use these tools to locate, organize, or create authoritative content, let alone select appropriate tools for collaborative academic work or other forms of real-world problem solving. They also may have difficulty evaluating content they locate through these media. Because their professors most likely do not have this training, and may even discourage students from using "distracting" social media for research, the students who use Web 2.0 and social media daily, from the time they could hold a device, may actually be social media illiterates. Digital natives still prefer to seek out a real person, whether face-to-face or online, for assistance over online how-to guides or video tutorials. Because of this, academic librarians should dust themselves off and show that they have skin in the social media game.

HOW ACADEMIC LIBRARIANS USE WEB 2.0 AND SOCIAL MEDIA

Academic librarians, like their undergraduate patrons, also use social media. Most academic librarians view themselves as early adopters of online communication systems and mobile technologies (Wexelbaum & Miltenoff, 2013, p. 437) and are more likely to use social media than teachers and professors (Bayliss, 2012). Academic librarians consider Web 2.0 and social media skills vital to providing relevant resources, services, and instruction to their patrons—second to mastery of online searching (Chawner & Oliver, 2013, p. 34; Pacheco, Kuhn, & Grant, 2010; Zohoorian-Fooladi & Abrizah, 2014, p. 164). Borrowing the term *Librarian 2.0* from Library Crunch blogger Michael Casey, Kumar (2013, pp. 29–30) spells out the Web 2.0 and social media competencies a librarian should have:

- Understand the power of [the] Web 2.0 opportunities;
- Learn major tools of Web 2.0 and Library 2.0;
- Is device independent, uses and delivers on everything from laptop to iPod;
- Develop targeted federated search and adopts the Open URL standard;
- Embrace nontextual information and the power of pictures, moving images, sight, and sound;
- Understand the "long tail" and leverages the power of old and new content;
- See the potential in using content sources like the open content Alliance, Google print, and Open WorldCat;
- Connect with everyone using their communication mode of choice—telephone, Skype, IM, SMS, texting, e-mail, virtual reference, etc.

Today academic librarians constantly evaluate apps for scholarly communication, collaboration, and research. At state and national library conferences, events such as "the appy hour" allow librarians from all generations to come together to learn about new apps for academic purposes, and to share their own experiences with apps that may be on the list. As most academic librarians either possess smartphones or tablets, they will upload the new apps right then and there, and try them out. Around the world, academic librarians enroll in fun professional development programs such as "23 Things on a Stick," an annual program where enrolled librarians and library staff must test out a list of new Web 2.0 and social media tools and blog about their experiences using them (Stephens & Cheetham, 2011). Each librarian enrolled in this program must follow one another's blogs, which leads to the creation of an informal support group. The support group, along with badges or prizes awarded for certain achievements, motivates enrollees to complete the program and take it again the following year.

As digital natives fill academic librarian positions, the expertise and motivation to use Web 2.0 and social media tools to teach information literacy skills increases (Emanuel, 2013). Digital native librarians view mobile technologies and social media as a necessary part of their lives and like to integrate technology and new media into their work whenever possible. As new librarians state that library school programs still do not provide them with sufficient training in technologies that they need for their positions (Emanuel, 2013), this new generation must have a high level of curiosity and motivation to learn and explore these technologies on their own, as well as a high comfort level with risk and failure.

Digital native librarians are very likely to follow blogs and news through Facebook and Twitter, and to have so many feeds that they will organize them using HootSuite or TweetDeck. To keep up with innovations in their field, librarians are more likely to follow Twitter feeds, blogs, or listservs rather than traditional journals (Terrill, 2014, pp. 194–99). At conferences, academic librarians will tweet to each other to exchange information during presentations, especially helpful during a large conference where multiple sessions are scheduled at one time. Digital native librarians also are likely to blog through WordPress, Tumblr, or Instagram, and share their posts through Facebook or Twitter. They will also have LinkedIn accounts, where they will network with other academic librarians and join discussion groups on topics related to their profession. They will also use Google Hangouts, Skype, or FaceTime to collaborate on projects. Digital natives also maintain YouTube accounts where they collect videos, or YouTube channels where they may create their own videos for classes and conference presentations. SlideShare is also a popular social media tool used by digital native librarians who wish to promote and share their conference presentations. Like their undergraduate patrons, academic librarians like to keep their personal and professional social media lives separate, but those lines often blur when using Facebook or Twitter to communicate with colleagues through organization and conference feeds (Terrill, 2014, p. 201).

Initially, Wikipedia challenged academic librarians' traditional beliefs about authoritative research resources (Wexelbaum, 2012, p. 9; Fitterling, 2014). At first, academic librarians did not include Wikipedia in library instruction sessions because they, like their full-time teaching faculty colleagues, were unaware of the evaluation process for Wikipedia articles, and did not feel empowered to edit the entries or create new ones. Today, major research university libraries in the United States either have a "Wikipedian in Residence" or a Wikipedia education team that includes at least one librarian and archivist. The team encourages faculty to build and improve Wikipedia content, as well as post primary source images and videos from local special collections and archives to drive researchers to those online collections.

ACADEMIC LIBRARY RESOURCES AND SERVICES AND SOCIAL MEDIA

In the workplace, academic librarians most likely use social media to promote library resources and services to undergraduates and other campus constituents (Abbott, Donaghey, Hare, & Hopkins, 2014; Dudenhoffer, 2012; Hagman, 2012; Hansen, Nowlan, & Winter, 2012; Milstein, 2009; Phillips, 2011; Salomon, 2013). Information shared through library social media channels may include instructions on how to access and use library resources, advertisements for new books and events, or fun multimedia. Academic librarians also have embraced social media tools to answer reference questions, which has resulted in more collaborative reference work across libraries (Carlson, 2007; Young, 2014, pp. 173–74).

Initially, academic librarians and faculty saw social media as a distraction from research. Students clogged up library computer labs to constantly check their MySpace and Facebook pages. Academic librarians got the idea to infiltrate Facebook and create library pages for students to like and share. Academic librarians encouraged interaction on the Facebook pages about all sorts of topics, from help with research assignments to shared decision making on whether or not the library should have more vending machines. Facebook success encouraged academic librarians to explore and implement other social media tools for outreach and student engagement, such as Twitter, to encourage students to ask questions and share information with one another (Junco, Heiberger, & Loken, 2010).

While research literature shows a gap of anywhere from two to four years between the launching of a social media tool and academic librarians embracing the tool to reach students, there are several reasons for this. Unlike individuals who have the freedom to develop personal social media accounts at their own pace and post whatever they wish, large academic libraries often create a team to manage each social media tool, identify best practices, make group decisions about policies and procedures, and so on. While these steps are necessary so that all library employees who post to social media represent the institution in a professional way, and they give all library employees the opportunity to master one or more social media strategies, they may take up to a year or more to complete. In small libraries, one librarian or staff member may handle all social media communication. If a solo librarian must do all reference, collection development, outreach, and library instruction, the odds that they will effectively master and manage all social media tools diminishes. Librarians also cite their institution's IT policies for restricting their Web 2.0 and social media exploration and implementation.

Educators and librarians have learned that the easiest, most acceptable way to reach Generations Y and Z is through social media. Both generations are open to the library sharing information with them through social media (McGough & Salomon, 2013, p. 283). While this may be the case, librarians sometimes have difficulty keeping a finger on what social media are most popular with their constantly changing student body. For this reason, they constantly have to survey and communicate with students about their social media habits, and learn new media all the time, to infiltrate the social and academic online spaces of their students. Academic librarians engaged in social media and emerging technologies will sometimes schedule informal workshops or "open sessions" where students can provide this input (Hensley, 2012).

FACULTY INFLUENCE ON WEB 2.0 AND SOCIAL MEDIA FOR ACADEMIC PURPOSES

While some Web 2.0 and social media tools are used across disciplines, humanities, social sciences, STEM, business, and education each have different online "cultures" that require specialization in particular information literacy skills. For this reason, academic librarians supporting specific programs find out from the faculty what they want their students to learn, and the librarians will share these tools with the faculty before sharing them in library instruction, online tutorials, or subject guides. If the faculty accept the new tools, the librarians can share those tools with the students.

College and university faculty are less likely to be active social media users than their students (Martinez-Alemán, 2014, p. 15; Seaman & Tinti-Kane, 2013). While the number of faculty engaging in social media usage increases every year, they are less likely to use social media for professional and instructional use than for personal (Seaman & Tinti-Kane, 2013). At the same time, faculty often express dissatisfaction with the features of the online course management systems (CMS) to which their institutions subscribe. An increasing number of faculty are breaking away from the CMS and organizing their course using wikis, blogs, or Facebook (Seaman & Tinti-Kane, 2013). Faculty discussions with academic librarians who support instructional design and emerging technologies often lead to these innovations in pedagogy. These successful collaborations often increase faculty motivation to learn more about social media and how to use it for teaching and research.

Faculty in all disciplines want up-to-the-minute, cutting-edge information from research in their respective fields. They are accustomed to receiving this information from commercially published peer-reviewed scholarly journal articles located in subscription-based databases. As library acquisitions budgets decrease and academic librarians must cut subscriptions to resources, faculty may perceive that they have access to less information than before. This becomes especially problematic when college and university faculty are expected to publish their research in peer-reviewed journals for tenure and promotion. Academic librarians have developed the field of "scholarly communication" in order to educate college and university faculty about open journals and open educational resources (OER) that cost nothing and are recognized as worthy, peer-reviewed media (Bueno de la Fuente, Robertson, & Boon, 2012, p. 31; Ho & Thomson, 2013). Most academic libraries have also established Google-searchable institutional repositories (IR) where faculty can give permission to make their publications available for free to all, and some engage in open access publishing (Ho & Thomson, 2013). Advancement of scholarly communication in academic libraries has pushed academic librarians to offer workshops to faculty on Creative Commons licensing; open-access, free ETextbook creation; and development of other open educational resources for curriculum (Bueno de la Fuente, Robertson, & Boon, 2012, p. 30). STEM and health science librarians in particular have also found that Twitter feeds provide more up-to-the-minute research information than journals, and they teach the faculty they support how to create and organize Twitter feeds in their disciplines (Giustini & Wright, 2009, pp. 13–14).

INTEGRATING WEB 2.0 AND SOCIAL MEDIA IN LIBRARY INSTRUCTION

Unfortunately, not all college and university faculty embrace social media tools for undergraduate research. Their requests for one-shot library instruction still focus on using traditional online resources—the library catalog, scholarly journal databases, and e-book collections. Faculty also still want librarians to teach students about proper research format and citation for papers and how to evaluate information for research purposes. While no one denies the value of foundational research resources, the truth is that most undergraduates—regardless of whether they receive library instruction or not—admit to using information gleaned from social media during their research process. Because of their "success" in finding information that is "just good enough," younger generations report a high level of confidence in their online search skills, even though they are poor (Achterman, 2005, p. 38). Because of this, academic librarians have had to find innovative ways to teach students not only how to use Web 2.0 and social media appropriately for research, as well as link them to social media specific to their disciplines, but show them why it is beneficial to do so (Margaryan, Littlejohn, & Vojt, 2011, p. 429).

One of the biggest challenges that faculty and students face during the research process is how to collect and organize the information that they find. Some undergraduates and faculty may already have experience with Google Drive, DropBox, or SkyDrive for file sharing for group projects, but more sophisticated collaboration calls for more powerful tools. Academic librarians have made the most inroads teaching Web 2.0 and social media through sharing information management tools such as subscription-based RefWorks, as well as the free WorldCat, Delicious, Diigo, Evernote, Zotero, and Mendeley (Farkas, 2012; Kapucu, Hoeppner, & Dunlop, 2008). Most of these tools employ folksonomy (also known as "tagging" or "social bookmarking") to help people categorize and relocate the resources they found for particular research projects. They also allow undergraduates—and faculty—to search for resources by tags within the information management tools themselves, in order to find what other resources researchers determined as relevant, as well as who else in the world is doing research on their topics. RefWorks, Evernote, Zotero, and Mendeley also help researchers organize their papers and format them using the appropriate research style for their chosen discipline. Academic librarians may also introduce students to Pinterest, Flickr, or any variety of RSS feed to show them how to gather images or organize and follow blogs that they find useful.

With the invention of the hashtag, academic librarians took the next logical step—showing faculty and students how to subscribe to Twitter feeds in their disciplines then conduct hashtag searches to find out what people have to say and share on those topics. Hashtag searching in Flickr, Pinterest, Tumblr, and Instagram also retrieves appropriate research resources, much to the delight of many undergraduates. Conversely, the librarians encourage students and faculty to create recognizable hashtags for their tweets, posts, and pins so that they can easily retrieve them at a later date.

During library instruction, academic librarians may engage students in discussions comparing information retrieved from traditional and new media sources. Undergraduates unfamiliar with Twitter often perceive it as a poor source for news or other research information, since they often hear that people tweet personal opinions there. Academic librarians surprise students by showing them how to locate Twitter feeds from government offices, non-profit organizations, professional associations, activist groups, and newspapers, magazines, and journals to boot, to get "the real scoop." In this way, students begin to pay attention to who tweets information and how they share links to articles, photos, and documents. Students doing research on living people can locate their Facebook, Twitter, or other social media accounts and use their posts as primary source documents (Coleman, 2013, p. 60).

During library instruction sessions, students may be asked either to work independently or in groups to determine the credibility and accuracy of news, blog, and journal articles. Some librarians will also facilitate discussions about bias in reporting and research, and will show students how to locate news articles on a topic from independent and international sources as well as from the media the students already follow. Academic librarians have also begun to introduce undergraduates to Digg and Reddit, to demonstrate why some news stories become more popularized than others, and to show that the most popular of the news articles are not always the most accurate.

Just as academic librarians have taught undergraduates how to conduct effective Google searches (since students are more likely to use Google as their starting point for research than the library website), they are stepping in to show undergraduates how to do effective research on Wikipedia, evaluate the entries, and even edit content if necessary (Jennings, 2008; Zlatos, 2014). Based on what they believe their professors and librarians want to hear, undergraduates often hold tight to two myths about Wikipedia: 1) that traditional encyclopedia entries are more authoritative and credible than Wikipedia entries, and 2) that no one monitors Wikipedia entries for accuracy, authority, or credibility. Academic librarians may ask undergraduates to locate an encyclopedia entry and a Wikipedia entry on a particular subject, and ask them to compare both for authority, credibility, accuracy, comprehensiveness, and bias. In doing so, librarians teach undergraduates how to "read" a Wikipedia entry by reviewing the "Talk" and "Edit" pages to discover how frequently the page is edited, as well as how it was rated and discussed by WikiProject groups in connected disciplines (Jennings, 2008, p. 433). They will discuss the strengths and weaknesses of the encyclopedia entry versus the Wikipedia entry, and when and how it is appropriate to use Wikipedia instead of an encyclopedia (Jennings, 2008, p. 434). Academic librarians are often the figures on campus to host Wikipedia "edit-a-thons" or "parties" open to the entire campus and surrounding community; interested faculty will often encourage students to attend for extra credit.

Infographics have become a popular source of statistical information. Students and faculty not only would like to use infographics discovered through social media in papers and presentations, but they also would like to make, use, and share their own. Academic librarians will not only build undergraduate awareness of how to evaluate the validity of information in infographics, but they will also teach students and faculty how to create infographics using Piktochart, info.gram, visual.ly, or even Microsoft Office tools, as well as how to cite the sources of data provided and how to apply a Creative Commons license if they would like to share their work. The librarians will encourage students to create pin boards on Pinterest for infographics, to give them the opportunity to collect good examples, as well as to save and share their own with others. As communication becomes more image-driven, it is expected that academic librarians will provide more assistance with infographic evaluation and creation in the future.

DISCUSSION AND FUTURE RESEARCH

The role of Web 2.0 and social media in academia will continue to advance with the rise of online schools and degree programs. The evolution of tablet and smartphone apps will eventually allow undergraduates to participate in online classes without using a single desktop computer. While fewer undergraduate students will go to the physical campus library for services, they will expect to communicate with librarians through their preferred social media channels. As faculty and undergraduate students will continue to depend on online resources for research and collaboration, academic librarians must always stay one step ahead of the trends in order to provide the most relevant guidance and service.

As faculty embrace emerging academic disciplines such as digital humanities and geographic information systems, academic librarians must keep up with using Web 2.0 and social media for content creation as well as research. Academic librarians providing research support for faculty and students in these new disciplines learn about creating infographics, maps, and other forms of data visualization. The librarians encourage students and faculty to credit sources of information used in these infographics, as well as to label them with Creative Commons licenses. They also teach faculty and students how to archive and organize data used for these projects.

More than ever, academic librarians and faculty must exchange their knowledge and work together to teach undergraduates information literacy skills through Web 2.0 and social media. Academic librarians knowledgeable about Web 2.0, social media, and other forms of technology should promote their existence across campus. Whether this happens through online tutorials, one-shot library instruction sessions, informal workshops, or credit-bearing courses, academic librarians must continue to share best practices with students, faculty, and other librarians. While faculty from all disciplines and academic librarians publish and present their work teaching information literacy skills with Web 2.0 and social media at conferences around the world, there is no single dedicated, globally accessible repository for this work. Academic librarians and faculty looking for successful activities or curricula would appreciate such a resource. During the time the authors wrote this book chapter, academic publisher Taylor & Francis conducted the first comprehensive international study of academic librarians and how they use and teach Web 2.0 and social media (Taylor & Francis, n.d.). Results of this study will be published in a white paper in 2015, and will provide librarians not currently engaged in social media instruction with some guidance and inspiration.

REFERENCES

Abbott, W., J. Donaghey, J. Hare, and P. Hopkins. (2014). "The Perfect Storm: The Convergence of Social, Mobile and Photo Technologies in Libraries." Conference paper presented at VALA 2014, Melbourne, Victoria, Australia. http://epublications.bond.edu.au/cgi/viewcontent.cgi?article=1033&context=library_pubs.

Achterman, D. (2005). "Surviving Wikipedia: Improving Student Search Habits through Information Literacy and Teacher Collaboration." *Knowledge Quest* 33, no. 5: 38–40.

Alter, C. (2014, Jan. 17). "Oversharenting Victims Rebel: The Quest for Online Anonymity." *Time.* http://time.com/2018/oversharenting-victims-rebel-the-quest-for-online-anonymity/.

Association of College & Research Libraries. (2014). "Information Literacy Competency Standards for Higher Education." http://www.ala.org/acrl/standards/informationliteracycompetency.

Bayliss, S. (2012, Dec. 13). "Librarians Use Social Networking Professionally More Than Teachers and Principals. According to Report." *The Digital Shift.* http://www.thedigitalshift.com/2012/12/k-12/librarians-use-social-networking-professionally-more-than-teachers-and-principals-according-to-report/.

Bercovici, J. (2010, Dec. 9). "Who Coined 'Social Media'? Web Pioneers Compete for Credit." *Forbes.* http://www.forbes.com/sites/jeffbercovici/2010/12/09/who-coined-social-media-web-pioneers-compete-for-credit/.

Bershidsky, L. (2014, June 22). "The Many Dimensions of Gen Z." *Pittsburgh Post-Gazette.* http://www.post-gazette.com/opinion/Op-Ed/2014/06/22/The-many-dimensions-of-Gen-Z/stories/201406220115.

Bolton, R. N., A. Parasuraman, A. Hoefnagels, N. Migchels, S. Kabadayi, T. Gruber, Y. K. Loureiro, and D. Solnet. (2013). "Understanding Generation Y and Their Use of Social Media: A Review and Research Agenda." *Journal of Service Management* 23, no. 3: 245–67.

Bueno de la Fuente, G., R. J. Robertson, and S. Boon. (2012). *The Roles of Libraries and Information Professionals in Open Educational Resources (OER) Initiatives: Survey Report.* [PDFfile]. Center for Academic Practice & Learning Enhancement (CAPLE) and the Centre for Educational Technology and Interoperability Standards (CETIS). http://publications.cetis.ac.uk/wp-content/uploads/2012/08/OER-Libraries-Survey-Report.pdf.

Calhoun, C. (2014). "Using Wikipedia in Information Literacy Instruction: Tips for Developing Research Skills." *College & Research Libraries* 75, no. 1: 32–33.

Carlson, S. (2007). "Are Reference Desks Dying Out? Librarians Struggle to Redefine—and in Some Cases Eliminate—the Venerable Institution." *The Reference Librarian* 48, no. 2: 25–30.

Chawner, B., and G. Oliver. (2013). "A Survey of New Zealand Academic Reference Librarians: Current and Future Skills and Competencies." *Australian Academic & Research Libraries* 44, no. 1: 29–39.

Coleman, V. (2013). "Social Media as a Primary Source: A Coming of Age." *Educause Review* 48, no. 6: 60–61.

Connaway, L. S., and K. M. Randall. (2013). "Why the Internet Is More Attractive Than the Library." *The Serials Librarian: From the Printed Page to the Digital Age* 64, no. 1–4: 41–56.

DiNucci, D. (1999). "Fragmented Future." *Print* 53, no. 4: 32, 221–22. http://darcyd.com/fragmented_future.pdf.

Dudenhoffer, C. (2012). "Pin It! Pinterest as a Library Marketing and Information Literacy Tool." *College & Research Libraries News* 73, no. 6: 328–32.

Emanuel, J. (2013). "Digital Native Academic Librarians, Technology Skills, and Their Relationship with Technology." *Information Technology and Libraries*, 20–33.

Farkas, M. G. (2012). "Technology in Practice. Tools for Optimal Flow: Technology-enabled Workflows." *American Libraries* 43, no. 7/8: 23.

Fitterling, L. (2014). "Wikipedia: Proceed with Caution." *The Journal of the American Osteopathic Association* 114, no. 5: 334–35.

Gangadharbatla, H., Laura F. Bright, and K. Logan. (2014). "Social Media and News Gathering: Tapping into the Millennial Mindset." *The Journal of Social Media in Society* 3, no. 1: 45–63.

Giustini, D., and M. Wright. (2009). "Twitter: An Introduction to Microblogging for Health Librarians." *Journal of the Canadian Health Libraries* 30: 11–17.

Hagman, J. (2012). "Joining the Twitter Conversation." *Public Services Quarterly* 8, no. 1: 78–85.

Hansen, K., G. Nowlan, and C. Winter. (2012). "Pinterest as a Tool: Applications in Academic Libraries and Higher Education." *The Canadian Journal of Library and Information Practice and Research* 7, no. 2. http://davinci.lib.uoguelph.ca/index.php/perj/article/view/2011#.U9IEX2PpVb0.

Hensley, M. K. (2012, 12 April). "Think Like a Librarian: Best Practices for Offering Open Workshops." Conference paper presented at Librarian's Information Literacy Annual Conference, Glasgow, Scotland. http://hdl.handle.net/2142/34765.

Ho, A. K., and M. B. Thomson. (2013, May 16). "Library as Open Access Publisher: An Overview for Technical Service Librarians." Presented at the 2013 OVGTSL Annual Conference in Richmond, Kentucky. http://works.bepress.com/akho/34/.

International Society for Technology in Education. (2007). "ISTE Standards: Students." [PDF file]. http://www.iste.org/docs/pdfs/20-14_ISTE_Standards-S_PDF.pdf.

Ipri, T. (2010). "Introducing Transliteracy: What Does It Mean to Academic Libraries?" *College & Research Library News* 71, no. 10: 532–67.

Jennings, E. (2008). "Using Wikipedia to Teach Information Literacy." *College & Undergraduate Libraries* 15, no. 4: 432–37.

Junco, R., G. Heiberger, and E. Loken. (2010). "The Effect of Twitter on College Student Engagement and Grades." *Journal of Computer Assisted Learning* 27, no. 9: 119–32.

Kapucu, A., A. Hoeppner, and D. Dunlop. (2008). "Getting Users to Library Resources: A Delicious Alternative." *Journal of Electronic Resources Librarianship* 20, no. 4: 228–42.

Kim, K., S. J. Sin, and T. Tsai. (2014). "Individual Differences in Social Media Use for Information Seeking." *The Journal of Academic Librarianship* 40: 171–78.

Kirschner, P. A., and I. G. J. H. Wopereis. (2013). "Do You Know the Way to . . . Web 2.0?" In J. M. Spector, B. B. Lockee, S. E. Smaldino, and M. C. Herring (Eds.), 88–104, *Learning, Problem Solving and Mind Tools: Essays in Honor of David H. Jonassen*. New York: Routledge.

Kumar, K. (2013). "Attentiveness of Librarian 2.0: A Survey of Engineering Educational Librarians in Andhra Pradesh." *International Journal of Academic Library and Information Science* 1, no. 2: 29–38.

Levinson, P. (2013). *New New Media*. Upper Saddle River, NJ: Pearson.

Lim, S. (2013). "College Students' Credibility Judgments and Heuristics Concerns Wikipedia." *Information Processing & Management* 49, no. 2: 405–19.

Mackey, T. P., and T. E. Jacobson. (2011). "Reframing Information Literacy as a Metaliteracy." *College & Research Libraries* 72, no. 1: 62–78.

Mao, J. (2014). "Social Media for Learning: A Mixed Methods Study on High School Students' Technology Affordances and Perspectives." *Computers in Human Behavior* 33: 213–23.

Margaryan, A., A. Littlejohn, and G. Vojt. (2011). "Are Digital Natives a Myth or Reality? University Students' Use of Digital Technologies." *Computers & Education* 56: 429–40.

Martinez-Alemán, A. M. (2014, Jan./Feb.). "Social Media Go to College." *Change Magazine*: 13–20.

McGough, B. L., and D. Salomon. (2013). "Engaging Students through Social Media." *Proceedings of the Charleston Library Conference*. http://docs.lib.purdue.edu/charleston.

Milstein, S. (2009). "Twitter for Libraries (and Librarians)." *Computers in Libraries* 29, no. 5: 17–18.

Pacheco, J., I. Kuhn, and V. Grant. (2010). "Librarians Use of Web 2.0 in UK Medical Schools: Outcomes of a National Survey." *New Review of Academic Librarianship* 16, no. 1: 75–86.

Paul, J. A., H. M. Baker, and J. D. Cochran. (2012). "Effect of Online Social Networking on Student Academic Performance." *Computers in Human Behavior* 28: 2,117–27.

PewResearch Internet Project. (2014). "Social Networking Fact Sheet." http://www.pewinternet.org/fact-sheets/social-networking-fact-sheet/.

PewResearch Internet Project. (2013). "Teens Fact Sheet." http://www.pewinternet.org/fact-sheets/teens-fact-sheet/.

Phillips, N. K. (2011). "Academic Library Use of Facebook: Building Relationships with Students." *The Journal of Academic Librarianship* 37, no. 6: 512–22.

Raspa, D., and D. Ward. (2000). *The Collaborative Imperative: Librarians and Faculty Working Together in the Information Universe*. Chicago: Association of College and Research Libraries.

Rheingold, H. (2010). "Attention and Other 21st Century Social Media Literacies." *Educause Review* 45, no. 5: 14–24.

Salomon, D. (2013). "Moving On from Facebook: Using Instagram to Connect with Undergraduates and Engage in Teaching and Learning." *College & Research Libraries News* 74, no. 8: 408–12.

Scholarly Publishing and Academic Research Coalition. (2014, March 13). "Libraries Leading the Way on Open Educational Resources." [Video presentation]. http://www.sparc.arl.org/resource/libraries-leading-way-open-educational-resources.

Seaman, J., and H. Tinti-Kane. (2013, Oct.) "Social Media for Teaching and Learning: Annual Survey of Social Media Use by Higher Education Faculty." Boston, MA: Pearson Learning Solutions.

Sohn, D. (2014). "Coping with Information in Social Media: The Effects of Network Structure and Knowledge on Perception of Information Value." *Computers in Human Behavior* 32: 145–51.

sparks & honey. (n.d.). "Meet Generation Z: Forget Everything You Learned about Millennials." [PowerPoint presentation]. http://www.slideshare.net/sparksandhoney?utm_campaign=profiletracking&utm_medium=sssite&utm_source=ssslideview.

Stephens, M., and W. Cheetham. (2011). "The Impact and Effect of Learning 2.0 Programs in Australian Academic Libraries." *New Review of Academic Librarianship* 17, no. 1: 31-63.

Taylor & Francis. (n.d.). White Paper: Social Media in the Library-Best Practice. http://www.tandf.co.uk/journals/pdf/white-paper-social-media-in-the-library-best-practice.pdf.

Tekulye, N., and K. Kelly. (2013). "Worth 1,000 Words: Using Instagram to Engage Library Users." Conference paper presented at Brick and Click Libraries Symposium, Northwest Missouri State University, Maryville, Missouri. http://ecommons.udayton.edu/roesch_fac/20/.

Terrill, L. J. (2014). "Catalogers' Perceptions and Use of Social Media and Conventional Information Sources for Professional Development." *Cataloging & Classification Quarterly* 52, no. 2: 181–228.

Thompson, C., K. Gray, and H. Kim. (2014). "How Social Are Social Media Technologies (SMTs)? A Linguistic Analysis of University Students' Experiences of Using SMTs for Learning." *Internet and Higher Education* 21: 31–40.

van Dijk, J. A. G. M. (2013). "Inequalities in the Network Society." In *Digital Sociology: Critical Perspectives*. 105–24. Edited by Kate Orton-Johnson and Nick Prior. New York: Palgrave Macmillan.

Wexelbaum, R. (2012). "Is the Encyclopedia Dead? Evaluating the Usefulness of a Traditional Reference Resource." *Reference Reviews* 26, no. 7: 7–11.

Wexelbaum, R., and P. Miltenoff. (2013). "The Role of Academic Libraries in the Development and Support of Mobile-learning Environments." In *Handbook of Mobile Learning*, 436–44. Edited by Zane L. Berge and Lin Y. Muilenberg. New York: Routledge.

Young, C. L. (2014). "Crowdsourcing the Virtual Reference Interview with Twitter." *The Reference Librarian* 55, no. 2: 172–74.

Zarro, M., and C. Hall. (2012). "Pinterest: Social Collecting for #linking #using #sharing." *ACM/IEEE Joint Conference on Digital Libraries*: 417–18.

Zlatos, C. (2014). "Still Not Ready for Prime Time: Academic Librarian Attitudes toward Wikipedia in a Networked Age." Presented at the 10th International Conference on Technology, Knowledge, and Society, Madrid, Spain.

Zohoorian-Fooladi, N., and A. Abrizah. (2014). "Academic Librarians and Their Social Media Presence: A Story of Motivations and Deterrents." *Information Development* 30, no. 2: 159–71.

Zurkowski, P. G. (1974, Nov.). "The Information Science Environment: Relationships and Priorities." Related paper No. 5. Conference paper presented to the National Commission on Libraries and Information Science. http://files.eric.ed.gov/fulltext/ED100391.pdf.

Chapter Thirteen

Library Instruction in the Age of Constructivism

Engaging Students with Active Learning Technologies

Anthony Holderied and Michael C. Alewine

INTRODUCTION

Recent trends in education reveal a new emphasis in the use of interactive technologies in the classroom as a positive and effective strategy aimed at enhancing learning through the promotion of student engagement and active learning. Student engagement through the use of technology has become a popular teaching strategy in the information literacy classroom, specifically due to the changing nature of the information-seeking environment and the attitudes and behaviors of modern library users. The idea of engaging students through active learning is not a new instructional strategy; however, recent development of a variety of technology-related teaching tools has enhanced the ability of librarians to engage students during instruction sessions like never before. This chapter will discuss the pedagogical uses of some of these technologies in the context of library instruction, including interactive whiteboards, clickers, and wireless slates. Emphasis is placed on the theoretical justification for learning with interactive technologies, practical examples of their usage in the information literacy classroom, and best practices drawn from the authors' experience.

STUDENT ENGAGEMENT AND ACTIVE LEARNING

Today's traditional college student, most likely a member of what is referred to as Generation Y, tends to look a little different than that of previous generations. With their lives significantly impacted by the Internet, social networking, mobile devices, and complex schedules, typical college students, also referred to as Millennials, seem to be constantly inundated with information and technology.

Millennials have seemingly changed the way educators look at the teaching and learning process, with more of the emphasis being placed on how students learn rather than how teachers teach. With renewed enthusiasm toward learning theories, brought on largely by the advent of technology-based teaching tools, academic librarians have witnessed a paradigm shift by which students are being actively engaged in the classroom, and the teaching tools geared toward them are becoming increasingly more interactive. Education research suggests that students prefer having a more active role in their own learning process, whether it comes in the form of a more interactive classroom environment, heavier use of instructional technology, or simply a more engaging instructor. Given this trend, educators are aiming to reach students in formats and mediums that are more familiar to them, which may include new technological platforms that resemble things they use in everyday life.

A good example of this transition can be found in the recent application of classroom clickers, also known as audience or classroom response systems—a technology that resembles the text messaging function of a cell phone. By using this technology to make the learning environment more interactive and appealing, teaching librarians can engage students in the classroom using nontraditional methods that incorporate active learning strategies.

So exactly how do these interactive technologies enhance the learning experience and student engagement in library instruction classrooms? To answer this question, one must have a basic understanding of what active learning is and why it is important. Active learning is essentially the antithesis of passive learning, which can be described as any educational experience that relies on one-way communication from teacher to student. This one-way avenue is most often associated with teaching styles that incorporate lecture, note-taking, and rote memorization of facts as a basis for student learning. However, this style of teaching and learning may no longer be optimal for today's learner. According to Bonwell and Eison, students prefer learning environments where active learning is employed over traditional lecture. They defined active learning as "instructional activities involving students in doing things and thinking about what they are doing." Active learning strategies have become popular because they are believed to increase development of thinking and writing in students who participate more actively in the learning process. It is also held that active learning offers teachers multiple ways of reaching learners that perform better in nontraditional lecture environments (Bonwell and Eison, 1991, p. 5).

Active learning is considered a pedagogical approach that is derived from Constructivism—a philosophical approach to learning that attempts to "create learning situations that promote the engagement or immersion of learners in practice fields." These learning environments should ideally include activities that are authentic to the discipline or content being learned (Reiser & Dempsey, 2007, pp. 42, 46). One of the ways in which the Constructivist approach is different from earlier learning theories, such as Behaviorism and Cognitivism, is that there is a change in the way content is transferred from the teacher to the student. In active learning, the focus of learning moves from an instructor-centric environment to one that is learner-centric, meaning the emphasis is no longer placed on how the teacher teaches but how the student learns. The student gains a far better understanding of the material when he or she is able to play a role in participating in the shaping of content, instead of simply having it dictated by means of one-way communication (Leonard, 2002, p. 3). Interactive technologies, such as whiteboards and clickers, for example, give learners the ability to actively participate in how they receive and retain information. Compared to traditional lecture, note-taking, and memorization, implementation of active learning technologies provides students the opportunity to become more involved in the learning process.

Social Constructivism is a brand of Constructivism whose proponents postulate that students perform best when placed in peer learning communities, whereby they can construct meaning of content through their collective individual experiences. Some of the principles used to design social constructivist environments include: focusing on learners not performance, viewing learners as co-constructors who actively work together to create knowledge and meaning, the idea of teacher as facilitator or guide, engaging learners with tasks that are seen as ends in themselves, and promoting assessment as an active process that is aimed at shared understanding (Adams, 2006, p. 247). These principles will naturally emerge by simply incorporating the use of interactive technologies and active learning exercises that promote peer-to-peer and peer-to-instructor interaction.

Fink outlined three strategies for implementing effective forms of active learning into the classroom. One of these strategies is to "find new ways to introduce students to information and ideas" (Fink, 2003, p. 114). By exploring with new technologies such as clickers and electronic whiteboards, students are experiencing a variety of delivery methods to engage with course content as an alternative to simply reading a text or passively listening to a lecture. This exploration of interactive learning mediums in the classroom increases the likelihood of reaching more students in an environment of pupils that possess varying learning styles. In the section to follow, the authors discuss a pedagogical approach to information literacy and how interactive technologies play a role in their students' learning environment.

PEDAGOGICAL OVERVIEW OF INSTRUCTION

In the Mary Livermore Library, there is a core instructional staff of three librarians, who for the most part share a fairly cohesive pedagogical philosophy for the delivery of information literacy instruction. Librarians have made a concerted effort over the last few years to add active learning elements of instruction into each session provided. Instructional sessions run the gamut of student levels; from new freshman to upper division courses to graduate students. Though many incoming freshmen are typical Generation Y students who are comfortable using an array of technologies, a significant number of students are nontraditional students, many of whom have a limited facility and experience with technology.

While the nature of the course instructor's request guides the initial instructional design, the authors have also been working to develop a tiered approach to teaching information literacy that incorporates scaffolding and widely accepted standards and learning outcomes for teaching information skills. The library wants to assure that students at each level (e.g., first-year students, students in the majors, and graduate students) receive some common instructional elements that lead to a progression of knowledge from basic to advanced information literacy skills.

In striving to create a learning environment that puts into use constructivist principles, it is necessary to foster collaboration and engagement among students inside the classroom. Most first-year courses receive instruction that requires team-based inquiry and problem solving. Upper division courses receive a more minimal instructional approach, with a significant portion of each session being devoted to actual information seeking whereby students are encouraged to collaborate and help one another. In this environment, the librarian acts more as a facilitator than lecturer, encouraging learners to construct meaning in a more authentic manner.

Over the last couple of years the library has been fortunate to be able to invest in interactive technologies, namely, an interactive whiteboard, one classroom response system, and a set of mobile wireless slates. It did so with the intention of reaching students using nontraditional mediums aimed directly at improving their understanding of information literacy concepts through active engagement. Librarians can use these technologies to effectively enhance pedagogy to better stimulate positive student attitudes and perceptions toward the research process. The following sections describe each of the technologies mentioned above, and how they can be utilized in the classroom to promote student engagement with learning content.

Interactive Whiteboards

An interactive whiteboard (IWB) is an interactive display surface that is used in conjunction with an instructor workstation and a mounted projection system. Interactive whiteboards can be attached to a wall or placed on a stand with castors, thus making them mobile. They come in various sizes and are manufactured by a variety of companies. For the purposes of this chapter the authors will discuss a specific IWB that was purchased for the Mary Livermore Library and manufactured by Smart Technologies. Known as a SMART Board, the IWB is a wall-mounted unit centered on the front wall of the electronic classroom. The library also has a special projector that came with the unit, which is attached to the whiteboard. The board itself measures four feet by five feet.

The hallmark of IWBs is the ability to interact with and manipulate the displayed content by using an electronic pen or a finger—in essence the pen or finger becomes a form of computer mouse. Most IWBs, along with the appropriate software applications, allow the instructor to annotate concepts being presented (using one of the electronic pens that come in different colors—or lifting one of the pens from its cradle and then writing or drawing with a finger). Accompanying software allows instructors and students the creativity to go beyond what is imaginable with traditional instruction tools. Instructor or student presentations can be recorded as static documents or as videos and saved to be uploaded to a course site. Such capabilities allow for the creation of valuable resources that can be referred to later when working on related assignments or utilized as pre-class assignments in a flipped classroom model. It also allows for the use of creative and dynamic documents, and the touch-screen technology allows for greater fluidity in the presentation of the materials. There are numerous bells and whistles that come with most IWBs, some of which the authors have not yet experimented with and can be used in powerful ways to attract the attention and interest of participating students.

Although originally designed with business applications in mind, IWBs have been used in educational settings for nearly a decade now in some classrooms. They can serve a variety of pedagogical purposes, although this chapter will concentrate on their specific use for enhancing information literacy instruction. The interactive capability of whiteboards make them wonderful teaching tools in the library classroom, bringing new energy and enthusiasm toward learning content simply by its ability to attract the attention of students. Learners are visually and emotionally engaged by the "wow" factor as the learning content is manipulated by a tap of the instructor's finger. For instance, in most library classrooms an instructor station is used for projection on a screen at the front of the classroom, while the instructor and station itself are typically off to the side or even behind the students. With the SMART Board, librarians are now more "front-and-center," actively engaging with the students instead of instructing from a far-off dark corner of the room. This especially makes a difference in larger classes where students tend to drift off or get distracted. Library research is likely not the most interesting academic topic that students encounter; therefore it is important to find ways to build intrinsic motivation to help them become good researchers. When instructors are more engaged with the audience, there is a higher chance that students will become interested in the material being presented.

Among the many ways to make use of the SMART Board is to gauge previous knowledge of the learner and to provide students with an opportunity for immediate reflection. Depending on the course and how much time is available (some course sections do come to the library for multiple instructional sessions, but many do not), students are asked to come up to the board to show some baseline process such as keyword searching using the library's online catalog. For courses that come to the library for multiple sessions, students can be selected to come to the board (the authors usually start with students from the back row) to present some piece of database functionality. This serves to gauge acquisition of skills from the previous session and also provides for some peer-to-peer learning opportunities. Other students in the class guide the student at the board through the process (whatever it may be), thus encouraging more students to participate in the learning activity. IWBs can be used for reflection even within fifty-minute, one-shot instruction sessions where students may be receiving their initial exposure to information literacy instruction. These sessions can move at breakneck speed and mostly cover keyword development and the functionality of a specific database. Again, in keeping with constructivist principles, a few students are called to the board to repeat some process they just learned, and students in the audience are asked to provide guidance to the students at the board. In this environment, everyone is participating and learning from one another.

A couple of the key issues that librarians face in teaching information literacy include working under time constraints and staffing limitations—two potential problems that have a tendency to prohibit instructors from teaching what is really important in information research. Due to these limitations, librarians may often find themselves relegated to simply teaching the use of specific electronic databases rather than concentrating on the basic concepts of information retrieval and evaluation, as well as the development of critical thinking skills. The SMART Board can be used to alleviate some of these problems by allowing instructors to teach the harder-to-grasp skills and concepts in a more efficient manner. For example, the SMART Board provides a visual learning canvas that can be used to present a kinesthetic representation of the more difficult concepts such as Boolean logic. When the instruction is thoughtfully and thoroughly planned in this manner, IWBs by their nature usually appeal to visual learners, especially in relation to exercises that involve processes (e.g., the steps necessary to narrow the focus of a search by adding keywords, etc.). The instruction of such skills can be difficult to express and carry out through traditional means such as lecture.

The SMART Board can also be used in conjunction with information literacy through sessions that are provided for English composition courses. As the instructional presentation in the classroom progresses, useful comments and notes are added to the slides to annotate further points of instruction, such as evaluating web resources or the functionality of a database. The presentations highlight concepts such as topic development, keyword strategies, selection of appropriate resources, as well as the critical evaluation of resources. Presentations are then saved in their entirety using the SMART Notebook software (much like a PowerPoint). The presentations then become, in effect, a useful research tutorial for students to refer to when working on their research assignments. By saving these presentations, best practices can be shared with other instruction librarians, thus improving the quality of sessions as they evolve over time.

The library also utilizes the SMART Board in the Freshman Seminar instruction, which takes students through a mini information literacy program. In the program, students work in groups to complete information-seeking tasks that are eventually submitted to the instructing librarian in the form of a worksheet. The interactive whiteboard is used by these students to present their group work findings (e.g., showing why a particular website is credible or not) to the rest of the class. This type of reflection allows librarians and students the ability to present research skills in different ways that appeal to students of varying or nontraditional learning styles. For this reason, IWBs in general are good tools for quick reflective activities that reinforce important concepts.

There are some practical issues with the positioning of IWBs in the classroom. They are not very effective with a lot of sunlight in the room; therefore blinds may need to be installed to counteract the weak display. Another challenge can be the size of the IWB itself. The classroom whiteboard is small and is centered at the front of the room, but because of the size of the room (thirty-one feet by twenty-nine feet), some students are unable to see the content from the back row of the classroom. To help alleviate this problem, there is a software application called NetOp School 6, which controls all student workstations, displaying the presentation content on each workstation. This is beneficial when presenting something in small font, or some particularly small but important feature of an electronic resource. These types of programs are particularly useful in larger lab settings.

The following is a brief list of best practices to consider when using interactive whiteboards in the information literacy classroom:

- Design the instruction so that the whiteboard is used in such a way that the instructor or teaching student is out in front of the class as much as possible.
- Use the whiteboard to break the ice, the authors play a variety of YouTube videos—usually those that are currently going viral and are at the same time appropriate in terms of classroom decorum.
- Have students from the back of the classroom come up to the front to use the whiteboard early in the session (e.g., have them show classmates how to locate a business-related article).
- If teaching using a multisession information literacy model, use the first few minutes of class to review what was learned in the previous session.
- If time is available, use group collaboration assignments, and have students use the whiteboard to engage in peer-to-peer instruction, such as dividing the class into small groups.
- There are a number of free sources for Smart instructional templates, including those specific to higher education and libraries. You can share your own templates or use others—or just look at them in order to get pedagogical and instructional design ideas.

Clickers

Clickers are a highly effective teaching and learning tool for the information literacy classroom. Student engagement, and to a degree student learning, can be greatly enhanced through the use of clickers (Holderied, 2011). "A great advantage to using an audience response system, especially in larger lecture classes, but also in smaller classes, is that it makes each student continually active in working with the material and the lecturer" (Webking & Valenzuela, 2006, p. 129). In the Mary Livermore Library, the SMART Technologies Senteo system (now called the SMART Response system) was purchased and adopted. The SMART Response software from the Senteo system works in conjunction with the SMART Board and the SMART Notebook software, which largely influenced the authors' decision to purchase the SMART clickers.

The primary focus of this technology is to have students learn by doing; even if just clicking, this is still a form of active learning. One beneficial aspect of employing clickers is that they allow students to give opinions in an anonymous, nonthreatening forum. Students who normally do not speak in class are able to lend their voices to the discussion, even if only to a limited degree. Assessment questions of all types can be quickly created at the instructor station (or anywhere the software is installed). Question types include true/false, yes/no, multiple-choice, numeric response, and multiple-answer. Questions can be easily imported from question banks and other software applications (e.g., Microsoft Word, PowerPoint, etc.). Students can respond anonymously or can be assigned a clicker that identifies the student. The clickers connect with the IWB and instructor workstation using a radio frequency wireless Bluetooth connection. The effective range is about a hundred feet.

Clickers are also useful for gauging prior student knowledge of skills and concepts. In sessions where clickers are utilized, the authors design one to two questions that examine students' baseline knowledge or general experience with research. This information will be useful in the case that the instructor may be able to save time by not having to cover content that was originally planned for if students already have a firm grasp of the skill or idea. Although the design of each session is based largely on course instructor input and previous teaching experience, there are a number of presumptions that are not always accurate when it comes to what students actually know, even with upper division or graduate students. By asking a multiple-answer survey question using the clickers, it is possible to get a reasonable idea of the previous experience students have using library resources. As stated before, these types of questions can give instructors the ability to quickly modify the content of the instruction on the fly if necessary.

It is important to note that it is necessary to put some thought into these questions, or else the instructor may find himself standing in front of the class realizing that the questions may be confusing to students or just plain useless. Just like all elements of instructional design, each question should serve a very specific purpose or be used to address a learning objective. Limit the use of questions to the essential concepts to be assessed and try to employ them to engender critical thinking. Use one or two questions in the beginning of the session, and then two or three more interspersed within the content of the presentation or as an assessment at the end of the session. In a fifty-minute class, having more than a few questions is not practical, and it is also possible to overuse the clickers to the point that they lose their novelty with the students.

Clickers can be used to spark debate and get students engaged in class discussion. They can be used to get students discussing the credibility of particular websites. As part of the information literacy program for Freshmen Seminar courses, students are required to work in groups to critically evaluate websites. During the initial lecture, a website is displayed that is likely to spark debate (e.g., climate change, military involvement, gun rights, etc.), and then students are asked to vote on the credibility of the site. After reviewing the results, a brief discussion is initiated as to why students voted the way they did. Hopefully, some peer-to-peer discussion and interaction will ensue that allows students to set aside their personal attitudes and give concrete examples of why they believe a website to be authoritative or not. This discussion can be a good bridge into other group activities, where each group must come to a consensus on the authority of a given resource.

Clickers can also be used for immediate reflection of information literacy concepts that have just been covered during the lesson. For example, a well-placed question can quickly gauge if students understand Boolean operators, truncation, wild cards, etc. One thing that often frustrates library instructors is to have covered a concept in-depth, and soon thereafter have a student fail to demonstrate understanding of the concept. By taking the most crucial aspects of an instructional presentation or module and posing a relevant question to students, the instructor can readily assess if students need more time with that particular concept. The question also provides a reflective moment that helps students to better commit the concept to memory. Clicker questions should incorporate specific examples related to the discipline—relevancy to their actual context proves to be more engaging than generic examples. Connor (2011, p. 247) found that using both clickers and subject-relevant case studies can help to engage and focus students in science and engineering classes while helping them to develop critical thinking skills.

Clickers can also be used for learning assessment. Historically, the authors have used a standard, paper-based assessment at the end of all of information literacy sessions, with the exception of Freshman Seminar and English Composition (which use special assessments). The paper-based assessments include five multiple-choice or true/false questions that assess acquisition of skills or information literacy concepts covered during the session. A question bank for selection of the five questions is useful, but often questions are tailored for specific courses, disciplines, and research assignments. In addition, there are some demographic indicator questions and a place for student comments. Audience response questions can also be used to "collect feedback from the students at the close of the session. Students were questioned about their level of interest in the session's content; the organization of the presentation; the preparation of the instructor; and the amount of 'new' material in the session" (Abate, Gomes, & Linton, 2011, p. 16).

The authors have also used the clickers for assessing multiple instruction sessions of an introductory economics course. The five questions used are the same as those on the corresponding paper assessment (at this time, there is no electronic means of collecting the demographic information or garnering student comments unless an additional paper-based instrument is used). The clicker software allows one to export the results of the assessments or polls into Excel; for the authors, this data is later included in the aggregate assessment reports compiled by the lead instruction librarian.

One advantage of using clickers versus paper-based assessment is that as students proceed through each question, the librarian can display the students' answers collectively to the class in the form of a histogram, thus indicating how many responses were given for each question. Students can be asked to discuss the results, especially problem questions, to get a sense of how the class did overall and what needs to be covered again and which individual questions were confusing and possibly need to be refined. Students at the back of the class cannot always see the questions well, so the instructor should read each question and possible answer choices (although it is important to be careful not to add inflection to your voice when reading the correct response). The NetOp software mentioned earlier is used to display the assessment questions on each workstation, for those having trouble seeing the SMART Board.

With the proliferation of multisession information literacy instructional models and semester-long credit-bearing information literacy courses, clickers can also be used to assess required reading assignments. "Reading quiz questions evaluate students' knowledge of material from assigned readings. Although any course material is fair game, this pedagogical model promotes assessing students' knowledge of the most important concepts and findings from assigned readings. With this approach, the dual purposes of motivating students to do the reading and teaching them to read carefully to identify major themes and concepts are met" (Mollborn & Hoekstra, 2010, p. 21).

The following is a brief list of best practices to consider when using clickers:

- Test the clickers and connections before the session begins. Software updates (e.g., SMART software) can remove all of your previous settings, so make sure that you save notes concerning your preferences, and be prepared to make changes on the fly.
- Provide students with instructions on how to use the clickers. Let students know up front why they are being used and what is to be expected. The SMART Response software includes a working virtual clicker (displayed on the SMART Board) that allows you to model powering up the clicker, selecting a class/session, and making answer choices.
- Keep questions to a minimum based on the duration and content of the session.
- When developing questions, make them precise, intuitive, and relevant to specific learning objectives. Do not create questions with more than a few choices.
- Use an initial question to gauge student attitudes or previous experience or simply to break the ice.
- Use a question to reflect upon important concepts—use results to illuminate misunderstandings and teachable moments.
- Use questions to spark discussion and debate. All questions should be used in conjunction with discussion, especially peer-to-peer discussion if possible.

- Read questions and possible answers aloud—not everyone can clearly see the screen.

Wireless Slates

Wireless slates are interactive classroom technologies that look a lot like small tablet PCs. Although tablet PCs have been around for a while, wireless slates seem to be a relatively new technology. They are thin, light, work in conjunction with the IWB and instructor workstation, and are designed to be distributed throughout the classroom. Using a tethered electronic pen (or a wireless mouse), participants can control any computer function or annotate any screen being displayed from remote locations within the classroom. Essentially, this allows multiple classroom participants to engage with one another and the instructor simultaneously while visually interacting from the same screen or application.

The Mary Livermore Library purchased the SMART Technologies WS 100-R1 Airliner, of which there are two in the classroom. The slate's display area corresponds to that of the IWB. The user simply hovers the pen or engages the wireless mouse, and a cursor appears on the IWB. Multiple slates can be circulated around the classroom and used simultaneously while connected to the IWB and instructor workstation using a radio frequency wireless Bluetooth connection. The effective range is about fifty feet. Controls are programmable through the SMART software loaded on the instructor workstation. The basic controls of the slates include the electronic four-color pen, mouse, eraser, and keyboard functions. The slates can be used to control all of the functions of the interactive whiteboard.

The slates have tremendous potential for active learning. The authors use them in two ways in the classroom. The first is to allow a few of the English composition instructors who take an active role in the information literacy sessions to participate in the lesson working alongside the librarian to add insight and keep students engaged and on task. Each of these instructors are library advocates and bring their course sections to the library for multiple sessions (anywhere from three to six sessions per course section). Each session is used to cover an in-depth information literacy concept/skill/standard with an accompanying workshop or group work component assigned by the course instructor. The course instructors use the wireless slates to interact with the librarian's on-screen lesson or the student group presentations. The wireless slates allow the instructor to add insight by controlling the screen navigation and making annotations when further analysis or feedback is needed. This is particularly useful for allowing the course instructor to be involved in the session while remaining at the back of the classroom or moving around from student to student.

The other way that the slates are used is for student engagement. Randomly chosen students are asked by the instructing librarian to interact in some way with the content being presented on the IWB in response to the librarian's specific prompts or questions. An example of this is when students may be asked to highlight a database function or parts of a website being critically evaluated. The librarian can move from student to student having each interact with the content right from their seats. Although this is just an anecdotal notation, one of the benefits of using the slates in this random fashion is that the students seem to be more alert and paying closer attention to the lesson, not knowing if he or she will be asked to play a part.

The slates are useful companions to the IWB. Both the IWB and the slates present good opportunities for engaging the students, as the instructor can have them come to the board or interact from their individual workstations. The slates can also be used for small group information literacy assignments where students working together make brief presentations of their findings from their workstations.

There are newer and more robust wireless slates that connect to most projection systems. Some institutions have even opted to use wireless slates instead of purchasing IWBs, because of lower costs and greater portability. As tablet PCs and iPads have become more ubiquitous in higher education, there are multitudes of free and low-cost apps that allow these devices to interact with and control IWBs. This also provides instructors with the ability to create instructional materials and learning objects at the office or home.

The following is a brief list of best practices to consider when using wireless slates:

- Encourage course instructors to play an active role in sessions that feature slates.
- Ask students who show up early to test the slates prior to the start of a session.
- Use slates sparingly but effectively to engage students during the session.
- Select students randomly from around the classroom to use the slates.

CONCLUSION

Two of the most important questions related to the use of interactive technologies are: 1) Do interactive technologies in the classroom increase student engagement?, and 2) Do interactive technologies actually improve cognitive learning? To the first question, based on the authors' experiences and what has been observed in the literature that is available, the answer is an unequivocal yes. While most of the evidence to this point is anecdotal or comes from the results of postsessions assessments, the authors can conclude that the three interactive technologies that were employed over the last several years have served to increase participation on the part of the students during information literacy sessions. Any survey of the literature regarding the use of whiteboards and clickers universally point to an increase in student engagement at some level or other. The authors have found few if any articles that describe an environment where interactive technologies did nothing to improve engagement. In the future, the authors will be working to collect affective data from students who participate in the sessions in order to measure to what degree they feel the use of the technologies has enhanced their engagement level as well as their understanding of instructional content.

As for seeing an increase in learning outcomes among students taught in technology-rich environments versus those in traditional lecture-based environments, the jury is still out. In one of the authors' studies, a brief comparison was made between test scores taken from economics students that participated in upper-level information literacy sessions. The sections that did not use the clickers scored 83 percent on the postsession assessment. The sections that used the clickers scored 87 percent on the same assessment. While these results are far from presenting a scientific case for improved learning, they do provide a rationale for continued investigation. The authors are considering using satisfaction survey data and assessment scores to compare how sections that make use (beyond simple presentation) of these interactive technologies stack up against the scores of students in those sections where interactive technologies are not employed. The authors' instructional sessions regularly include peer-to-peer learning and group work based on Constructivist principles. Based on these initial discussions, IWBs, clickers, and wireless slates will play a significant role in that transformation.

REFERENCES

Abate, Laura E., Alexandra Gomes, and Anne Linton. (2011). "Engaging Students in Active Learning: Use of a Blog and Audience Response System." *Medical Reference Services Quarterly* 30, no. 1 (2011): 12–18.

Adams, Paul. (2006). "Exploring Social Constructivism: Theories and Practicalities." *Education 3–13* 34, no. 3: 243–57.

Bonwell, C. C., and J. A. Eison. (1991). "Active Learning: Creating Excitement in the Classroom." ASHE—ERIC Higher Education Report No. 1. Washington, DC: George Washington University, School of Education and Human Development.

Connor, Elizabeth. (2011). "Using Cases and Clickers in Library Instruction: Designed for Science Undergraduates." *Science & Technology Libraries* 30, no. 3: 244–53.

Fink, L. Dee. (2003). *Creating Significant Learning Experiences*. San Francisco, CA: Jossey-Bass.

Holderied, A. (2011). "Instructional Design for the Active: Employing Interactive Technologies and Active Learning Exercises to Enhance Library Instruction." *Journal of Information Literacy* 5: 123–32.

Leonard, David C. (2002). *Learning Theories A to Z*. Westport, CT: Greenwood Press.

Mollborn, Stefanie, and Angel Hoekstra. (2010). "'A Meeting of Minds': Using Clickers for Critical Thinking and Discussion in Large Sociology Classes." *Teaching Sociology* 38, no. 1: 18–27.

Reiser, Robert A., and John V. Dempsey. (2007). *Trends and Issues in Instructional Design and Technology*. 2nd ed. Upper Saddle River, NJ: Pearson Prentice Hall.

Webking, Robert, and Felix Valenzuela. (2006). "Using Audience Response Systems to Develop Critical Thinking Skills." In *Audience Response Systems in Higher Education: Applications and Cases*, 127–39. Hershey, PA: Information Science Publishing.

Index

Contributors

Hannah Alcasid is electronic information and data support technician in the Ruth Lilly Law Library, Indiana University Robert H. McKinney School of Law Library. She earned a B.A. from the New School in New York City.

Michael C. Alewine is the Outreach/Distance Education librarian at the University of North Carolina at Pembroke. He has more than fifteen years of experience teaching information literacy and is always looking for new ways to more effectively motivate students. His research and publication interests are centered on learner engagement, online teaching and learning, and distance and military education. Michael holds a Master of Library Science from North Carolina Central University; a Master of Science, Instructional Technology, from East Carolina University; and he is currently finishing a Master of Arts, English, at East Carolina University.

Mladen Cudanov is assistant professor of organizational sciences at the University of Belgrade. He has ten years of experience in teaching at one of the leading institutions of higher education in southeastern Europe. He has done research in various fields of management. He is published regularly in national and international journals, and presents at international conferences.

Michelle Currier began her work in academic libraries as an assistant librarian in public services. She developed an interest in, and began to move professionally toward, the area of digital initiatives librarianship, beginning an iPad program at her college. She is presently the director of the Southworth Library Learning Commons at SUNY Canton College of Technology. She holds an MLIS from Florida State University.

Susan David deMaine is a research and instructional services librarian in the Ruth Lilly Law Library, Indiana University Robert H. McKinney School of Law Library. She earned a J.D. and an M.S.L.S. from the University of Kentucky.

Antonio DeRosa, MLIS, is a reference librarian at Memorial Sloan Kettering Cancer Center where he provides timely and accurate research support services to a range of clients including attendings, fellows, residents, nurses, students, allied health professionals, and other administrative support staff. He is also the clinical medical librarian for the Department of Radiology's Breast Imaging Service where he provides current awareness literature updates on a regular basis as well as training, roving reference, and one-on-one research consultation. His other duties consist of LibGuide development, bibliographic and research methods training, collection development, systematic reviews support, and pursuing emerging mobile apps and technologies. Antonio obtained his undergraduate degree from the State University of New York at New Paltz and his Masters of Library & Information Science degree from Pratt Institute in New York.

John A. Drobnicki, M.A., M.L.S., has been a faculty member in the library at York College/CUNY since 1995. Currently the Head of Acquisitions & Collection Development, Drobnicki was the Chief Librarian/Chair of the Library when the School Media Specialist position was created at York. He has published several articles on the presence of controversial items in library collections, especially Holocaust-denial materials.

Bradford Lee Eden is dean of library services at Valparaiso University. He is editor of *OCLC Systems & Services: Digital Library Perspectives International*; *The Bottom Line: Managing Library Finances*; *Library Leadership & Management*, the journal of the Library Leadership & Management Association (LLAMA) within the American Library Association; and *The Journal of Tolkien Research*, a new, open-access peer-reviewed journal. He has a masters and Ph.D. degrees in musicology, as well as an MS in library science. His recent books include *Middle-earth Minstrel: Essays on Music in Tolkien* (McFarland, 2010); *The Associate University Librarian Handbook: A Resource Guide* (Scarecrow Press, 2012); *Leadership in Academic Libraries: Connecting Theory to Practice* (Scarecrow Press, 2014), and *The Hobbit and Tolkien's Mythology: Essays on Revisions and Influences* (McFarland, 2014).

Helen Fallon is Deputy University Librarian at the National University of Ireland Maynooth. She has worked in libraries in Ireland, Saudi Arabia, Sierra Leone, Tanzania, and Namibia. Her professional interests include libraries in developing countries, African women writers, staff development, academic publishing, creativity, and the leadership and marketing of academic libraries. She has published extensively and runs workshops on academic publishing, and maintains a blog for library staff who wish to write for publication at http://academicwritinglibrarian.blogspot.com.

Teri Oaks Gallaway is the library systems and web coordinator at Loyola University New Orleans. In addition to her work on user-experience studies, she participates in the library's reference and instruction programs as the liaison to the Sociology, Criminal Justice, and Honors Departments. She has published and presented on topics including selection of a web-scale discovery system, promoting electronic resources, and using web services APIs.

Cynthia Harbeson is the processing archivist in Belk Library at Appalachian State University. She is responsible for accessioning and processing the archives and manuscripts from three of the library's four special collections: the W. L. Eury Appalachian Collection, University Archives, and Rare Books & Manuscripts. She has an M.S. in Library and Information Science with an archival science concentration and an M.A. in History, both from Simmons College in Boston, Massachusetts.

Marisol Hernandez, M.L.S., M.A., senior reference librarian at Memorial Sloan Kettering Cancer Center, provides reference, research, and instructional services to nurses, clinicians, researchers, patients, and caregivers. Ms. Hernandez is also clinical librarian liaison to the Memorial Sloan Kettering Nursing Department, providing customized training on evidence-based practice resources, bibliographic management, and mobile technology. Ms. Hernandez obtained her degrees from the University at Buffalo State University of New York and William Smith College.

James B. Hobbs is the online services coordinator at Loyola University New Orleans. He participates in the library's reference and instruction programs as the liaison to the Biological Sciences, Chemistry, Mathematics, Physics, and Psychological Sciences Departments. He also oversees contracts for electronic abstracting and indexing services and provides research assistance online and at the library's Learning Commons Desk.

Anthony C. Holderied is the assistant director of the library at the Environmental Protection Agency in Research Triangle Park, NC, under the contract of the School of Information and Library Science at the University of North Carolina at Chapel Hill. Anthony has ten years of experience leading information literacy and instruction initiatives at a variety of academic institutions, and has also worked as an instructional technologist. He has published and presented in the fields of information literacy and educational technology and holds a Master of Library Science and Master of Arts in Educational Media.

Benjamin J. Keele is a research and instructional services librarian in the Ruth Lilly Law Library, Indiana University Robert H. McKinney School of Law Library. He earned a J.D. and an M.L.S. from Indiana University.

Rebecca Kuglitsch is the interdisciplinary science librarian at the University of Colorado Boulder. She completed her MLIS at the University of Washington and an M.A. in the history of science at UCLA, which sparked her interest in how scientists work. Her research focuses on information literacy in the sciences and on developing relevant, usable library spaces and services for the sciences.

Catherine A. Lemmer is head of Information Services in the Ruth Lilly Law Library, Indiana University Robert H. McKinney School of Law Library. She earned a J.D. from the University of Wisconsin and an M.S. from the University of Illinois.

James Lund is library director and professor of Theological Bibliography at Westminster Seminary California. He is currently researching and writing on library administration, trends in library service, and the future utilization of information resources.

Mike Magilligan is the librarian for Digital Learning for SUNY Canton. Mike was working as a musician in New York City for over a decade before obtaining his M.L.S at Pratt Institute. Although he began his "second career" as a music archivist, he quickly accumulated varied experiences in the field of librarianship including: working in technical services, earning a fellowship at the Metropolitan Museum of Art, and working as a prison librarian. His focus at Canton is to instruct innovative research techniques that blend digital and traditional resources.

Christina Miller, M.L.S., M.S. Ed., is a faculty member in the York College Library with dual responsibilities as an academic librarian and a high school librarian. Miller provides library services for the Queens High School for the Sciences at York College, one of New York City's specialized high schools, that shares the York College Library. Miller is an NYS-certified School Media Specialist and an NYS-certified Literacy Specialist (grades 5–12), a member of several library and literacy associations, and a reviewer for *Voice of Youth Advocates* (*VOYA*).

Plamen Miltenoff is an information specialist and professor at St. Cloud State University in St. Cloud, Minnesota. His professional interests include social media, new technologies, web development and multimedia, and use of new media and technologies in education. Plamen is currently teaching the for-credit social media class offered through Learning Resources Services, and has a leadership role on the library's Social Media Committee, as well as the library's YouTube channel. He has published and presented extensively on the impact of emerging technologies on learning, pedagogy, and higher education.

Anne O' Brien works as a television producer and academic with Kairos Communications Ltd. She coordinates the provision of production modules for NUI Maynooth's degrees in Media Studies, Digital Media, and their MA in Radio and Television Production. She has published a number of articles on gender and media as well as a book *The Politics of Tourism Development.* She has produced documentaries for broadcast in Kenya and Sierra Leone and was delighted to work on the production of an audio archive on the life of Ken Saro-Wiwa and the activist work of Sr. Majella McCarron and Owens Wiwa.

Diana Parlic (1989) holds an MSc in management in the department of organizational sciences at the University of Belgrade. She is researching the application of gamification in business contexts. She is employed at Coca-Cola, Hellenic, Serbia.

Scott Rice is the coordinator of Technology Services in Belk Library at Appalachian State University. He has an M.A. in Philosophy from Tulane University and an M.S. in Information Sciences from the University of Tennessee Knoxville. His research interests include e-learning, educational gaming, and information literacy. He is also a coeditor of the book *Gaming in Academic Libraries: Collections, Marketing, and Information Literacy.*

Adam Sofronijevic (1973) holds an MSc in management, an MSc in LIS, and a BSc in IT. As of July 2014, he is a PhDc in LIS in the faculty of Philology at the University of Belgrade. He has five years of experience in the management of a department in a main Serbian university library — university library Svetozar Marković. He publishes regularly in national and international journals, and presents at international conferences.

Loren Turner earned her law degree from American University in Washington, D.C. After law school, she practiced family law litigation in a boutique firm in Chicago before transitioning to law librarianship and joining the UF Law faculty in 2012 as a reference librarian and adjunct professor of law. She teaches legal research to first-year law students and provides research support to faculty, students, and guests of UF Law. Her scholarship focuses on instructional methodologies and in foreign, comparative, and international law.

Alexander Watkins works at the University of Colorado Boulder as the Art & Architecture Librarian. He graduated from the double Master's program at Pratt Institute in Library Science and Art History. Originally from California, he is a Boulder transplant by way of New York City. His research focuses on meeting the changing needs of art researchers and engaging art library users through space design, instruction, and outreach.

Rachel Wexelbaum is collection management librarian and associate professor at St. Cloud State University in St. Cloud, Minnesota. She has developed and taught a for-credit social media class for undergraduates that focuses on critical thinking and information literacy skills. Since then, Rachel has taken a leadership role on her library's Social Media Committee. Although she continues to write encyclopedia entries for academic publishers, Rachel has joined the Wikipedia Education movement and is working on creating and editing entries about prominent LGBT and Jewish people.

Jennifer L. Wondracek is senior law librarian and assistant director of Instructional Technology at the University of North Texas, Dallas College of Law.